*Touring the
Coastal South Carolina Backroads*

Books by Nancy Rhyne

The Grand Strand: An Uncommon Guide to Myrtle Beach and Its Surroundings
Carolina Seashells
Tales of the South Carolina Low Country
More Tales of the South Carolina Low Country
Coastal Ghosts: Haunted Places from Wilmington to Savannah
Murder in the Carolinas
Once Upon a Time on a Plantation
Plantation Tales
More Murder in the Carolinas
Alice Flagg: The Ghost of the Hermitage

Other Titles in John F. Blair's *Touring the Backroads* Series

Touring the Western North Carolina Backroads, by Carolyn Sakowski (1990)
Touring the Eastern Tennessee Backroads, by Carolyn Sakowski (1993)

Touring the Coastal South Carolina Backroads

by
NANCY RHYNE

JOHN F. BLAIR, PUBLISHER
™WINSTON-SALEM, NORTH CAROLINA

Third Printing, 1996

Printed and Bound by R. R. Donnelley & Sons
Photographs by Sid Rhyne
Designed by Debra L. Hampton
This book is printed on acid-free paper.

Photographs on front cover, clockwise from top left:
North Beach Lighthouse, Witch Doctor Tour
Tidalholm, Historic Beaufort Tour
Pelican and Fish from Brookgreen Gardens, Southern Grand Strand Tour
Diana from Brookgreen Gardens, Southern Grand Strand Tour
French Huguenot Church, Charleston Walking Tour
Basket weaver's stand near Mount Pleasant, Swamp Fox Tour
Hurl Rock, Myrtle Beach Tour
"The Three Sisters," Charleston Walking Tour

Photographs on back cover, top to bottom:
Ironwork from John Rutledge Home, Charleston Driving Tour
Church of the Cross Episcopal at Bluffton, Hilton Head Tour

Library of Congress Cataloging-in-Publication Data
Rhyne, Nancy, 1926–
Touring the coastal South Carolina backroads / by Nancy Rhyne.
p.   cm.
Includes bibliographical references and index.
ISBN 0-89587-090-8 (trade pbk. : acid-free paper) :
1. South Carolina—Description and travel—1981– —Tours.
2. Automobile travel—South Carolina—Guide-books. I. Title.
F267.3.R48   1992
917.5704'43—dc20   91-41378

"What is the use of a book,"
thought Alice, "without pictures or conversation?"
Alice's Adventures in Wonderland

For Sid
His pictures make this book more useful.

Contents

Preface   ix
Acknowledgments   xi

The Calabash to Bucksport Tour   3

The Northern Grand Strand Tour   23

The Myrtle Beach Tour   37

The Southern Grand Strand Tour   55

The Georgetown Tour   85

The Santee Plantations Tour   107

The Swamp Fox Tour   123

The Charleston Driving Tour   141

The Charleston Walking Tour   159

The Charleston Plantations Tour   181

The Witch Doctor Tour   205

The Historic Beaufort Tour   223

The Hilton Head Tour   243

Appendix   259
Bibliography   263
Index   265

Preface

I am always a little disappointed when I hear of people who travel to the coast of South Carolina intending to do no more than lie on the beach and soak up the sun. How much they stand to miss! Coastal South Carolina provides a rich mixture of ocean beaches, barrier islands, marshland, forests, rivers, and farmland. Spectacular new resort communities exist alongside historic homes and villages. And all of it is easily accessible.

This book offers thirteen tours that attempt to give a taste of the variety of people, places, and lifestyles that exist along the coast of South Carolina. The tours also present a look at days gone by. Much of the Low Country's past revolved around the plantations that had their golden era about 150 years ago. For example, my home county, Georgetown County, once hosted more than two hundred plantations. Many of the Low Country plantations no longer exist, but many of the ones that remain are treated in this book. You will see rice plantations so prosperous that they surpass the plantations in *Gone With the Wind*. You will visit the sea-island cotton plantations that made millionaires out of families living on some of the Palmetto State's barrier islands. And you will tour the only tea plantation in the United States.

It is my hope that history and architecture buffs will enjoy viewing the classic homes of Georgetown, Charleston, and Beaufort; that students of our nation's wars will benefit from visits to Revolutionary War and Civil War sites; and that fans of folklore will appreciate the many tales presented here. Indeed, every backroad in the Low Country seems to have a plantation gate, an old church, an eerie graveyard, or an interesting house, each with a story to tell.

For one reason or another, famous people from George Washington to George Gershwin and from Francis Marion to Mickey Spillane have been drawn to the coast of South Carolina. Their stories are told here, and so are the stories of coastal residents who ought to be better known than they are, like the woman who pioneered indigo planting in the United States and the former slave from Beaufort who went on to become a legislator at the state and national levels. The little people get their turn, too, like the witch doctor from Frogmore and the sixteenth-century French dwarf who haunts a fabulous mansion.

The tours in this book range from 25 city blocks to 140 country miles. You may want to combine some of the shorter tours or divide some of the longer ones. There is no way I could possibly take you down every dirt road or out-of-the-way lane that offers an interesting site or story. In each case, I have had to make a judgment whether the payoff was worth the effort expended. I hope you will feel encouraged to pursue roads outside the bounds of these tours whenever the mood strikes you.

The backbone running through this book is U.S. 17. While hardly a backroad, it is certainly a starting place for getting to the backroads, and it is difficult to cover the entire length of the South Carolina coast without encountering it from time to time. Likewise, I understand that Ocean Boulevard in Myrtle Beach and the avenues in Charleston's historic district can hardly be considered backroads. But my feeling is that it would be a grave injustice to write a tour guide about coastal South Carolina and neglect such important places. Even when dealing with popular vacation spots like Myrtle Beach and Charleston, I have always made an effort to cover people, places, and stories that are little-known and outside the mainstream. I hope you will find that effort a success.

Acknowledgments

Some of the people who helped with this book are new friends, while others have helped me many times before. My deep gratitude goes to C. B. Berry of Crescent Beach; Catherine Lewis of Conway; Emory Campbell with Penn Community Services on St. Helena Island; Ralph and Catherine Chandler of Charlotte, North Carolina; John Monroe Holliday of Gallivants Ferry; Tom Garrison of Myrtle Beach; Dr. James L. Michie, the associate director of the Waccamaw Center for Historical and Cultural Studies at Coastal Carolina College in Conway; Glen Stapleton of Francis Marion National Forest; and Betsy Veronee, the public-relations director at Magnolia Gardens.

I owe a special thanks to the staff of the Chapin Memorial Library in Myrtle Beach: Cathy Wiggins, the library director; Shirley Wayland, the assistant director; Mary Owens, Linda Maher, and Grace Kicidis in the Circulation Department; Lesta Sue Hardee, Libby Spivey, and Leona Lewis in the Technical Services Department; Patty Cox, the children's services coordinator; Cindy Herrington, reference assistant; and Ernestine Overby, children's room assistant. The people at the Chapin Memorial Library sometimes answer my questions before I am certain what information I am seeking. They are not only my helpers, but my friends as well.

Some people have helped me to such an extent that I feel this book could not have been written without them. Jack Leland of Charleston—the man who in my opinion knows more about the South Carolina Low Country than anyone else—is one such person. Bert Lippincott of the Newport (Rhode Island) Historical Society is another; he offered to send me valuable information I didn't even realize existed.

Willis J. Keith, the program supervisor of the Shellfish Management Program for the Office of Fisheries Management on James Island, was generous in sharing his extensive research on Fort Johnson and the local marshlands. Mack Fleming of Charleston Tea Plantation, Inc., took the time to give me a detailed explanation of the unbelievable amount of work involved in the processing of tea; he even served me a slice of pound cake with my glass of iced tea. Beverly Donald, the superintendent with Magnolia Cemetery Trust in Charleston, made me aware of the painstaking work done by architects in crafting the ornate symbols of death on display in historic cemeteries. Stewart J. Pabst, the assistant director and curator of the Horry County Museum, provided me with some excellent photographs. And Stephen Hoffius of the Charleston Historical Society brought me more old books from the archives than I thought to request; I used them all. Anyone who has to make inquiries for information on a regular basis knows what a treat it is to encounter friendly, interested, and professional people like these.

Again, Steve Kirk, Carolyn Sakowski, and Margaret Couch at John F. Blair, Publisher, guided me over a tedious course without giving up hope. And my agent, Sally McMillan of Sally Hill McMillan and Associates, advised me on contractual and bookkeeping matters.

For the eleventh time, I end my acknowledgments with Sid. He deserves a whole page of praise for taking the photos, for driving me to all the sites covered in this book at least three times, and for keeping me straight.

Touring the
Coastal South Carolina Backroads

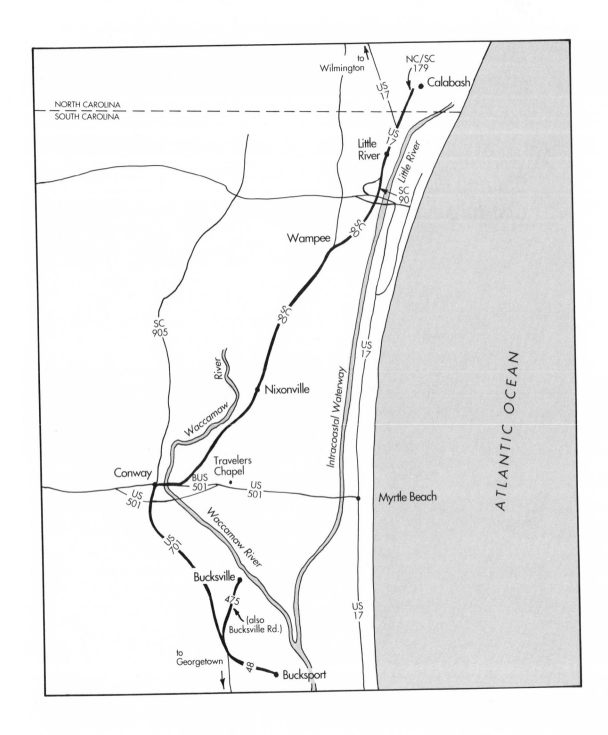

The Calabash to Bucksport Tour

This tour begins just across the North Carolina state line in the restaurant-rich village of Calabash considered the gateway to South Carolina's Grand Strand. It then heads to Marsh Harbour Golf Links and across the South Carolina line to the community of Little River. Next, the tour veers inland to visit the Travelers Chapel and explore the city of Conway. It travels to Hebron Methodist Church, near the former site of the village of Bucksville, before ending at Bucksport.

Total mileage: approximately 56 miles.

One of the first things visitors to the beaches of North and South Carolina learn is that U.S. 17 is the main artery along the coast of both states. N.C. 179 runs to the east of, and roughly parallel to, the section of U.S. 17 just above the South Carolina border. This tour starts at the intersection of N.C. 179 and River Road near Calabash, North Carolina. Drive down River Road, following the signs for Calabash.

The word *calabash* has been used for gourds and pumpkins since the end of the sixteenth century. Early settlers in this area probably applied it first to the Calabash River, which takes the distinct shape of a gourd. The word also gained fame from another source. Comedian Jimmy Durante always ended his radio and television shows by saying, "Good night, Mrs. Calabash, wherever you are." A woman from Calabash once wrote Durante asking him if there was any significance to his famous closing statement. The comedian responded with a photograph of himself bearing a brief greeting, the kind of throw-away line he probably wrote to thousands of fans: "It has been a pleasure, believe me. Jimmy Durante." So the question remains unanswered.

The reason why Calabash has come to be a mecca for seafood lovers is another mystery. You'll notice that River Road is virtually lined with restaurants from N.C. 179 to the Calabash River. Huge oysters and a variety of other edible creatures of the sea flourish in the local sounds, but the supply is really no more plentiful than at some other locations along the coast. Why should a restaurant boom have come to such an isolated area? No one seems to know for certain. Perhaps local residents are right not to question success, preferring to just sit back and enjoy the food.

The humble beginnings of the restaurant trade in Calabash are known, even if the reasons for the subsequent explosion aren't. When dredging for the

*The local fleet at rest
on Calabash River*

construction of the Grand Strand section of the Intracoastal Waterway started prior to World War II, a prodigious amount of mud was thrown onto the banks of the Calabash River. The Beck family was the first to open a seafood restaurant on the reclaimed soil. Seeing the Becks' early success, other entrepreneurs built restaurants on the knoll, and the trade began to gain a momentum of its own shortly thereafter. Most restaurants operated their own shrimp boats.

Today, a number of restaurants in the village make the claim that they, not their competitors, serve the original "Calabash-style" seafood. There seem to be enough hungry seafood enthusiasts from far and wide to support them all. Calabash Seafood Hut, 0.2 mile from N.C. 179, is a local favorite. It is an additional 0.1 mile to the river, where other memorable restaurants are clustered. Depending upon the time of day you pass through, you may not be able to resist overindulging at one of the sumptuous buffets.

You may also notice the local fleet at rest on the Calabash River. Half-day deep-sea fishing excursions, as well as ocean and scenic cruises, are offered on ships with names like *New Capt. Jim, Capt. Sam's*, and *Mary B II*. The shrimp boats, battered by wind and water, usually bear the names of their skippers, such as the *Hank*. Sea gulls customarily perch on the pilings under huge moss-festooned oaks. The odor is a mixture of fried fish and marsh mud.

The Calabash River runs into the Intracoastal Waterway a short distance south of the village. The Intracoastal Waterway is an important source of commerce throughout this area. The Grand Strand section of the waterway is 95.5 miles long, twelve feet deep, and ninety feet wide. It supports a considerable volume of commercial shipping, principally barge traffic moving in interstate commerce. But it is also heavily used by pleasure craft of all types; hundreds upon thousands of yachts with their beautiful white sails travel the route on their various migrations.

Today's Intracoastal Waterway stretches 3,000 miles from Maine to Key West, Florida. It is a far cry from the tidal streams, bays, and sounds that local Indians once used as a means of transportation, though the principle is the same. The network of streams and rivers all along the east coast of the United States was of such obvious commercial value that it caught the attention of George Washington, who went so far as to formulate plans for a canal in the Great Dismal Swamp area around the North Carolina–Virginia border.

The historic Indian route through the northern part of South Carolina traversed an area of uninterrupted marshland. The completion of the waterway brought improved drainage. Now, the land bordering the waterway is used for farming, residential development, and golf courses. Not so many years ago, it was only the land above the flood plain that was considered suitable for residential use, but today fine homes border the waterway much of the way from the state border south to Georgetown.

After you have enjoyed Calabash, retrace your route to N.C. 179 and turn left. It is 0.6 mile to the entrance to Marsh Harbour Golf Links. Turn left into the entrance and drive approximately 0.8 mile to the clubhouse area.

Marsh Harbour Golf Links was opened for play in 1980. The course's director of golf made a statement around that time that Marsh Harbour might well be the most scenic of the hundred-plus courses on the Grand Strand. He was probably right. When they least expect it, Marsh Harbour golfers may see the mast of a sailing yacht moving into their fairway from among the giant oak trees shrouded in moss. The effect is startling. At first glance, there appears to be no way a boat could have gotten there. However, a closer look reveals a network of inlets snaking their way through the vast marshlands that border the fairways and greens. Boats sometimes enter the inlets for protection from ocean winds and high tides; skippers may drop anchor and elect to stay

Marsh Harbour Golf Links

*A giant oak on
Marsh Harbour Golf LInks*

This six-hundred-pound granite monument marks the spot where the Boundary House once stood.

overnight. Although no facilities are afforded those seeking shelter, Marsh Harbour is known among boaters as a lovely, private place. Most vessels that find their way into the channels on the golf-course property are travelers on the Intracoastal Waterway.

Marsh Harbour lies squarely on the North Carolina–South Carolina border. It is said that on the tenth hole, a good drive with a slight fade will pass from North Carolina over a historic boundary marker into South Carolina before landing safely where it belongs back in North Carolina. Although most visitors come for the excellent golf, the spectacular sights—the dark lagoons, the live oaks draped in Spanish moss, the passing boats laden with tourists, the shrimp boats moving through the marsh grass as silently as mirages—are a photographer's delight.

Besides being one of the Grand Strand's finest golf courses, Marsh Harbour is situated on some of the area's most historic land. The six-hundred-pound granite monument you will notice in front of the clubhouse marks the spot where the Boundary House once stood. The oldest house recorded in South Carolina's Horry County (pronounced O-ree), the Boundary House was so named because it was divided in half by the North Carolina–South Carolina line. In colonial days, it served as a resting place for travelers on the Kings Highway, an important route between the two states. Isaac Marion, the older brother of Francis Marion, the legendary Swamp Fox of Revolutionary War fame, was dining in the Boundary House in 1775 when he received word of the Battle of Lexington. (For more information on Francis Marion and his family, see The Swamp Fox Tour.) The Boundary House was also well-known as a dueling place. Benjamin Smith, who briefly served as governor of North Carolina from 1810 to 1811, was badly wounded here when he took a bullet to the chest.

Return to the Marsh Harbour entrance and turn left. You will cross the border into South Carolina almost immediately. Approximately 1.2 miles from the Marsh Harbour entrance, N.C./S.C. 179 merges with U.S. 17. On the left just where the roads merge are the Vereen Memorial Historical Gardens, recognizable by their split-rail fence. If you care to tour the gardens on a nature trail that follows part of an old road used in George Washington's day, turn into the parking area. The self-guided walk features many interesting native plants and trees that are labeled for easy identification; the trail has been left as natural as possible. The old cemetery of the Vereen family is located at the end of the trail.

The Vereen name is a prominent one along the Grand Strand today.

According to local surveyor and historian C. B. Berry, the tract on which the gardens are located was once owned by a Frenchman named Varin. By the time of George Washington's tour of the area in 1791, the spelling had been corrupted to Vereen, and that was the way Washington noted it in his diary and the way it has come down through the years.

The South Carolina Welcome Center is located on the opposite side of U.S. 17 from the Vereen Memorial Historical Gardens. It is an excellent place to obtain brochures and information about the area.

Drive south on U.S. 17 for 1 mile to a traffic light at the corner of Mineola Avenue. Turn left. It is 0.5 mile into the heart of the fishing village called Little River.

C. B. Berry says that the town has gone by the name of Little River from the earliest records, no doubt in reference to the abbreviated, 5-mile-long river of the same name located nearby. There was once an effort to change the name to Mineola, an Indian word that translates as "little waters," but the new name failed to stick.

Unlike early settlers farther to the south, the first inhabitants of Little River had neither large tracts of land nor slaves to work them. They depended upon the river for a plentiful supply of fish and the pine woods for lumber and

South Carolina Welcome Center

firewood. Theirs was a hand-to-mouth existence, but it seems that they still managed to find their pleasure. It has been recorded that an English missionary by the name of George Whitfield visited Little River on New Year's Day in 1740. He found the residents singing and dancing so boisterously that he felt obliged to chide them for irreverence.

On April 17, 1791, George Washington visited Little River during his tour of the coastal South. He traveled in a light coach drawn by four horses and was accompanied by a valet and four men who served as groomsmen and drivers. As with all his other stops along the Kings Highway, the meticulous Washington noted in his diary the names of people who offered him hospitality. At Little River, he had lunch at the home of James Cochran, a Revolutionary War veteran, after which he and his party continued down the road to the beaches that today comprise North Myrtle Beach. (For more information on George Washington's visit to the area, see The Northern Grand Strand Tour.)

In the nineteenth century, Little River became an active port for the export of lumber, pitch, tar, and turpentine. The port could accommodate vessels of up to 150 tons. Lumber was the mainstay of the local economy. In fact, old piles that mark the former site of sawmills are still in evidence along the shoreline. A newspaper article from December 1868 gave a thorough catalog of the village's principal businesses and civic attractions—four stores, a steam-operated sawmill, two gum stills, an academy, and a church. Little River was recognized as something of a commercial center.

The early part of this century saw relatively few changes. The first telephone in the village was installed in 1907 by a man named Willie Stone, the owner of a general store. Stone wanted to know in advance when the boats bearing his goods were to arrive, so he ran a line from his store to a house at Little River Neck, where he had a lookout who dutifully phoned him whenever a supply boat appeared at the mouth of the river.

Little River remained isolated until the 1930s, when roads throughout the area were improved; the local section of U.S. 17 was completed by 1941. The most profound change affecting the village was brought about by the gradual decline of the logging industry. Local people turned to the sea to fill the void in commerce. A man named Tom Bessent was operating an oyster farm around the turn of the century; in those days, oysters sold for about ten cents a bushel. When the town docks were constructed, they carried a lofty price tag of $10,000. However, the boost they gave the economy more than justified the

Little River

expense. By the 1950s, Little River was catering to sportfishermen. Local advertisements promoted sixteen small boats for hire, as well as three hotels, several tourist homes, and a motor court, all of which catered to visiting anglers.

Captain Frank Juel has been an important figure in the rise of the village's fishing industry. It is Juel who started the Hurricane Fishing Fleet. After serving in the United States Coast Guard during World War II, he bought a PT boat and brought it back to Little River for use on fishing excursions. The story goes that Juel wanted to name the vessel the *Tornado* but that he didn't know how to spell the word *tornado*. He settled instead upon the *Hurricane*, a name he *did* know how to spell. Over the course of time, the other vessels in the local fleet came to be recognized by that name. Juel no longer owns the fleet, though he still works for current owner Steve Speros.

What Mardi Gras is to New Orleans and the Kentucky Derby is to Louisville and race day is to Indianapolis, the Arthur Smith King Mackerel Tournament is to Little River. In his younger days, Arthur Smith was a nationally known country-and-western singer and a popular radio and television personality in Charlotte, North Carolina. He has since retired to the Little River area, where he came upon the idea of sponsoring a fishing tournament. The tournament has succeeded beyond anyone's expectations. During the two days of the autumn event, billed as the world's largest fishing tournament, boats leave Little River at eight o'clock in the morning and return at three-thirty in the afternoon. Any boat at least eighteen feet in length can be entered for a fee. Prize money totaling in the hundreds of thousands of dollars is awarded to those who catch the largest specimens of king mackerel. In previous years, boats have entered from more than half the states in the country, with fishermen from nearly every state and crews from as far away as Japan.

The waterfront section of Little River is only 1 block long, but it boasts a lively collection of seafood restaurants and ticket shacks for the fishing and sightseeing excursions that depart the docks. Riding at anchor just offshore are boats with names like *Goodfoot, Capt. Juel II, South Wind*, and *New Billy Boy*. After the boats return from fishing, it is a customary sight to see men and women standing on the docks and cleaning their catches, throwing fish parts into the water. Today's Little River is an ideal place for people who can sense when there is a large fish stirring the water and who are able to cast a line artfully.

Once you have explored Little River, retrace your route to U.S. 17 and turn left. After 1.9 miles, exit onto S.C. 90, heading toward Conway; you will actually have to bear left and cross U.S. 17 to join S.C. 90, which then veers inland almost immediately.

As you travel the 4.1 miles to the tiny community of Wampee, you will notice that you are driving through a transitional area. The sparsely populated agricultural country you are entering is a far cry from South Carolina's popular beach communities. Wampee is so small that it doesn't even have a crossroads. It is probably best known for hosting a school called the Pig Pen Bay Schoolhouse. Troops were readied for battle at the school during the Civil War, at which time the name was changed to the Muster Shed School.

In the 18.5 miles from Wampee to the outskirts of Conway, you will pass through communities whose names aren't even posted—Mill Swamp, Poplar, Hand, and Red Bluff. You may recognize Nixonville, approximately midway between Wampee and Conway, by the lovely homes bordering the highway and the Tilly Swamp Baptist Church, on the right.

S.C. 90 follows the route of a railroad line built in 1905 between Little River and Conway. The bordering area is rich with soybean fields, sweet potato fields, and pecan trees. Depending upon the time of year of your visit, you may see signs advertising the sale of blueberries and strawberries on a pick-your-own basis. Some local farmers maintain beehives that are more than a hundred years old.

Abundant as they are, soybeans, sweet potatoes, and the other crops have to compete for second place in Horry County, where tobacco is king. Horry County produces more tobacco than any other county in South Carolina. The first tobacco crop in the county was planted around 1869 by Gallivants Ferry resident J. W. Holliday. Today, John Monroe Holliday, J. W. Holliday's grandson, sits on several tobacco boards and is nationally known in tobacco circles. He probably grows more tobacco than anyone else in the state, and he was kind enough to outline the process for me:

A tobacco barn

> During an earlier time, the seeds were planted between "Old Christmas" and "New Christmas" from December 25th to New Year's Day. The seeds are now planted in January and covered with plastic covers. The heat is held in, and the seeds grow faster. In late March or April, the seed is transplanted in the field. Sometimes, tobacco is planted as late as mid-May.
>
> After the seed has been planted, the cultivation begins, and the leaves are carefully looked after until the bottom leaves turn yellow. Bottom leaves are called lugs, and they are the first to be gathered. The middle leaves make the best-quality tobacco, and the top leaves, called tips, are picked last.

After the tobacco leaves have been gathered, they are put in automated gas curing houses, which cost from $15,000 to $20,000 each. Well within a week you can get a barn cured out. Then the tobacco is taken to market.

You will see a good many old tobacco barns between Wampee and Conway. Located in fields, in wooded areas, and right beside the road, they are tall and narrow, with a porch and tiny chimneys. Weeds have overtaken the majority of them, as they have been abandoned in favor of the automated gas curing houses.

S.C. 90 ends at U.S. 501 Business just outside Conway. Don't head into Conway just yet, but rather turn left onto U.S. 501 Business and drive approximately 1.3 miles to where it joins U.S. 501. Follow U.S. 501 toward Myrtle Beach for about 0.4 mile to see the tiny Travelers Chapel, on the left. The Travelers Chapel is not the only place of worship of its kind in the

Travelers Chapel

TOURING THE COASTAL SOUTH CAROLINA BACKROADS

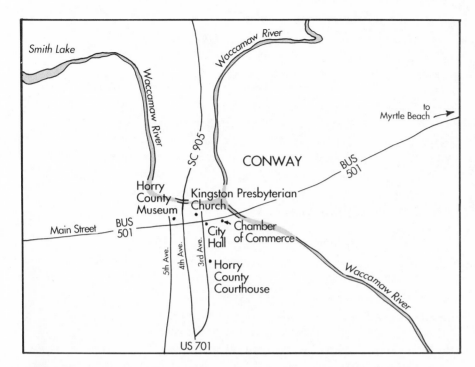

country, but it must certainly be among the prettiest. The story goes that a local chiropractor by the name of Dr. Kelley conceived the idea of a miniature chapel for coastal South Carolina after he came upon just such a structure while vacationing in Hawaii.

The Travelers Chapel was constructed in 1972 by the Reverend Emory Young, his son Bruce, and some volunteers. It measures just sixteen feet by ten feet and sits among towering pines. All visitors and worshipers are welcome. The building has six pews and can seat about twelve people. It is a popular place for weddings. If you will take the time to glance at the register, you'll notice that travelers from across the country have jotted down complimentary remarks, such as "What a quiet, restful place this is, beside a busy highway," and "We never expected to find such a wonderful place to have a quiet moment." You may feel inspired to sign the register and add a comment of your own.

After you have seen the Travelers Chapel, retrace your route along U.S. 501 and U.S. 501 Business. This time, continue on U.S. 501 Business past the junction with S.C. 90 and into Conway. You will cross two bridges, the second of which leads over the Waccamaw River. U.S. 501 Business becomes Main

---

Conway City Hall

Kingston Presbyterian Church

Street entering town. At the foot of the second bridge, on the left 3 miles from the Travelers Chapel, is the Conway Chamber of Commerce, a good place to pick up information about the area.

Horry County was named in honor of Brigadier General Peter Horry, a Revolutionary War hero. The man who succeeded Horry as brigade commander of the state militia was Colonel Robert Conway, another Revolutionary War soldier. Robert Conway became an important local landowner in 1784, when he acquired a grant covering a considerable portion of the present town. He then proceeded to sell pitch, tar, and turpentine to the firm of Bird, Savage, and Bird of London. The roots of the town of Conway go back even farther than that. The town was actually laid out by Alexander Skene and a partner in 1734 and called Kingston, but the name was changed to Conwayborough in 1802.

In the town's early days, mail arrived just once a week from Georgetown, South Carolina, or Wilmington, North Carolina. It wasn't until a railroad was built in the 1880s—the Wilmington, Chadbourn & Conway Line—that mail began to be delivered on a daily basis. The transition was not entirely smooth. In 1887, the railroad company obtained permission from the Horry County Board of Commissioners to lay about fifteen hundred feet of track along Main Street in Conway. During construction, a local woman named Mary Beaty walked from her house on Main Street, raised a gun, and ordered the crew to redirect the right of way so that a pair of live oak trees might be preserved. Her gun was loaded. The workmen began to see her point of view, and the route of the track was hurriedly altered.

Continue on Main Street 1 block past the Conway Chamber of Commerce. The Conway City Hall, dating from 1824, is on the corner of Main Street and Third Avenue. The building was designed by Robert Mills, the same man who designed the Washington Monument and other public buildings in our nation's capital. The brick structure has vaulted record rooms. The rod ties on its exterior were designed to hold the structure together in the event of an earthquake. First used as a courthouse, the building was converted to a town hall in 1907. It is listed on the National Register of Historic Places.

Turn right onto Third Avenue and drive 1 block to Kingston Presbyterian Church, on the left. The meeting house for Conway's original Presbyterian congregation, formed in 1756, was located on this site; that congregation apparently disbanded by 1795. A proposal to reestablish a Presbyterian church in town was favorably received in 1855, and the present Kingston Presbyterian Church was built and officially organized in 1858.

One of the saddest moments in the long history of the church occurred in 1870, when funeral services were held for two young sisters, Cora and Freddie Beaty. Upon seeing a maid trying to rescue little Freddie from a lake in back of the family home, Cora had hurried to help, but all three lives were tragically lost. The Beaty children's tomb can still be seen in the church cemetery. Colonel Robert Conway is also believed to be buried nearby.

Return to Main Street, turn right, and proceed 2 blocks to the Horry County Museum, at the corner of Fifth Avenue. The museum's central theme concerns environmental conditions in Horry County and how inhabitants have adapted to those conditions from ancient times to the present. On exhibit are age-old artifacts, farming tools, household items, clothing, wildlife specimens, and information on old-time methods of logging and the making of turpentine and tar. A not-to-be-missed exhibit is the 490-pound black bear struck dead by an automobile on U.S. 501 in 1981.

The most popular photograph in the Horry County Museum must certainly be that of Edmund Bigham. The Bighams were a wealthy local family that owned some 30 miles of land along the Pee Dee River. They were a talented group, with a congressman, a senator, and a physician counted among their

Edmund Bigham
Courtesy of Stewart Pabst,
Horry County Museum

members. But the Bighams were also murderers.

Beginning in the late nineteenth century, Leonard Smiley Bigham taught his children that there were two kinds of murder—clean and messy. Subsequent generations of Bigham children were instructed in murder of the clean variety; in other words, they were taught how to murder without getting caught. The Bighams were highly successful in that endeavor, though the exact extent of their murderous "success" will probably always remain a mystery. No Bigham ever served time in jail until the 1920s, when, in a case that attracted national attention, Edmund Bigham was sentenced to a thirty-nine-year term for the murder of all the remaining members of his family, save for one brother. In the end, the Bighams' twisted philosophy turned upon the family itself. As J. A. Zeigler, author of *The Last of the Bighams*, wrote, the Bighams' story "proves how easily children can be trained by successive steps to look upon the worst of crimes as but their right in the battle of life and how this hate turns and twists in its own hot bed, destroying the very elements that gave it life." The story of the Bighams is etched into the consciousness of local people.

Retrace Main Street to Third Avenue and turn right. The Horry County

Horry County Courthouse

Hebron United Methodist Church

Courthouse is on the left after 3 blocks. Constructed in the 1820s and extensively renovated in 1966, it is the courthouse where Edmund Bigham was tried for murder.

Continue along Third Avenue for 0.5 mile to a junction with U.S. 701. Turn left to head out of town. You will probably see horses grazing in pastures carved from large stands of Horry County pine trees. If it happens to be springtime and the yellow jessamine is blooming, you'll witness the blossoms spreading through most of the trees. On February 1, 1924, the South Carolina General Assembly officially named the Carolina Jessamine the state flower. From Virginia to Florida and westward to Texas, yellow jessamine brightens the countryside during the months of March and April.

After 10.3 miles on U.S. 701, turn left on Bucksville Drive, also known as S.C. 475. You are heading toward the site once occupied by the community of Bucksville. It is 2.5 miles to Hebron United Methodist Church, on the right.

Buck Cemetery

The old brick and wrought iron fence surrounding Buck Cemetery

TOURING THE COASTAL SOUTH CAROLINA BACKROADS

This simple Greek Revival church was built in 1848 of heart cypress and pine, with interior walls of oyster plaster; the original floorboards extend the entire width of the building. The windows, doors, and shutters—gifts from a sea captain—came from New England. The pulpit is of mahogany from Honduras. Note the unusual layout of the church, with the front doors opening into the area *behind* the pulpit. As in other churches of the era, partitions divided the pews in half, since it was the custom for men to sit on one side and women on the other. The red-painted church is listed on the National Register of Historic Places. Services are still held in the building, which has survived the Civil War, the Depression, and the ravages of coastal storms, most recently Hurricane Hugo in September 1989.

No visit to Hebron Methodist Church can be complete without a stroll through the Buck family cemetery, located across the road and enclosed by a fence of old bricks and wrought iron. A tablet on the back wall of the fence assures visitors that the Bucks are "securely enshrouded in the historic soil of South Carolina."

In the days when turpentine and timber ruled the Horry County economy, Henry Buck arrived from Bucksport, Maine, a town founded by his father. Buck established three sawmills in Horry County and named them Upper Mill, Middle Mill, and Lower Mill; Middle Mill later became Bucksville, while Lower Mill became Bucksport. It is likely that Henry Buck was Horry County's first important entrepreneur.

Under Buck's direction, oaks and pines were squared in the forest, pulled to the river, and floated down to the sawmills for finishing and shipping. Much of the lumber went to New England, where it was used in the construction of sailing vessels. The abundant forests of Horry County made Henry Buck such a wealthy man that he imported governesses and tutors from the North to care for and educate his children. Among the tutors was Sarah Delano, a distant cousin of Franklin Delano Roosevelt's. Buck also brought in shipwrights from the North and offered them the services of his slaves. His construction projects included several boats, a two-story barn, about twenty cabins for employees, an icehouse, and Hebron Methodist Church.

Nothing is left of Bucksville today. The town is best remembered for a ship constructed there. In September 1874, Captain Jonathan Nichols and master builder Elishua Dunbar arrived from Maine with 115 carpenters, blacksmiths, joiners, and riggers to begin work on the *Henrietta*, the largest ship ever built locally. The venture was an experiment. A vessel of the same dimensions was to be constructed simultaneously in Maine, the objective being to determine where ships could be built more economically. The *Henrietta* required 1,300,300 feet of lumber. She was built for $90,000, while her sister ship cost $115,000. Bucksville appeared to be the winning location. However, the *Henrietta* was so large that her crew had great difficulty warping her down the river to Georgetown, which was her first stop en route to having her masts installed in Charleston. Indeed, she never returned to Georgetown or Charleston, as she drew too much water for their harbors. Bucksville turned out the loser.

The *Henrietta*'s career was brief. She operated in trade with the Orient and Australia, and her passages were considered superb for a ship classified as a carrier. In November 1890, she sailed from New York to Portland, Oregon. In May 1891, she was loaded with lumber for Melbourne, Australia. Subsequent trips saw her carrying wool for Boston; lumber for Buenos Aires, Argentina, a trip of 49 days; and oil for Singapore. She sailed for Japan in 1894. In Yokohama that August, the *Henrietta* was loaded with eight hundred tons of manganese ore, a tricky cargo that is prone to shifting. Entering the harbor at Kobe, Japan, where she was to take on more cargo before sailing for New York, she encountered a violent typhoon. The pilot ran her back to an area consid-

The dock at Bucksport

TOURING THE COASTAL SOUTH CAROLINA BACKROADS

ered secure for anchoring, but the turbulent winds continued to tear wildly at her masts, and the vessel was a total loss before the storm subsided. Fortunately, all hands were saved. The *Henrietta* is listed on the National Register of Historic Places *in absentia*.

Retrace Bucksville Drive to U.S. 701 and turn left. Travel 0.8 mile to Bucksport Road and turn left again. Proceed 3.1 miles into the little village of Bucksport, on the Waccamaw River.

This tour ends at Bucksport, as does the story of the Bucks. You can't help noticing the old house on the right at the end of Bucksport Road, just before the restaurant overlooking the Intracoastal Waterway. The house is named Road's End, appropriately enough, and it was built by Henry Buck. His son, Henry Lee Buck, lived at Road's End with his wife, Georgia, from the time of their marriage in 1866 through the birth of their six children. Today, the house stands unoccupied and neglected.

Retrace Bucksport Road when you have seen the village. Turning left on U.S. 701 will take you south to Georgetown. If you prefer to head toward Myrtle Beach and the Grand Strand's other major beaches, turn right onto U.S. 701, then transfer to U.S. 501 when you reach Conway.

The Intracoastal Waterway

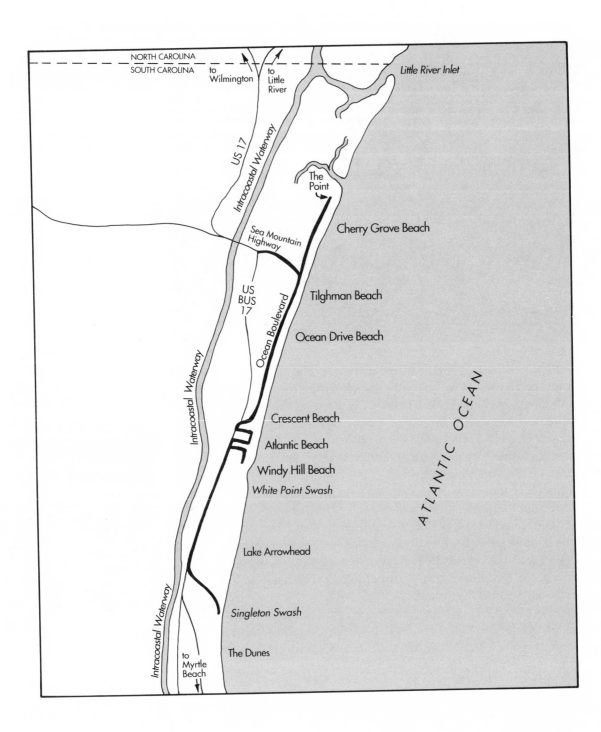

The Northern Grand Strand Tour

This tour concentrates on the union of beaches known as North Myrtle Beach. It begins on Ocean Boulevard in Cherry Grove Beach. Next, it visits Ocean Drive Beach—famous for its beach-music tradition—Crescent Beach, Atlantic Beach, and Windy Hill Beach. It then proceeds to the Meher Spiritual Center before ending at Singleton Swash.

Total mileage: approximately 15 miles.

Cherry Grove Beach is the northernmost beach in the state of South Carolina; most visitors reach it by traveling east off U.S. 17 on Sea Mountain Highway. To begin this tour, find your way to the far northern end of Ocean Boulevard in Cherry Grove Beach, just above 60th Avenue North. Head south on Ocean Boulevard for an extended look at the northern portion of the Grand Strand.

With the exception of Atlantic Beach, the beaches north of Myrtle Beach—Cherry Grove Beach, Ocean Drive Beach, Crescent Beach, and Windy Hill Beach—are collectively known as North Myrtle Beach. You will quickly get an idea of the heavy concentration of beach development along this section of the 75-mile Grand Strand. It is a unique phenomenon on the entire east coast that so many beaches so close together should have undergone development almost simultaneously.

Colonel Daniel W. Jordan was a pioneer in the production of naval stores in the area today occupied by Cherry Grove Beach. In the 1840s, he acquired a tract of 375 acres adjoining Little River at its junction with Cedar Creek, an astute transaction that elevated him into the elite planter aristocracy, quite a social jump for a man who had made his living from pine trees. Jordan adapted smoothly to the aristocratic lifestyle, even becoming a member of the exclusive Hot and Hot Fish Club, where planters met to socialize. (For more information on the Hot and Hot Fish Club, see The Southern Grand Strand Tour.) The heirs of a subsequent owner developed Jordan's original tract into a recreational area and named it Cherry Grove Beach in honor of the abundant local crop of cherry trees.

The development of South Carolina's beaches didn't really begin in earnest until after World War II, when Horry County boys, their horizons broadened, returned home with ideas of property and wealth. Earth-moving machines,

"The Point"—the end of the road in Cherry Grove Beach

pile drivers, cranes, and concrete mixers started to take up residence in Cherry Grove Beach. Motels and private cottages rose from the sand.

They all became a hodgepodge of rubble and broken furniture when Hurricane Hazel slammed into the coast on October 15, 1954. Radio and television forecasters had been predicting that Hurricane Hazel would come ashore somewhere in South Carolina, but no one was quite prepared for the tidal surge that swept in at high tide during a full moon. Oceanfront buildings were left looking as if some giant had picked them up and tossed them about at random. It is a wonder that developers were not discouraged. The cranes and concrete mixers returned, but this time the buildings boasted a higher quality of construction. The local skyline was changed all the way to "the Point"—the end of the road in the northern section of Cherry Grove Beach.

The spring of 1975 saw construction proceeding more rapidly than ever. At that time, a private yacht basin was dug at Cherry Grove Beach, and some clamshells were found that scientists believed dated back to 1200 B.C. Some of the shells weighed five pounds and were between six and seven inches across.

Cherry Grove Beach gained in popularity partly because of the local fishing. A pier that formerly stood toward the northern end of the beach became famous in 1964 as the site where a world-record tiger shark—13 feet, 10.5 inches long and 1,780 pounds—was taken. The catch belonged to Walter Maxwell, a bricklayer from Charlotte, North Carolina, and it topped the old record by a whopping 350 pounds. A cry went up as soon as Maxwell's 1,400 yards of line began to fly out to sea, and before the shark's three runs were over, a crowd of 3,000 had gathered to watch the contest between man and shark. It took Maxwell three hours to claim his prize. The pier was destroyed in 1989 by another memorable hurricane—Hurricane Hugo.

It is 2.5 miles on Ocean Boulevard to the Cherry Grove Pavilion, at the southern end of Cherry Grove Beach. Shortly thereafter, you will leave the high-density development behind and enter an area of expensive homes with a notable absence of motels, restaurants, and other commercial interests. Though there is no sign to inform you of it, you are traveling through a section called Tilghman Beach. The high-density development resumes 1.8 miles past the Cherry Grove Pavilion, at the outskirts of Ocean Drive Beach.

The beaches in many parts of the world are as soft as loaves of bread, but the Grand Strand is blessed with hard-packed sand that will support good-sized vehicles. During winter, when cars are allowed on Ocean Drive Beach, those who choose to take a spin on the sand experience a unique, wide-open feeling. The view is fabulous. Some people claim that the beach is the widest in the

*Houses along
Cherry Grove inlet*

Cherry Grove Pier

world at low tide. Ocean Drive Beach got its name before World War II, when automobile races were held on the strand. Some property owners were hoping that Ocean Drive Beach would become another Daytona Beach, which boasts a 23-mile beach of hard-packed sand five hundred feet wide at low tide. However, Ocean Drive Beach has never managed to rival its Florida counterpart in popularity. For the benefit of sunbathers, cars are now prohibited on the strand during summer.

In spring and summer, the main drag in Ocean Drive Beach is packed with people. The entire community is a kind of shrine to the popularization of beach music. Those who knew the place during its heyday in the fifties and sixties are likely to be overcome by a wave of nostalgia.

Beach music and its accompanying dance, the shag—an elegant version of the jitterbug—go hand in hand. The Grand Strand and Ocean Drive Beach in particular are often credited as being their birthplace. Beach music evolved from black rhythm-and-blues seldom played on white radio stations until the mid-fifties, when songs like "Gee" by the Crows were written to cross over into the white market. Before that, white kids had to go to the beaches, away from Mom and Dad, to hear the black jukebox music they preferred. Hence the name

"The Horseshoe" at Ocean Drive

TOURING THE COASTAL SOUTH CAROLINA BACKROADS

beach music.

Since the late 1940s, college students have flocked to "O.D."—Ocean Drive—to experience beach music firsthand. Upon returning to their campuses, they then spread the word about shagging and songs like "Miss Grace" and "Be Young, Be Foolish." Beach-music lovers remained true to their cause during the rock-'n'-roll of the fifties, the protest songs of the sixties, the disco craze of the seventies, and the country and gospel of the eighties. Now it seems that their music is getting more play than ever. Every year, hundreds of members of the Society of Shaggers (S.O.S.) come to North Myrtle Beach from all over the country for the S.O.S. Weekend, which includes shag contests offering thousands of dollars in prize money. Levi Crawford, spokesman for the Fat Jack Band, once said that "beach music has no age to people. The stuff today has a beat like the stuff of yesterday. It's great as long as you can shag."

If beach music has an ageless quality about it, then so do beach music lovers. In September 1980, alumni of the University of South Carolina chose North Myrtle Beach as the site of one of their largest class reunions ever. Gray-haired and balding "teenagers" arrived by the thousands to party with old friends, to dance, and to reminisce about the blue-sky days of the forties and fifties, when they came to play at Ocean Drive Beach. Some of the same old hangouts that attracted crowds to "O.D." back in those days are still in existence today, like Fat Harold's Pad. A sign over the door of that establishment encourages

Fat Harold's Pad at Ocean Drive

Ocean Drive Pavilion

customers to "Boogie in the Pad cause yo' Momma did."

It isn't the easiest thing in the world to tell when you leave Ocean Drive Beach and enter Crescent Beach; Crescent Beach begins about 1.6 miles south of the start of Ocean Drive Beach. Sixty years ago, a cornfield known as "the Swamp Field" stood where Crescent Beach is today. Since the corn was surprisingly free of infestation by weevils, farmers assumed that any corn grown in proximity to salt water would prove to be likewise, an assumption that has yet to be verified by agricultural research.

Crescent Beach is named for the crescent-shaped arc of Long Bay. If you look at a map, you'll notice that the northern section of the South Carolina coast has a curved shape. It is believed that the beaches that are within the curve are likelier to be spared the ravages of hurricanes than those that are not.

Property in Crescent Beach has passed through the hands of several well-known coastal families, but credit for local development belongs to J. W. Perrin and I. C. Jordan. Perrin, the first mayor of Crescent Beach, owned large tracts of land subsequently developed by others; Jordan served on the city council and was the moving force behind the Crescent Beach Corporation. Another important local figure is surveyor, historian, and writer C. B. Berry, who served two terms as mayor of Crescent Beach in the fifties and sixties. Ask virtually any local resident a question about Horry County history and you will be referred to Berry. His articles appear in many publications, and he is a recognized authority on the production of pitch, tar, and turpentine.

Unlike Georgetown County to the south, Horry County was not blessed with the tidal rivers and low-lying bottoms essential for the production of rice. During the time when Georgetown County rice planters were becoming millionaires, farmers in Horry County were making their living, though not their fortune, off pine trees. The resinous products of the pine forests were called naval stores, since their primary commercial use was in building and maintaining wooden ships. The principal naval stores were pitch, tar, and turpentine. Horry County was an important producer of naval stores during the nineteenth century and the early part of the twentieth century, in the days when 70 percent of the nation's yield came from the Southeast.

The first step in the production of naval stores was to test pine trees for their resin content by chopping into them with an ax. Trees containing a high percentage of resin were called lightwood. Lightwood was cut into pieces about four feet long; the pieces were placed in a hole and arranged around a pipe so that when the resin began to run downward, it would flow into the pipe and from there into a barrel. The wood was lit by a torch and covered with dirt so that the fire would not burn too quickly, but would last for several days. Holes were opened at certain locations to allow the entry of air.

The second day after the fire was started, tar—a thick, black, combustible liquid—began to run into the barrel. As soon as a barrel was filled, another was set in its place. Pitch was made by boiling tar in iron kettles and distilling it to its dark-colored remains. Turpentine was made by combining resin with a volatile oil; the resulting mixture was called oil of turpentine or spirits of turpentine. The sites where tar kilns once operated can still be seen around North Myrtle Beach today. They seem to be particularly abundant on the area's golf courses.

It was local geography, rather than the production of naval stores, that was chiefly responsible for making Horry County distinct from its neighbors. Entirely separated from the rest of South Carolina by the Lumber and Little Pee Dee rivers and their swamps, Horry County was left out of many of the changes occurring around the state, and its people developed a distinctive lifestyle and a characteristic temperament that are evident even today. As early as 1856, Horry County was being called "the Independent Republic of

Horry." Horryites have always been autonomous.

A new crop introduced in the latter part of the nineteenth century promised to make the area even more distinct. When J. W. Holliday arrived in Horry County in 1869, he came with the idea that the local soil would be excellent for the growing of tobacco. Holliday proved to be a man of foresight, as his tobacco venture turned the county's economy in a new direction. Within the span of a couple of generations, Horry County was known far and wide for its production of flue-cured tobacco. "We make as good tobacco as is made anywhere in the world," John Monroe Holliday, grandson of J. W. Holliday, once boasted. (For more information on the Holliday family, see The Calabash to Bucksport Tour.)

However, the expected period of affluence did not follow. In the mid-1890s, the annual per capita income in Horry County was said to be $2.50. Most local people were out of work during the Depression, and those who found work made only pennies a day. But the citizens of Horry County persevered, practicing frugality and even returning to the barter system of earlier days. It wasn't long before another source of revenue emerged, one that erased the hard times experienced during the first third of this century and that promises to continue to bring prosperity for the foreseeable future—tourism. Just twenty-five years after the Depression, Crescent Beach and the neighboring beaches were so popular that they were already experiencing traffic tie-ups on holiday weekends.

Continue on Ocean Boulevard for 0.7 mile through Crescent Beach to S.C. 65. Turn right and follow S.C. 65 for 0.3 mile to U.S. 17. Turn left and proceed 0.2 mile, then turn left onto South Atlantic Street to see Atlantic Beach.

Atlantic Beach is an intriguing place. Its Ocean Boulevard has never been connected to its counterparts in Crescent Beach to the north and Windy Hill Beach to the south, necessitating the roundabout route back to U.S. 17. Atlantic Beach has been, is now, and seems destined to remain a strongly independent entity.

In 1933, developer George Tyson purchased a tract of oceanfront land and named it Pearl Beach; the name was subsequently changed to Atlantic Beach. Times were tough during the Depression and World War II. Beaches were segregated in those days, with the prime locations reserved for use by whites. The Atlantic Beach Company decided to set aside part of its oceanfront property for use by blacks, the objectives being to boost the local economy and to provide a rare beach haven for the enjoyment of the black community. A charter of incorporation was granted on June 30, 1966. A year after that, when

Cherry Grove Beach, Ocean Drive Beach, Crescent Beach, and Windy Hill Beach joined to form North Myrtle Beach, Atlantic Beach rejected all efforts to be annexed.

"We didn't want to be swallowed up and squeezed out by the white beaches," explained Saudi "Doc" Kuka, the proprietor of an Atlantic Beach lunch counter. Today, a large percentage of the year-round residents of Atlantic Beach are black.

Local residents have long had to weigh their proud independence against the prosperity that following the trends at neighboring beaches might bring. "We're in bad shape and everybody knows it," said James Lewis, owner of Atlantic Beach's biggest motel. "That's why the tourists drive through, stay a few hours, and go someplace else."

There are some who believe that Atlantic Beach can have both independence and prosperity. "Actually, we see it as the pearl of the Grand Strand," said Mayor Cleveland Stevens. "We're just waiting on the pearl to develop.... Let's face it. Despite all the court-ordered integration, blacks and whites are born

Fishermen seining at Atlantic Beach

and raised in different cultures. If we work hard to enhance what we already have, we can create something that's unique on the Grand Strand . . . something akin to Bourbon Street in New Orleans, a separate entity with a unique lifestyle built around ethnic food, jazz, and entertainment."

The going hasn't been easy for Atlantic Beach, as the sixty-year-old black-owned resort remains pitted in a motionless tug of war against its more affluent neighbors.

Every fall, Atlantic Beach is mobbed by visitors who come to see local fishermen stretch their nets into the breakers and draw in a variety of fish. Sometimes, residents pull a big, black pot out over the dunes and deep-fry a portion of their catch right on the strand, serving up the fish on slices of bread. Sea gulls enjoy the seining process, too; they get to eat whatever remains on the sand after the nets have been dragged back into the sea. All of this is quite a spectacle if you're lucky enough to stroll the beach on a day when the fishermen are seining. They work with lightning speed, yelling instructions to each other and concentrating so completely on pulling in their catch that you're

White Point Swash with Windy Hill Beach in the background

TOURING THE COASTAL SOUTH CAROLINA BACKROADS

likely to get tangled in their nets if you don't watch out.

Retrace you route on South Atlantic Street. Turn left on U.S. 17 and head south for 1.4 miles until you reach 48th Avenue South at Windy Hill Beach. Turn left and continue 0.5 mile to White Point Swash. Until recent years, White Point Swash was a place of wild beauty and a prime spot for shrimping and crabbing. Today, the bluffs overlooking the inlet are lined with shops, cottages, and hotel complexes, but you can still drop in a line with a fish head tied to it and catch yourself a blue crab of considerable size. Marsh grass and plankton provide the food for the sea creatures that make their home in the inlet—shrimp, oysters, and even flounder, in addition to crabs.

If you care to drive along the few blocks that make up Ocean Boulevard in Windy Hill Beach, you may be interested to learn that the buildings on the ocean side were all constructed after Hurricane Hazel crashed the coast in 1954. The buildings on Ocean Boulevard were either washed away or left in shambles. An immediate cleanup was begun, and some local residents went so far as to speculate—or perhaps rationalize—that the hurricane could only be blamed for removing the old construction that should have been destroyed anyway. People who live along the Grand Strand are perpetually concerned with the prospect of hurricanes, but they refuse to be frightened away by them.

Retrace 48th Avenue South and turn left onto U.S. 17. The Meher Spiritual Center, a secluded area that stretches from U.S. 17 to the sea, is on the left after 1.6 miles. A narrow dirt road begins at a mailbox by the highway and meanders through a virgin hardwood forest to a group of wood cabins nearer the ocean. Travelers should note that reservations are necessary to enter the gate.

Meher Baba, whose name means "compassionate father," was a spiritual leader who established a colony in India to provide shelter and free hospital care for the poor. He encouraged his followers to establish other spiritual colonies, directing that any such centers should be built on virgin land with ample water; that they should have good soil and a moderate climate; and most important, that their land should be "given from the heart." The late Elizabeth Patterson lived in India for an extended period of time and was a disciple of Meher Baba. In 1943, she visited her father, Simeon B. Chapin, at his home in Myrtle Beach and told him that she had found a local tract of land that would be an ideal site for a spiritual center. Chapin was able to acquire the land, which he then "gave from the heart" to his daughter. The facility organized by Elizabeth Patterson was not long in gaining popularity. It has numbered among its patrons rock superstar Pete Townshend of The Who.

You are likely to see the name Chapin in many places throughout Myrtle

Beach. Among the local institutions named for philanthropist Simeon B. Chapin are the Chapin Memorial Library, the Chapin Foundation of South Carolina, Chapin Memorial Park, and the Chapin Department Store. In the days before he started investing in the Grand Strand, Simeon B. Chapin owned brokerage firms and family homes in Chicago and New York, as well as an additional home in Pinehurst, North Carolina. When he came to South Carolina in 1912, he went into partnership with Frank and Don Burroughs to create the Myrtle Beach Farms Company, still one of the leading forces on the Grand Strand. Stories of Chapin's generosity continue to be told in the area today.

Approximately 1.2 miles past the Meher Spiritual Center, you will reach Restaurant Row, a stretch of highway several blocks long with a heavy concentration of fancy restaurants featuring a variety of cuisines. Shortly after entering Restaurant Row, you will notice a chairlift rising high above the Intracoastal Waterway. The chairlift carries golfers to Waterway Hills Golf Course, the only course in the world reached by a tram over such a waterway. The time involved in crossing is just about right for golfers to change into their golf shoes.

There is a traffic light at the corner of Lake Arrowhead Road approximately 0.3 mile from the chairlift. Turn left onto Lake Arrowhead Road and drive 1.1 miles to Shore Drive, at the ocean. Turn right. After you weave among the high-rise buildings for about 0.5 mile to Shore Drive's terminus, you will reach Singleton Swash, where this tour ends.

In 1791, when George Washington was making a tour of the South Carolina Low Country, he dined with Jeremiah Vereen, who lived near Singleton Swash. After the meal, Vereen transported Washington and his party by ferry. As Washington noted in his diary, "Mr. Jeremiah Vereen piloted us across the Swash (which at high water is impassable, and at times, by the shifting of the sands is dangerous) on the Long beach of the ocean, and it being a proper time of the tide we passed along it with ease and celerity to the place of quitting it." Washington recorded his impressions of other places along the Grand Strand, but it is believed that his tour of the area began here, and Singleton Swash has long been considered a special place for that reason. (For more information on George Washington's visit to the area, see The Calabash to Bucksport Tour.)

On the opposite side of the swash, on the present site of the Dunes Golf and Beach Club, is the place that is believed to have been the first campsite used by Myrtle Beach vacationers. Today, the Grand Strand is sometimes referred to as the camping capital of the world; you may have already noticed signs for some of the hundreds of campsites in the area. In the old days, the first order of business for campers upon their arrival was to get a supply of fresh water from one of the nearby residences. Men slept in wagons or on the sand, while women and children bedded down on mattresses brought from home. Fathers and sons fished by dropping lines into the surf or seines into the swash; as the sun went down, the aroma of fish frying on open fires rose among the pines. Mothers and daughters spent their time salting fish for winter use or washing clothes in salt water and spreading them in the sun to bleach.

Singleton Swash was also the site of a saltworks during the Civil War. A large tank for storing salt water sat near where the eleventh fairway of the Dunes Golf and Beach Club is today. The brick foundations for salt-boiler evaporator pans can still be seen along the banks of the inlet. More than thirty buildings made up the Singleton Swash salt-making operation. The factory's warehouses could accommodate some 2,000 bushels of salt. There was also a horse-powered mechanical lift that pumped seawater from the swash to the 200,000-gallon storage tank. Despite precautions taken by the operators, Union mariners destroyed the factory in April 1864. Recent excavations have revealed ceramic grinding balls, whose presence suggests that there may also have been a Confederate gunpowder factory on the site.

Singleton Swash

Singleton Swash is a place with a long, rich history, yet it is located among tall hotels and ultramodern development. With its rich mixture of the old and the new, it comes awfully close to capturing the essence of today's Grand Strand.

If you plan to head into the heart of Myrtle Beach after your visit to Singleton Swash, retrace your route to U.S. 17 and turn left, heading south.

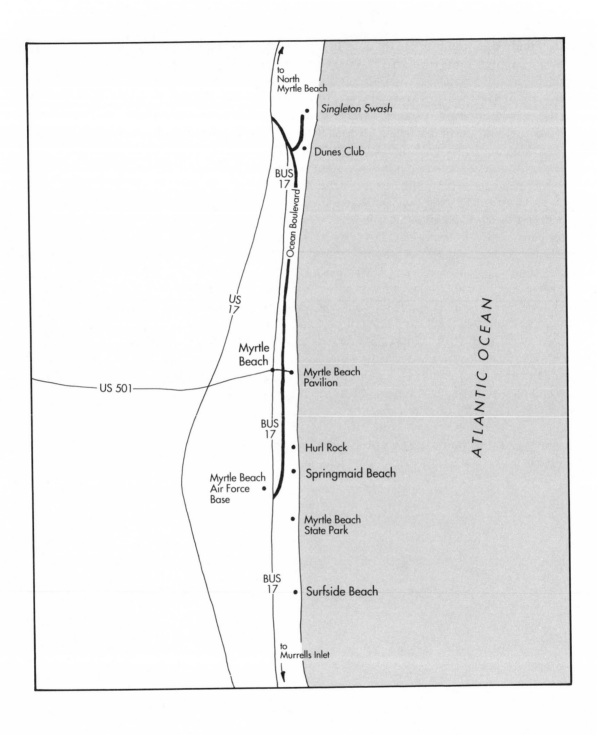

to
North
Myrtle Beach

Singleton Swash

Dunes Club

BUS
17

Ocean Boulevard

US
17

Myrtle
Beach

US 501

Myrtle Beach
Pavilion

BUS
17

Hurl Rock

Springmaid Beach

Myrtle Beach
Air Force
Base

Myrtle Beach
State Park

BUS
17

Surfside Beach

to
Murrells Inlet

A T L A N T I C   O C E A N

The Myrtle Beach Tour

This tour explores some of the popular attractions and some of the hidden treasures of Myrtle Beach, the centerpiece of the Grand Strand. It begins at the Dunes Club, considered the northern entrance to Myrtle Beach. It then heads south on Ocean Boulevard to explore such attractions as Caravelle, the Ocean Forest Hotel's former site, the wreck of the *Freeda A. Wyley*, and the Myrtle Beach Pavilion, with its historic merry-go-round. The tour then visits Hurl Rock before ending at Myrtle Beach Air Force Base, the southern terminus of the city.

Total mileage:
approximately 10 miles.

This tour covers the entire length of Myrtle Beach's Ocean Boulevard from north to south, discovering en route the origins of the Grand Strand's golfing and recreational boom. Ocean Boulevard runs roughly parallel to, and just to the east of, U.S. 17 Business. It begins at the Dunes Club, where travelers can catch a glance of historic Singleton Swash, believed to have been George Washington's first stop on his tour of the South Carolina coast in 1791. (For more information on Singleton Swash, see The Northern Grand Strand Tour.)

Head south on Ocean Boulevard. It is 1.9 miles from the Dunes Club to the oceanfront complex called Caravelle, on the left. Caravelle was built by George Miller "Buster" Bryan, the first man in the area to envision offering package deals combining golf, lodging, and meals. With a push from merchants, bankers, the city council, and the golf clubs themselves, it wasn't long before Bryan's dream began to be realized. Six outstanding courses constructed in the 1960s got the ball rolling by attracting some of golfing's all-time greats. Jimmy D'Angelo, golf pro at the Dunes Club, became the administrator of Golf Holiday, a firm that worked to combine the interests of local motels and golf courses. The advent of the "golf package" brought phenomenal growth and helped make the Grand Strand a kind of "golf coast."

With the possible exception of Fort Lauderdale, Myrtle Beach has experienced the most rapid growth in golfing of any region in the nation. It has been estimated that the proliferation of new courses will continue through the year 2000. Golfing brought a new lifestyle to this section of the coast, as condominiums were constructed on every available inch of land and it became the "in" thing to own a condo at Myrtle Beach.

On the right opposite Caravelle is the former site of a World War II prisoner-of-war camp. Conway resident Walter Luff was a prisoner at the camp. At the

Dunes Club

age of eighteen, the German-born Luff was flying his forty-eighth mission as a Luftwaffe fighter pilot when his plane took a direct hit from a British antiaircraft gun and crashed in Tunisia. He was kind enough to talk to me about the wartime atmosphere in Germany and his experiences at the Myrtle Beach camp:

> In June 1944, 250 of us were sent to Myrtle Beach, and our camp was exactly where 71st Avenue is today. We cleared out live oaks and myrtle bushes and built a camp between the A&P and the Caravelle and put up tents to accommodate 4 people to a tent. The compound was fenced in and 30 guards and the captain were outside. My captain, Captain Fleming, was about 30 years old.
>
> We started working at Myrtle Beach Lumber Company and Myrtle Beach Farms, in the lumber business. Out of 250 men, I would estimate that at least 100 worked in cutting pulpwood. Only a very few prisoners were unskilled labor. Most were highly skilled technicians. The toughest part was adjusting to the heat, but we finally became accustomed to it.
>
> It was while I was in Myrtle Beach that it came to me just what Hitler had led Germany into. We were not loved, as he had said, and we were not the people of salvation. He was evil, self-serving for the Nazi ideal.
>
> We had all, as youngsters, been required to join the Hitler Youth, and it was a must—premilitary training pure and simple. For one who was born free, to go to a Hitler Youth meeting, it would seem regimented, unreal.
>
> I hate to say it, but Hitler was a powerhouse. Magnetic. Someone with tremendous power. I was from Nuremberg, and I first saw him at a Nazi party rally. You would not believe how that man affected people. Highly educated people. Perhaps mass hysteria took over. Everyone was anticipating him, and then he arrived. It was like a Hollywood production. Bands played, flags waved. Hollywood could never have done any better. And Hitler must have known exactly how a mass of people would react. He gave them hope, hate, and all human feelings. He was simple enough for the uneducated, and yet not too simple for the educated. *Germany above all.* It's amazing how gullible I was.

Luff was interned at the Myrtle Beach camp until March 1946. He even saved a man's life during the course of his imprisonment. He was working at a pulpwood camp one day when an army bomber crashed nearby; Luff hurried to the scene and pulled the pilot from the wreckage.

After his release, Luff returned to Nuremberg to find what he estimated to be 80 percent of his hometown destroyed—"rubble over rubble," as he put it.

He may have left Myrtle Beach and returned to his native land, but local people didn't forget him. In fact, the late E. Craig Wall of Conway remembered Luff's work in the pulpwood trade so well that he visited him in Germany in 1955 and offered him a job in the United States. Luff took him up on the offer; Luff's son is still employed by Wall's organization, Canal Industries, Inc. It must be highly unusual for former prisoners of war to want to return and set up homes near the place of their internment. But the fact is that other World War II prisoners at the Myrtle Beach camp now count themselves as local residents, too. Perhaps that says something about Grand Strand hospitality.

Cabanas along Ocean Boulevard

Outside terrace of Ocean Forest Hotel
Courtesy of Ralph Chandler

Continue south on Ocean Boulevard. It is another 1.1 miles to the Ocean Forest Villa Resort, on the right, the former site of the Ocean Forest Hotel. In the 1920s, the late Woodside brothers of New York and Greenville, South Carolina, purchased a large parcel of Myrtle Beach land. They planned to develop what they vowed would be the finest recreational facility in the world, better even than those in the south of France. The Woodsides were mill owners. They had already constructed the Poinsett Hotel in Greenville, and they were acknowledged to be South Carolina's master builders. The first phase of their Grand Strand complex was the Ocean Forest Hotel, built in 1929 at a cost of well over $1 million. Next came the Ocean Forest Country Club—now Pine Lakes Country Club—with an eighteen-hole golf course designed by Robert White. However, times turned tough during the Depression, and ownership

Lavish buffet at Ocean Forest Hotel
Courtesy of Ralph Chandler

of the Ocean Forest Hotel passed through a number of hands.

In September 1974, a large hotel chain offered a considerable sum of money for the land on which the Ocean Forest Hotel sat. The owners were eager to get rid of the acreage, so they hired a demolition company from Atlanta to take down the hotel. Their mistake was in not finalizing the deal with the hotel chain *before* making arrangements for demolition. The demolition company came to town, threw up a chain-link fence around the property, and advertised a major liquidation sale to be held the day before their iron ball smashed the historic hotel. People arrived from several states to buy window sashes, light fixtures, lamps, and every other item auctioned off. But by the time the iron ball had done its work and the owners of the property contacted the hotel chain to formally agree to the sale, the hotel chain had changed its mind. The owners were left with thirteen acres, a sizable bill from the demolition company, and no hotel. However, the story has a happy ending, as Ocean Forest Villa Resort was eventually constructed on the property. It is one of the most popular condominium complexes on the Grand Strand.

Continue south on Ocean Boulevard. Beginning at about 51st Avenue North, you will be traveling along a 20-block stretch that is one of the few residential beach areas on the ocean; the Myrtle Beach city fathers are firm in their conviction that it shall remain that way.

It is 1.2 miles from Ocean Forest Villa Resort to 43rd Avenue North, where you can park at the beach-access area and walk a few steps on the beach to the remains of the shipwrecked *Freeda A. Wyley*.

In August 1893, a hurricane struck the coast of the Carolinas. The *Freeda A. Wyley* was sailing from Pascagoula, Mississippi, to New York with a load of yellow pine lumber when she was apparently struck by lightning, according to the late Dr. Reinhold Engelmayer, archaeology professor at Coastal Carolina College. The ship was reported on fire 30 miles north of Frying Pan Shoals at the mouth of the Cape Fear River, off the southern part of North Carolina. The crew escaped on lifeboats and survived the raging storm, but the *Freeda A. Wyley* did not. She was last reported burned to the water line off Myrtle Beach. Many years later, receding sand on the beach at 42nd Avenue North exposed the hull and a portion of the superstructure of the 507-ton vessel. It is said that people came with chain saws to remove the remaining superstructure and patches of copper sheathing. But there is still enough of the skeleton left on the beach to excite anyone interested in old ships.

Continue south on Ocean Boulevard. If you care to make a short side trip to the Myrtle Beach Convention Center and its South Carolina Hall of Fame, turn

Remains of the shipwrecked
Freeda A. Wyley
Courtesy of Tom Garrison

The South Carolina Hall of Fame is housed in the Myrtle Beach Convention Center.

right on 21st Avenue North and follow it 1 block across U.S. 17 Business. The South Carolina Hall of Fame honors past and contemporary citizens who have made outstanding contributions to the heritage of the Palmetto State.

It is 2.2 miles on Ocean Boulevard from 43rd Avenue North and the *Freeda A. Wyley* to the Gay Dolphin gift shop. The Gay Dolphin opened for business in 1944 on the boardwalk at 910 North Ocean Boulevard in a building about half the size of a mobile home. It is in the same location today, but it has been expanded to include the three-story building extending from the boardwalk to the ocean, another building across the street facing Ocean Boulevard, and the nearby Straw Cove building. And two huge warehouses are entirely off the premises. On any summer day, the Gay Dolphin's customers number in the thousands. From its humble beginnings, the store has grown into one of the largest gift shops you are ever likely to see. According to owner Justin Plyler, more than sixty thousand different items are available on the premises.

It is only 1 block from the Gay Dolphin to the Myrtle Beach Pavilion; abundant parking is available nearby. The pavilion is the most popular attraction at Myrtle Beach aside from the beach itself. Indeed, many people feel that a trip to the Grand Strand isn't complete unless you've "hung out" at the Myrtle Beach Pavilion. The present pavilion is not the first one to attract crowds to the area. In fact, one way to trace Myrtle Beach's history is to take

The old Myrtle Beach Pavilion, built in 1923, was destroyed by fire in 1944.
Courtesy of Stewart Pabst, Horry County Museum

A shorefront scene in early Myrtle Beach
Courtesy of Stewart Pabst, Horry County Museum

a look at its pavilions, the first of which was attached to the Sea Side Inn, the town's first hotel, which was located less than 1 block inland from the present pavilion and amusement park.

There was nothing on the beach before 1900, save for a farm and a cotton gin operated by the Conway firm of Burroughs and Collins. Under the direction of Frank A. Burroughs, a railroad line was built from Conway to the seashore in 1900. People from Conway took a ferry across the Waccamaw River, then boarded a little train called the Black Maria for the trip. Once tourists began

Myrtle Beach in the 1920s
Courtesy of Stewart Pabst, Horry County Museum

Early vacationers at Myrtle Beach
Courtesy of Stewart Pabst, Horry County Museum

Florence Theodora Epps, pictured here on a friend's shoulders, was the first woman to have a lifesaving certificate.
Courtesy of Stewart Pabst, Horry County Museum

riding the rails, it seemed the perfect time to give the beach area a name other than New Town, as it was known in contrast to Conway's traditional nickname of Old Town. A contest was held in 1900 to choose a name, and Adeline Cooper Burroughs submitted Myrtle Beach in honor of the region's abundant wax myrtle bushes. Myrtle Beach it became.

The Sea Side Inn was operating by 1901. It was gray with a red roof, and its windows were framed in white. Rates at the well-kept country inn were $2 a day for a room and three meals. The facility had no plumbing or electricity. Fishing boats belonging to the inn took to the water each morning and headed for an underwater rock formation 10 or 12 miles offshore. They returned in late afternoon, usually with an abundant catch of rockfish, blackfish, and other species. The fish were served in the inn's dining room. When the catch was larger than needed for the guests, buckets of fish were sold to the people who owned cottages near the beach.

A boardwalk led from the Sea Side Inn to the original octagonal pavilion. Local fiddlers and other musicians entertained guests in the evenings. Couples came to dance. One night, it was learned that a certain man in the audience could play the piano; the story goes that the man was pressed into service and

Sea Side Inn, Myrtle Beach's first hotel
Courtesy of Stewart Pabst, Horry County Museum

TOURING THE COASTAL SOUTH CAROLINA BACKROADS

made to play until dawn, even though he repeatedly complained of being too tired to continue. By 1922, the pavilion was so popular that it could no longer accommodate all the dancers. It was enlarged to double its original size, and notices were sent out that a splendid string orchestra had been engaged by the management.

The following year, a new pavilion was constructed on the site of the current pavilion. The wooden structure was built high off the ground, and it was so large that it filled an entire block. The new facility had even greater success in luring people to Myrtle Beach. Between 1930 and 1944, the area experienced population growth of 500 percent; in a story published in the local newspaper on Thursday, April 14, 1944, it was boasted that Myrtle Beach's growth percentage exceeded that of any other community in the state of South Carolina. The second pavilion was destroyed on December 28, 1944, in a fire of undetermined origin.

By 1949, young people were enjoying a brand-new pavilion on the site of the one that burned. They were also getting their first taste of a new style of music and a new dance. The Grand Strand is synonymous with beach music and the shag, which were born in the late forties and began to gain in popularity during the fifties and sixties. (For more information on beach music and the shag, see The Northern Grand Strand Tour.)

One of the hand-carved horses on the Myrtle Beach merry-go-round

Even if you aren't in the mood to zoom up, out, around, upside down, or sideways, you might take a minute to observe the rides at the amusement park before you leave the pavilion area. The first ride ever installed at the pavilion was a small merry-go-round. The current merry-go-round is the most popular ride at the Myrtle Beach Pavilion today. As one of fewer than a hundred hand-carved carousels in existence, it is a real treasure.

The carousel was built by the Herschell-Spillman Company of New York in 1912, though the two elephants on the ride date back to 1890. The company actually built five hand-carved, custom-finished merry-go-rounds at the same time, but the one at the Myrtle Beach Pavilion is the only one still in existence. The animals on the carousel present a striking array of colors, everything from the most delicate pastels to the most flamboyant primary shades. An Indian pinto pony, a medieval armored steed, lions, zebras, pigs, giraffes, ostriches, frogs, cats, storks, llamas, mules, camels, goats, sea monsters, dogs, roosters, and a pair of chariots provide fifty seats. The figures are arranged three abreast on a bi-level platform. Some are stationary, while others move up and down as the carousel rotates to the music of its 1920-vintage Wurlitzer organ.

The German organ built for the 1900 World Exposition is now a feature attraction at the pavilion.

TOURING THE COASTAL SOUTH CAROLINA BACKROADS

You may notice a little white building within the amusement park with a small grandstand arranged around it. The building houses a second organ, built by the German firm of A. Ruth & Sohn. The German organ is a story unto itself. After being featured at the World Exposition in 1900, it was pulled from village to village around the German countryside by a team of six horses. People gathered from far and wide to listen and dance. The organ was brought to a Massachusetts home on Martha's Vineyard some years after that. In 1954, it was sold to the Myrtle Beach Farms Company, which made it a feature attraction at the pavilion. The organ continues to play to standing-room-only crowds from June through Labor Day. Some of its original music sheets are still used. The organ has four hundred pipes and ninety-eight keys. One of its most identifiable features is the collection of eighteen figures displayed across its front side; twelve of the figures actually move in rhythm to the music. Many people come to see the organ just to appreciate the workmanship of its cabinet.

The pavilion is still owned by the Myrtle Beach Farms Company. The firm was started in the 1920s when New York stockbroker Simeon B. Chapin came to Myrtle Beach to look at some property offered for sale by Burroughs and Collins, the Conway firm. Chapin hit it off so well with Burroughs and Collins that they decided to consolidate interests to form the Myrtle Beach Farms Company. The company is a vital one on the Grand Strand today, with Myrtle Square Mall counted among its properties.

Continue south on Ocean Boulevard. It is 1 block from the pavilion to the Chesterfield Inn, on the left, one of the oldest hotels on the beach. The earliest cottages in Myrtle Beach were constructed on the site where the Chesterfield Inn sits today. The first was built by a Conway pharmacist named Dr. Epps, and it was followed in 1907 by a cottage belonging to the Barrett family, also of Conway. The Barretts paid $25 for their oceanfront lot and $75 for the construction of their cottage, prices that probably wouldn't buy a house made of matchsticks on a lot the size of a postage stamp in today's Grand Strand realty market.

Annette Epps Reesor, Dr. Epps's daughter, spent many vacations at the family cottage, called Brightwaters. She recorded her memories of the old days in a piece included in *The Independent Republic of Horry, 1670–1970*, published by the Horry County Historical Society:

> About four-thirty in the afternoon the fish boats came in. It was my great pleasure and responsiblity to buy the large string of blackfish (about twelve) from (the fisherman) Sump. The fish cost a quarter, and I shined my coin in the wet sand to make it exceedingly bright.
>
> . . . Looking for shells was second only to swimming. The rough walls of "Brightwaters" . . . were gay with garlands of sea biscuits, devil's pocketbooks, and other treasures from the deep.
>
> Watermelons were delightful mid-afternoon snacks, and a chilled one was usually cut when we returned from swimming. Rinds were thrown in the back yard for the chickens to pick clean. Billy Barrett's August birthday was always celebrated with cake, candles and a watermelon!
>
> . . . Evenings were glorious starlit wonders. All the children and dogs in the neighborhood gathered on the sand dunes between our house and the Barretts' to gaze at the stars and tell ghost stories.

There were several rows of dunes between the cottages and the sea during the first years of this century, and the ocean gave up fine specimens of seashells every day. Some descendants of the people who settled Myrtle Beach still have collections of those old seashells. As late as 1935, shells of exceptional quality could be found in abundance along the Grand Strand.

Local roads were greatly improved by 1912, though they were not yet paved. More and more visitors came for a dip in the ocean—a practice that was said to be therapeutic as well as pleasurable—and more and more beach cottages were built. Myrtle Beach was no longer South Carolina's best-kept secret.

Continue south for 0.5 mile from the Chesterfield Inn to the Second Avenue Fishing Pier, newly erected since it was destroyed in 1989 by Hurricane Hugo. During Prohibition, whiskey was shipped into Myrtle Beach from the Bahamas and Cuba, and one of the unloading sites was in the vicinity of the present Second Avenue Fishing Pier. One local story tells of a whiskey-running vessel that ran aground on a nearby sand bar during a particularly blustery night. The vessel's crew had to toss all the whiskey overboard to get the ship back afloat before they were discovered. When dawn came, the breakers were well-stocked with kegs of the contraband. Word spread quickly, and people arrived to help themselves to the bounty. One man was said to have collected and sold enough whiskey that day to buy himself a car.

It is 1.3 miles on Ocean Boulevard from the Second Avenue Fishing Pier to 20th Avenue South and Hurl Rock, a formation of rocks by the sea. Hurl Rock is an excellent place to look for seashells. Some unusual items have been known to wash up on this spot as well.

Just after the turn of the century, area citizens learned that a whale large enough to swallow Jonah had washed ashore at Hurl Rock. People came from Conway by train and over the dunes by wagon to see it, some of them carrying picnic baskets. The onlookers found the spectacle well worth the trip. Local resident Frank Burroughs, a tall man, stood next to the whale holding a hoe as high as he could, and the hoe did not reach the top of the whale. A day or

Hurl Rock

two later, a group of whalers arrived to claim their catch, explaining that they had harpooned the whale but were forced to cut the rope when a storm blew up. The whalers set to work removing the meat from the bones, after which they returned to their ship, leaving the whale's skeleton on the beach. Children played on it for months.

Continue 1 mile south to Springmaid Beach, developed in 1948 by Colonel Elliott White Springs and currently owned by Leroy Springs & Company. The development of Springmaid Beach was planned to accommodate the employees of Springs Mills, most of them residents of the South Carolina communities of Lancaster, Fort Mill, and Chester. Springs Mills workers get first choice of the facilities during June, July, and August. The beach is open to the public the rest of the year. Its principal patrons are church groups and senior citizens from the Palmetto State. Rates are considerably lower than at other oceanfront facilities. Springmaid Beach's thirty-four acres offer over four hundred motel units and campsites, a cafeteria, and a fishing pier. Springmaid Villa, once the beach home of the Springs family, is now owned by the Waccamaw Arts and Crafts Guild.

It is 0.5 mile from Springmaid Beach to where Ocean Boulevard ends at U.S. 17 and Myrtle Beach Air Force Base.

The armed forces began using local facilities in June 1940, when the United States Army Air Corps flew photographic and charting missions in the area and practiced gunnery along the beaches comprising the Grand Strand. Activity picked up rapidly with the approach of American involvement in World War II. The 112th Observation Squadron arrived in early 1941 to aid in coastal defense. A movement then began to establish a bombing and gunnery range. That range was officially designated Myrtle Beach Army Air Field on November 8, 1943. By that time, the armed forces were operating on a hundred thousand acres of owned and leased land in the area. Five air-to-ground ranges were located around Myrtle Beach, with a demolition range and three bombing ranges near Conway and a demolition range and two bombing ranges near Georgetown.

World War II was an unsettling time along the Grand Strand. Early in the war, the surf and sand were sometimes dirtied by oil from sunken tankers, the victims of the highly successful German U-boat campaign off the east coast.

Springmaid Villa

Beachfront residents might occasionally catch a faint glimpse of ships headed north, as convoys stayed close to shore for protection. When local people stepped outside their homes at night, they were likely to encounter Coast Guard patrols on horseback along the tide line; German saboteurs were believed to be trying to enter the area, and the patrols were on the lookout for them. Later in the war, the windows of houses on Ocean Boulevard were covered with black shades, and automobiles traveling at night had to be equipped with headlights painted black on their upper halves.

Local residents were edgy. An article that appeared in the *Horry Herald* on Thursday, April 9, 1942, speculated that "Hitler is trying to send along our shores the men he wants to spy and work for him. It must be so because it has been reported so many times, and because some of them have been caught." E. Craig Wall, the lumberman who convinced former prisoner of war Walter Luff to take up residence in the United States, remembered that "cigarette smoking outside the house was a memory and it was risky to walk outside after dark. Coast Guardsmen meant business, and they frequently fired warning shots overhead of someone who took instructions lightly."

The training of airmen at Myrtle Beach Army Air Field continued through the end of the war. Some of the men who flew with Lieutenant Colonel James Doolittle's famous raid on Tokyo were trained at the base. Meanwhile, some 114 buildings were being constructed and connected by a network of roads and runways. When personnel was short, Germans were brought in from Myrtle Beach's prisoner-of-war camp and given housekeeping detail.

Military activity in the area fell off after the war. The Department of Defense rehabilitated the base in 1953. The first commanding officer in the postwar period was Colonel (later General) Robert Emmons. During those years, men and planes from the base played a role in crises in Lebanon, Cuba, and the Dominican Republic, among other operations.

When professional observers discussed the United States Air Force's formidable night-fighting capability in the months before Operation Desert Storm, no one seemed to mention the A-10 Thunderbolt II—otherwise known as "the Warthog"—a unique lizard-green single-seater that had been in residence in Myrtle Beach since 1977. But the Warthogs were ready nonetheless. For several months, the 355th Tactical Fighter Squadron had been quietly practicing night fighting in the skies around the Grand Strand. And when the air war over Iraq and Kuwait began in the predawn hours of January 17, 1991, the A-10s had an important role to play. They destroyed enemy tanks and other armored vehicles with cannon shells and Maverick missiles; they struck targets to the rear before they could get to the battle lines; and they provided close air support for troops once the ground war finally began. By all accounts, they acquitted themselves admirably.

For years, the A-10s were a common sight around the Grand Strand as they took off in pairs, rose over the pines and the beach, and headed out on their training runs over the Atlantic. Those days became numbered in 1991, when Myrtle Beach Air Force Base was placed on a list of military facilities to be closed. However, it should be noted that the base served as Myrtle Beach's municipal airport throughout the time the Warthogs were in residence. It seems likely that its prominent role in the local economy will continue regardless of the fate of its military operations.

This tour ends at Myrtle Beach Air Force Base. If you would like to continue with the next tour, it begins nearby at Myrtle Beach State Park, on the opposite side of U.S. 17. If you are traveling south, make sure you take a glance back over your shoulder as you leave Myrtle Beach. It may seem difficult to believe that at the turn of the century all the area lying behind you was farmland.

Myrtle Beach in the 1960s
Courtesy of S. C. Dept. of Parks, Recreation, & Tourism

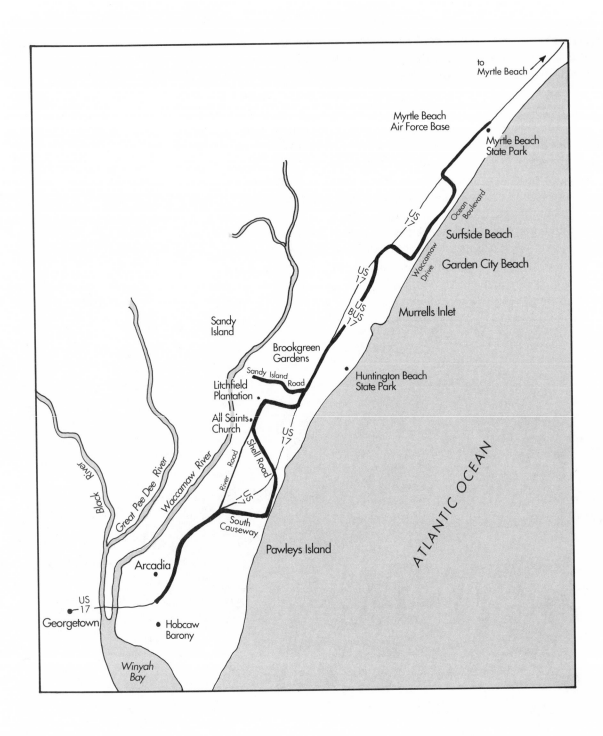

The Southern Grand Strand Tour

This tour covers the portion of the Grand Strand from Myrtle Beach south to the outskirts of Georgetown, taking frequent detours off U.S. 17 to the beaches and to the plantations inland. It begins at Myrtle Beach State Park and travels to Surfside Beach, Garden City Beach, Murrells Inlet, Brookgreen Gardens, and Huntington Beach State Park, which boasts Atalaya and the former site of the Hot and Hot Fish Club as two of its main attractions. It then heads past Sandy Island to Litchfield Plantation, Pawleys Island, and Arcadia before it ends at Hobcaw Barony.

Total mileage: approximately 43 miles.

This tour begins at Myrtle Beach State Park, just south of Myrtle Beach Air Force Base on the east side of U.S. 17. Though the state park is only a couple of miles removed from the hustle and bustle of Myrtle Beach, it seems closer in spirit to the old plantations to the south, thanks to its wide-open spaces and its relaxed atmosphere.

Myrtle Beach State Park was constructed by the Civilian Conservation Corps during Franklin Roosevelt's administration. It is currently the most popular park in the South Carolina state parks system. The park boasts the well-traveled Sculptured Oak Nature Trail and a wooded 350-site camping area that survived Hurricane Hugo in surprisingly good shape. If you happen to be passing through the area around mealtime, the park is an ideal place to organize a picnic and enjoy the breeze whipping off the ocean.

Drive south on U.S. 17. Approximately 2.4 miles from Myrtle Beach State Park, turn left onto Seventh Street North, just beyond Ocean Lakes Campground. You are now in Surfside Beach. Drive 0.7 mile to the ocean, then turn right onto Ocean Boulevard for a look at the village.

Like many other small towns, Surfside Beach has a rich tradition of local lore. In the nineteenth century, residents had to depend upon observations of animal behavior for their weather forecasting. It is said that when Surfside Beach people saw hogs running around and picking up sticks and trash, they knew cold weather was coming. Other signs of impending cold were birds fluffing their feathers and chickens clustering together late in the afternoon. A rooster crowing while standing on a fence was a sign of fair weather, while a rooster crowing on the ground meant rain. It was believed that killing a snake during hot, dry weather and hanging the skin belly side up in a tree brought rain.

In 1920, a man named George Holliday purchased a parcel of oceanfront land in the area and christened it Floral Beach in honor of his wife, Flora. The

*Pavilion at Myrtle Beach
State Park*

name was changed to Surfside Beach in 1950. For many years, Surfside Beach was a favorite among servicemen from Myrtle Beach Air Force Base. It is also known as a prime place for finding shark's teeth. The shiny, three-cornered teeth are sold in countless gift shops, but if you look closely enough, there's a chance you might find one right in the sand at Surfside Beach.

After traveling 2.5 miles on Ocean Boulevard, you'll notice that the name of the street has changed to Waccamaw Drive. That means that you are now in Garden City Beach, located on the line between Horry and Georgetown counties.

Oyster beds line much of the marshland around Garden City Beach. Well-known former slave Ben Horry spent the later years of his life in the area roasting oysters and serving them to the public. In the 1930s, the Federal Writers' Project undertook an ambitious program of recording the memories of elderly ex-slaves. Ben Horry took the opportunity to describe how he made his living from oysters: "Tide going out, I go out in a boat with the tide. Tide bring me in with sometimes ten, sometimes fifteen or twenty bushels. I make white folks a roast. White folks come to Uncle Ben from all over the country— Florence, Dillon, Mullins—every kind of place. Same price roast or raw, fifty cents a bushel." Groups from Myrtle Beach were among those who came to visit Ben Horry and his wife, Stella, at their property near Garden City Beach.

With its hundreds of oceanfront and creekside cottages and its mobile-home sites, Garden City Beach is a one-of-a-kind place. It will never be mistaken for Miami Beach or a New England seaside village. Rather, it offers a way of life that is unique to coastal South Carolina. And so many people have taken to that lifestyle—returning year after year to the same rental cottage or mobile home—that they are almost a migratory species.

Approximately 1 mile after Ocean Boulevard changes to Waccamaw Drive, you will reach an intersection with Atlantic Avenue in the heart of Garden City Beach. Turn right onto Atlantic Avenue. Drive 1 mile to U.S. 17 and turn left, heading south. Leave U.S. 17 for U.S. 17 Business after 0.9 mile, taking the left fork in the road at the South Strand Chamber of Commerce building—you'll notice a sign that says "Visitor Information." You will soon arrive in the center of Murrells Inlet, a creekside village that is known as South Carolina's seafood capital. Hurricane Hugo ravaged this area, but it is now back to normal. Restaurants await you on both sides of the road.

Murrells Inlet is the oldest fishing village in the state. Legend has it that Blackbeard and other pirates sailed into the inlet under the skull and crossbones and buried their treasure nearby, though none has ever been found. The village was established by, and named for, John Morrall, who purchased 610 acres in the area in 1731; the spelling of his name was corrupted over the years. Later, in the days when every inch of land along the Waccamaw River was planted in rice, Murrells Inlet proved to be a summer haven for rice-growing families trying to escape the heat and the mosquitoes of the plantations. Descendants of plantation owners still live in the village.

On the left 1 mile from the South Strand Chamber of Commerce is the former site of the Hermitage. Perhaps the best way to identify the site is to say that if you come to Chandler Avenue, you have gone 1 block too far. The property is best known for being the home of the ghost of Alice Flagg.

The Hermitage has just recently been moved a couple of blocks inland. To find it, turn right onto Chandler Avenue and drive 1 block. The Hermitage is the two-story white house just beyond the intersection of Chandler Avenue and Flagg Street.

Alice Flagg's story is a famous one. Her brother, Dr. Allard Flagg, was the owner of Wachesaw Plantation. He moved into the Hermitage in the late 1840s, and he generously invited Alice and his widowed mother to live with him. But

The Hermitage

family troubles were on the horizon. Alice committed the unpardonable sin of falling in love with a common lumberman, considered by Dr. Flagg and his mother to be well beneath their social station. They gave Alice a mandate not to see the lumberman again, but she disobeyed, letting her heart rule her actions. It was then decided that she should be sent to a boarding school in Charleston in hopes that she would come to her senses. However, the move only served to intensify her love to the point that she became physically ill. Word was sent to Dr. Flagg to go to Charleston and bring her home.

Alice died during her first night back in Murrells Inlet. She was buried beneath an oak tree in the garden at the original site of the Hermitage. Many times since her death, there have been reports of Alice's ghost roaming the house. Her apparition has been seen in the garden during thunderstorms, in her bedroom, and on the stairs—both ascending and descending.

The Hermitage remains a beautiful home, though it is not open to the public. It boasts twelve-foot ceilings, pine floors, and hand-blown window glass. The

Sea-going craft tied up at Murrells Inlet before a day of deep-sea fishing
Courtesy of S. C. Dept. of Parks, Recreation & Tourism

TOURING THE COASTAL SOUTH CAROLINA BACKROADS

Oliver's Lodge

status of Alice Flagg's ghost has yet to be determined since the house was moved.

Retrace your route to U.S. 17 Business and continue south. After 0.1 mile, you will pass a marina on the left. It is from that marina that Murrells Inlet's fleet of commercial fishing boats makes its daily run to the Gulf Stream in pursuit of snapper, grouper, sea bass, and other fish.

Another 0.1 mile brings you to Oliver's Lodge, the most historic of Murrells Inlet's restaurants. "Cap" William L. Oliver purchased the property in 1893 and first operated Oliver's Lodge as a fishermen's lodge and boardinghouse, according to Mike Andrews, a fifth-generation member of the Oliver family. His mother, Maxine Hawkins, is the current owner, and visitors can usually find her working as the cashier. The fifteen-room, two-story house looks much the same as it did when it opened.

On October 30, 1983, Oliver's Lodge hosted the wedding of popular detective writer Mickey Spillane and the former Jane Rogers of Marion, South Carolina. "It was a simple service—I do, let's eat," Spillane later quipped. "Then I took my wife on a honeymoon to the islands—Pawleys Island. We had a good time. There was nobody down there. And we'd come back to the house every day to check our mail and feed the cats and dogs." The Spillanes still have a home in Murrells Inlet. It was nearly washed away by Hurricane Hugo, but they have since rebuilt. It would be unfair to the Spillanes to tell the exact location of their house. Suffice it to say that it is precisely the kind of place you'd expect a famous writer to own in Murrells Inlet—a spacious Low Country house facing the sea, with a porch going all the way around it.

Continue on U.S. 17 Business for 0.3 mile from Oliver's Lodge to Spivey Avenue. Turn left onto Spivey Avenue, then right onto Creek Drive after 1 block. Creek Drive is an unpaved, extremely narrow street that meanders along the creek, hanging on the bank in front of the houses that face the marsh. The first impression most visitors have upon seeing Creek Drive is that there is absolutely no room for two cars to pass.

The houses along Creek Drive are expensive, though they are not elaborate. One of the most interesting of them, a home called Woodland, was built in the mid-1800s; it burned in the 1980s. Visitors from inland often don't have a full appreciation of the fury of coastal storms. The late Corrie Dusenbury lived at Woodland during her childhood, and toward the close of her life she was kind enough to tell me about the grave danger she experienced in a storm in 1893:

> Papa, a businessman, had gone to Georgetown that day and had left Mama in charge with the help of a hired man named Zack. When Zack came running up to Mama and said the waves had risen over the creek bank and were headed toward the house, she responded, with no emotion at all in her voice, "Place the flour barrel on the stove and all lower dresser drawers on the bed." After Zack had done this, he ran to the front door to bolt it. "Don't lock the door," Mama said quietly. "Open the door so when the water reaches it, it won't break the door down." It was Mama's lack of alarm that kept the children from becoming anxious. As long as she went about and spoke with such composure, we were not afraid. Mama called to the children and informed us that we should find a place on the stairs to sit. "Take the dog with you," she said, "and don't sit on a step too near the top nor too near the bottom."
>
> As we sat there, the water rushed through the house. On the water

were many things bobbing up and down, including some white chickens.

When the steamboat reached the landing at Wachesaw in the evening, Papa got on his mount and picked his way along the road, which was blocked by fallen trees. He met someone on the road who told him we were safe.

You may notice mounds of shells under some of the large trees on the bank of the creek. They are believed to date back to the time when Indians occupying what is now Murrells Inlet hosted the first cookouts ever held in this part of the country. Through the centuries, shells have been put to a variety of uses along the coast. Conch shells with holes knocked in them are believed to have been used as hoes by Indian women. And slave children on some plantations are said to have carried mussel shells for use as spoons.

Follow Creek Drive for 2 blocks, then turn right onto Vaux Hall Avenue. After 1 block, Vaux Hall Avenue brings you back to U.S. 17 Business at the location of a landmark restaurant called Lee's Inlet Kitchen, on the right. Eford and Pearl Lee's seafood eatery had only ten tables when it opened for business in 1948. The restaurant has been operated by the Lee family ever since that time, and its dining room has been enlarged to four times its original size. Credit for the success of Lee's Inlet Kitchen goes to the family's original recipes, some of which have been handed down for three generations.

Turn left onto U.S. 17 Business and continue south for 1.9 miles to a junction with U.S. 17. Bear left and drive 1.5 miles to Brookgreen Gardens. Anna Hyatt Huntington's sculpture entitled *The Fighting Stallions* stands at the entrance to this not-to-be-missed attraction. Drive onto the grounds and prepare yourself for an outdoor art experience like none you've ever seen before.

The plantations in the vicinity of Brookgreen Gardens have had a rich history. Nearby Laurel Hill, for example, was once owned by Gabriel Marion, nephew of legendary Revolutionary War figure Francis Marion. (For more information on Francis Marion, see The Swamp Fox Tour.) And the plantation called The Oaks passed through the hands of Joseph Alston, a South Carolina governor and the husband of Theodosia Burr, the only child of Aaron Burr.

The story of Theodosia Burr Alston is a well-known and tragic one. On December 30, 1812, disconsolate over the death of her ten-year-old son, she boarded a small vessel at Brookgreen Plantation and sailed down to Georgetown, where she in turn boarded the *Patriot*, a larger vessel bound for New York. It was hoped that a visit with her father in New York would be a

The Fighting Stallions *at Brookgreen Gardens*

The Visionaries
by Anna Hyatt Huntington

tonic to Theodosia in her depressed state. A gale was blowing as the *Patriot* set sail, and the talk on the wharf was that a violent storm was raging off Nags Head, North Carolina. Soon after the ship's sails were out of sight, rumors also began to spread that there were privateers active along the coast. The *Patriot*, Theodosia Burr Alston, and all the rest on board were never heard from again. Their exact fate has never been determined. (For more information on Theodosia Burr Alston and her family, see The Georgetown Tour.)

Brookgreen Plantation had its share of history, too. It once hosted a visit by George Washington, an event noted by Washington in his diary. By the middle part of the nineteenth century, the plantation had passed into the hands of Joshua John Ward, the grandest of all the Low Country rice planters. In 1838, Ward's overseer accidentally discovered a high-yield strain that came to be called "big-grain rice." By 1850, Brookgreen Plantation and its many slaves were producing nearly four million pounds of rice a year, the largest yield in the area.

Ward had a reputation as a stern taskmaster. His female slaves were expected to work at least a half-acre of rice per day in whatever task was assigned to them—planting, hoeing, or cutting and tying sheaves. And it was

Wood Nymph *by Henry Hering can be seen at Brookgreen Gardens.*

said that the women were not allowed to straighten up as they worked their
way from the beginning to the end of a row. Ward also raised sugarcane and
vegetable gardens at Brookgreen Plantation. His saltworks at Murrells Inlet
produced up to forty bushels of salt a day.

When Joshua John Ward died, he left his property to be divided among his
three sons, with no land or slaves going to any of his seven daughters. Real-
estate values plummeted during and immediately after the Civil War.
Brookgreen Plantation was sold to Dr. Lewis Hasell for the fire-sale price of
$10,000. The plantation passed through several owners through the early part
of this century, until it came into the hands of the Huntington family.

Archer Milton Huntington was the son of Collis P. Huntington, the man who
built the Southern Pacific Railway; the elder Huntington also ran several
important steamship lines and was considered one of the twelve richest men
in the United States during his day. In 1930, Archer Milton Huntington and his
sculptor wife, Anna Hyatt Huntington, were sailing their yacht, the *Rocinante*,
from New York to the West Indies when they received a communication from
their friend Isaac Emerson of Arcadia Plantation. Emerson informed them that
there were four prominent South Carolina plantations—Brookgreen, Laurel
Hill, The Oaks, and Springfield plantations—up for sale. The Huntingtons

Pelican and Fish
by Bruce Moore

sailed into Georgetown and disembarked to examine the properties. They then continued to the West Indies and back to New York, where they made the decision to buy the four properties.

Shortly after the purchase, the new owners were chatting with artist C. Paul Jennewein about Brookgreen Plantation. Jennewein suggested that they consider using the plantation as a setting for Anna's artwork. The idea immediately began to take root. Anna decided to transform the entire plantation into a garden that would serve as a background for her work, much of which was animal sculpture.

The late folklorist Genevieve Chandler told me about Archer Milton Huntington's role in the project: "Oh, he was a country gentleman, in his knickers, his high socks and his size thirteen shoes, which were made in London. He rode through the garden on a fine horse and supervised the work. Wild boars ran around, and deer were also in the forest. Then he would return to his office and sit by a fire of oak wood. He was very extravagant with oak wood, as there was plenty of it."

Huntington spread word that he was looking for a gardener who specialized in collecting and planting native wildflowers. Officials at Clemson University told him there was no better man in the whole state of South Carolina than Frank G. Tarbox, Jr. Tarbox was promptly hired. He spent many subsequent years searching the local woods for native plants and the variety of milkweeds found in the Low Country. Tarbox's influence on the landscaping and cultivating of Brookgreen Gardens is still visible today.

The South was in the depths of the Depression when Archer Milton

Duck and Turtle
by Albert Laessle

TOURING THE COASTAL SOUTH CAROLINA BACKROADS

Huntington arrived. Those who managed to find work earned only pennies a day. The transformation of Brookgreen Plantation brought a sudden upswing in the local economy, as Huntington gave area residents jobs in the gardens. When the rumor began to circulate that Huntington's income was $80,000 per *day*, requests for financial assistance increased. Huntington was sensitive to the people's needs. Among his gifts were such things as brick for a church building, flooring for the home of an employee, and a tombstone for an old man nearing his hundredth birthday. That tombstone was inscribed with the old man's name—Welcom Beese—but the date had to be left incomplete, reading 1833–19——. Welcom Beese didn't die until 1942, and the inscription was never finished. His remains rest in a graveyard administered by Faith Memorial Episcopal Church, located 3.8 miles south of Brookgreen Gardens on U.S. 17 at Pawleys Island.

As for Archer Milton Huntington, he died on December 11, 1955, at the age of eighty-six. His father had once said of himself that he would never be traced by the quarters he dropped or the money he gave away, but his son's obituaries noted that the younger Huntington had given away much of his multimillion-dollar fortune in founding and supporting museums.

It may have been Archer Milton Huntington's family money that bankrolled the transformation of Brookgreen Plantation, but it was the imagination of Anna Hyatt Huntington that made the gardens what they are today. As a close friend once said, "Mrs. Huntington was the boss [of the gardens' design] and Mr. Huntington had the money. He gave her $10 million to play with, to use in doing her sculpture."

The manor house occupied by Joshua John Ward and his family was gone by the time the Huntingtons bought Brookgreen Plantation, but Anna designed the gardens with the old Ward kitchen in the center. In fact, a boxwood garden that dates back to the Wards can still be seen outside the kitchen. Anna then set about acquiring notable works of sculpture and setting them against the rich backdrop of Frank G. Tarbox's gardening.

The main attraction at Brookgreen Gardens is the sculpture of Anna Hyatt Huntington herself. Anna was a pioneer in the use of aluminum as a sculpture medium. She was particularly fond of creating works featuring horses. As Genevieve Chandler recalled, "Mrs. Huntington was famous for her statues of horses. She always said she could carve anything if a horse were a part of the design."

One story about the gardens concerns the time that Anna summoned an employee to her studio and asked him to search the countryside for a horse scrawny enough to serve as a model for a statue featuring Don Quixote on his exhausted mount, Rocinante. The employee did his job well, returning to the studio with a horse that surely was dying, with its bones showing sharply through its rough coat, its heavy head hanging down nearly to its knees, and its mouth dripping foam. Anna made a sling to hold the emaciated horse upright so it could be used as a model. She was also moved by genuine sympathy. She fed the animal and nursed it back to health as she worked. "She wouldn't let anyone else care for the horse," noted George Besselieu, a former employee. "She let others clean the stable, but that was all."

The resulting statue of Don Quixote and Rocinante has been recognized as a masterpiece of detail. When he learned of it, C. Paul Jennewein—the man who first recommended turning Brookgreen Plantation into a sculpture garden—suggested to Anna that she next sculpt Sancho Panza, Don Quixote's rustic companion. Anna turned the tables on her friend by convincing *him* to undertake the rendering of Sancho Panza. In September 1971, Jennewein's vision of Sancho Panza joined Don Quixote and Rocinante in the garden near the visitor's pavilion. Another sculpture of Jennewein's, *Nymph and Fawn*, is also exhibited on the property.

Brookgreen Gardens is listed on the National Register of Historic Places. It is recognized as the earliest public sculpture garden in the United States and the model for others that have come since, and it remains the finest and largest collection of American sculpture on permanent outdoor exhibition. It is also

Don Quixote riding Rocinante, followed by Sancho Panza

TOURING THE COASTAL SOUTH CAROLINA BACKROADS

the largest grouping of the sculpture of Anna Hyatt Huntington, with works dating from 1901 all the way to 1973. Many pieces of historic and artistic significance make their home at Brookgreen Gardens, among them *Joan of Arc*, by Anna Hyatt Huntington; *Diana*, by Augustus Saint-Gaudens; *The End of the Trail*, by James Earle Fraser; and *The Fisher Boy*, by Hiram Powers, which was the recipient of important awards from the National Sculpture Society and the South Carolina Arts Commission. Some twenty-seven pieces of aluminum sculpture representing the work of twelve artists are on the site. Brookgreen Gardens is open every day except Christmas, with special events scheduled year-round. A fee is charged.

Anna Hyatt Huntington spent her last years at her home in Connecticut. When she died in October 1973 at the age of ninety-eight, her sculpture was being displayed all over the world. And the legacy she left at Brookgreen Gardens was gaining wider and wider recognition.

When you have finished enjoying the sculpture, retrace your route off the grounds and head across U.S. 17 to Huntington Beach State Park, located on the opposite side of the highway from Brookgreen Gardens. Huntington Beach State Park offers the best-preserved beach on the Grand Strand. It also offers alligators, which can often be seen patrolling or lounging around the banks of the marsh. The alligators are fed chicken, pork, and beef scraps about five o'clock each summer afternoon, a spectacle that may be viewed from the

Diana,
by Augustus Saint-Gaudens

A boardwalk at Huntington Beach State Park

relative safety of the park's boardwalks.

It is a drive of 1.4 miles on park property to Atalaya, a seaside home built by the Huntingtons that is now part of Huntington Beach State Park. For a small fee, visitors can explore this unusual structure. Atalaya was designed to serve as a winter residence, but the Huntingtons actually occupied the house for only a few weeks, as the cold and damp conditions there aggravated Anna's tuberculosis.

It's a shame that the Huntingtons didn't get more use out of their winter residence, because Atalaya was more than three years in the making. Building materials arrived at the railroad dock in Georgetown and were brought up the Waccamaw River by tugboat. Atalaya means "castle in the sand," and the name is not an overstatement. An inner courtyard surrounded by the four wings of the mansion contained fifty palm trees; two identical stairways rose from the courtyard to a flat roof affording a panoramic view of the sea. The living quarters at Atalaya consisted of thirty rooms, with additional space for servants, cooks, laundresses, housekeepers, and secretaries. An oyster-shucking room faced the ocean. A twenty-five-foot skylight allowed natural light to flood Anna's studio, located in the south wing. There were twenty-five fireplaces, and wrought-iron grillwork specially designed in Miami guarded the windows. The maids and laundresses were brought in from Scotland. "The little Scottish maids ran around, talking in their Scottish accent," one observer recalled. "They changed linens on the beds every morning. That was a luxury none of the rest of us could afford."

Anna had a great love of animals. A stable and cages for bears were located outside her studio at Atalaya. She was also the first American to import Scottish deerhounds; an elaborate five-room house was constructed on the property for the comfort of her two dozen dogs. It was a familiar sight during the middle part of this century to see Anna racing her Scottish deerhounds on the beach. Indeed, the dogs appeared to be as large as their owner. One was thirty inches tall at the shoulder and weighed nearly a hundred pounds. "They would put their paws on your shoulders and look you in the eye," remembered a close friend of the Huntingtons. "If they didn't like you they could be quite vicious."

Leaving Atalaya, drive another 1.3 miles along the park road to the northern end of the park. You'll notice a marker commemorating the Hot and Hot Fish Club. The club actually occupied several different locations over the course of its life, one of which was at the site of the marker. The other locations were in the general vicinity as well.

Views of Atalaya, the seaside home of the Huntingtons

Historical marker commemorating the Hot and Hot Fish Club

South Jetty at Huntington Beach State Park

The Low Country rice planters were a wealthy and close-knit group. One of the ways they set themselves above the rest of society was by organizing the Hot and Hot Fish Club. Robert Francis Withers Allston, the owner of Chicora Wood Plantation and a governor of South Carolina, recorded that the club was well-established in 1816. Joshua John Ward of Brookgreen Plantation later became a member. At that time, the clubhouse was on Drunken Jack Island in Murrells Inlet; Drunken Jack Island itself no longer exists, as hurricanes have reshaped the land and caused the island to disappear.

The rice planters were said to have enjoyed the happiest hours of their lives at the Hot and Hot Fish Club. They usually arrived at the club bearing covered dishes prepared at their plantations. A "fish boy" would then be sent out into the ocean to catch a boatload of fish, and as soon as he returned his catch would be cooked and served hot. While the fish were still being cooked, the fish boy would have to row back out into the breakers for another boatload, which would then be cooked and served hot as a second helping. Hence the name Hot and Hot Fish Club, for the two separate servings.

The facilities at the club included a racecourse, a billiard table, and a tenpin alley, but the real purpose behind the club's organization was to enable the planters to enjoy food, wine, and talk among their own kind. After the Civil

War, freed slaves tore down the clubhouse, but no one seemed to care. The way of life represented by the Hot and Hot Fish Club had already perished.

If you care to take an enjoyable stroll on the beach, leave your car in the parking lot just beyond the historical marker for the Hot and Hot Fish Club and head north on the strand. A walk of 1 mile brings you to the South Jetty, where many people come to fish or to sit on the rocks and watch the sea. The South Jetty's companion, the North Jetty, is located at the southern tip of Garden City Beach. The jetty project was initiated to stabilize the inlet so that commercial and recreational boats from Garden City Beach and Murrells Inlet could navigate the channel at all times, regardless of the tides. The project was completed in January 1979. The rocks that comprise the jetties weigh up to two hundred pounds. The South Jetty extends 3,445 feet from shore and has a top elevation of 9 feet above the low-water level.

After you have seen the former site of the Hot and Hot Fish Club, return to U.S. 17. The exit road bypasses Atalaya, so it is only 2.2 miles off the Huntington Beach State Park property. Turn left onto U.S. 17, heading south, and proceed 1 mile to Sandy Island Road. Turn right onto Sandy Island Road and drive 2.3 miles to the channel.

Sandy Island lies inland from Murrells Inlet and Brookgreen Gardens; it is encircled by the Waccamaw and Pee Dee rivers. You can't visit Sandy Island unless you arrange to go by boat, as there isn't—and never has been—a bridge connecting it to the mainland. If you're lucky, you might see the school boat, the *Prince Washington*, which carries island children across the water before and after their school day. If you want to make the trip yourself, you might contact a local marina, or you might ask someone to direct you to a Sandy Island resident who happens to be on the mainland.

All islands stake their claims to uniqueness, but Sandy Island's claim is indisputable. There are no gracious homes or spacious lawns here. In fact, there are no lawns at all. There is only sand covering the ground in front of the houses, so much of it that walking can prove difficult. During summer, residents always advise visitors to wear shoes, because the sand gets awfully hot and there is no way of escaping it. Electricity didn't come to Sandy Island until the mid-1960s, and telephones until about ten years after that. There is no ferry; residents make the five-minute trip to and from the mainland in their own boats. Some of Sandy Island's residents have spent eighty years on the island and seen very little "progress."

There is a rumor that developers are now looking to bring modernity to what has always been a changeless place. Such rumors are not new. In the early

A view of the North Jetty from the South Jetty at Huntington Beach State Park

1970s, a development company made plans to build houses on Sandy Island, but difficulties with permits and zoning laws led them to drop the project. Around the same time, Georgetown County laid the groundwork for instituting a local ferry. The islanders were overjoyed with that prospect, as crossing the river can be a major difficulty at times. One resident put it plainly: "When it rains, we get wet. If the wind's a-blowin', it'll blow you out of the boat." However, the ferry project proved too costly, as did plans for a bridge that would have connected the island to the mainland.

How Sandy Island came to be the way it is today makes an interesting story. For many years, the 24,000-acre island was the site of nine plantations owned by wealthy whites. But after the Civil War, Philip Washington, an ex-slave who had worked at a plantation named Pipe Down, bought land on the island from his former owner, Thomas Petigru. Washington then went on to establish a self-sufficient community of some thirty-two former slaves. Now, more than a hundred years later, the residents, who are descendants of Philip Washington's colony, still call sections of the island after the names of the old plantations. For example, there is a crossroads area in the center of the island that is known as Pipe Down.

Today, the 150 residents of Sandy Island resent being portrayed as primitive

The Sandy Island school boat

people who are not a part of the modern world. "We have houses and cars and are just like everyone else," said islander Hattie Mae Tucker. Sandy Islanders do face daily inconveniences, like having to leave their cars on the mainland, at Sandy Island Road. But they also enjoy a level of privacy and independence that is rare in contemporary society. Only time will tell whether their way of life will be preserved or whether forces beyond their control will drag them into the mainstream.

Retrace your route to U.S. 17 and turn right. It is 1.9 miles on U.S. 17 from Sandy Island Road to the entrance to Litchfield Country Club, on the right. Drive through the gates and continue 1 block, then turn left onto Cypress Drive. You are now in the middle of what was once Litchfield Plantation. When the Low Country rice planters reached the peak of their wealth, power, and influence between 1800 and 1860, they were among the wealthiest people in the entire nation. Litchfield Plantation was one of the most prosperous of the rice plantations. In recent years, inflation and rising taxes have led Georgetown County developers to transform many of the old plantations into residential communities.

After approximately 0.7 mile on Cypress Drive, turn left onto Pine Drive. Follow Pine Drive for 0.9 mile, then turn left back onto the meandering Cypress Drive. It is approximately 0.2 mile on Cypress Drive to a junction with River Road at the impressive Litchfield Plantation gate. The Litchfield manor house is located at the end of the avenue of oaks, and it looks much the same as it did when the Tucker family was planting rice 150 years ago. The manor house is now a bed-and-breakfast inn open only to guests.

The Litchfield Plantation property was purchased by Dan Tucker in the late eighteenth century, but it was under the supervision of his son, John Hyrne Tucker, that local rice-growing operations reached their peak. Some 1,140,000 pounds of rice were gathered by 201 slaves at Litchfield Plantation in 1850.

John Hyrne Tucker was most noted for his ugly nose, which had been badly pitted by smallpox. But his looks didn't stand in the way of a good love life— Tucker married four times. His third marriage produced seven children, one of whom was Dr. Henry Massingberd Tucker. There is a ghost story involving Dr. Tucker and Litchfield Plantation. Whenever Dr. Tucker returned from a sick call at night, he would strike the gatehouse bell with his riding crop, and the gateman would come to take the reins and lead the horse the rest of the way to the manor house. It is said that on certain nights—especially nights with a rain dripping through the Spanish moss—the sound of a riding crop tapping a bell can still be heard.

Turn left off Cypress Drive onto River Road and drive 0.5 mile to All Saints Church, on the right. It will be well worth your while to park your car and take a stroll through the burial ground.

Churches played a central role in the lives of plantation people during the first half of the nineteenth century. In this area, many residents attended All Saints Waccamaw Episcopal Church. The original church burned to the ground on December 12, 1915. The exterior design of the present All Saints Church is much like that of its predecessor, though the interior is different. Straight pews were installed rather than the old box pews, and there is of course no slave gallery as before.

All Saints Church has had many loving rectors down through the years, but none is remembered more fondly than Dr. Alexander Glennie. In 1829, a wealthy planter brought Glennie over from England to serve as a tutor. However, it was when his interest turned to the ministry that Glennie found his true calling. He was well-respected by both rich and poor, and his down-to-earth message was especially valued by the members of the congregation who were slaves.

Some of the grave markers in the cemetery at All Saints Church hint at high drama, like those of Arthur and Georgeanna Flagg of Wachesaw Plantation, who perished in a hurricane in October 1893. Others are decidedly humble, like that of Plowden Weston, whose inscription says merely that he fell asleep on January 25, 1864, at age forty-four. A monument in memory of George Pawley, the man who donated the land for the church, sits under an oak tree, while the markers for the family of Joshua John Ward of Brookgreen Plantation are at the back of the cemetery. Many believe that the stone inscribed *ALICE* marks the resting place of Alice Flagg, she of the famous ghost. In fact, there have been sightings of the ghost in this cemetery. But others claim that Alice Flagg was buried elsewhere.

Continue driving on River Road in your original direction. Approximately 0.3 mile from All Saints Church, you will reach an intersection with Shell Road; note your mileage carefully, as Shell Road is not clearly marked. Turn left onto Shell Road and travel 1.9 miles to a traffic light at U.S. 17. Turn left onto U.S. 17 and drive 0.3 mile to the collection of businesses called the Hammock Shops, on the right. A brief word about the local tradition of hammock making is a necessary introduction to Pawleys Island.

Joshua Ward, the grandson of Joshua John Ward of Brookgreen Plantation, is credited with being the first area resident to design a rope hammock. People who tried it found it so cool and comfortable that a relative of Joshua Ward's, A. H. Lachicotte, and his wife began to make hammocks and sell them in a building by the roadside, which they called the Hammock Shop. The Lachicottes' son, A. H. "Doc" Lachicotte, Jr., returned home after World War II and added a nursery beside the Hammock Shop; it was later phased out to make room for additional shops.

Hammocks have always been the most popular item on the premises, but all of the associated shops are uncommonly successful. Part of the credit goes to Doc Lachicotte for his insistence that each store have a distinctive Low Country rice-plantation feel about it, with a high-pitched roof of shingles or tin, whitewashed wood, and walls made of lumber and brick taken from plantation manor houses or rice mills. An authentic tobacco barn and a plantation schoolhouse are also part of the complex. Over a hundred years after Joshua Ward designed his original hammock, tourists still have a fever for hammocks made in the Pawleys Island area.

The tour now heads to Pawleys Island proper. Retrace your route 0.3 mile to the traffic light and turn left. You will cross a causeway almost immediately. Approximately 0.5 mile from the traffic light, bear right to enter the village of

The beach at Pawleys Island

A Pawleys Island hammock
provides the ultimate in relaxation.
Courtesy of The Hammock Shops

Pawleys Island.

Pawleys Island was named for the three sons of Percival Pawley, a mariner who purchased land in the Waccamaw River region in 1711 but continued to reside in what is now Berkeley County, farther south on the South Carolina coast. In his will, Pawley left his three sons all the land he owned "from the Waccamaw River to the sea," including a piece of property he referred to as "one great Isle." Historians have never been able to pinpoint the exact location of that isle willed to Percival Pawley II and his brothers, George and Anthony, but all indications are that it must have been the place now known as Pawleys Island.

Rice plantations in the area were going strong by the latter part of the eighteenth century, but there was one problem that seemed to defy solution. During the hot months, Low Country dwellers were plagued by an illness they called "country fever" or "summer fever," which they believed to be caused by the hot, humid, stagnant air. Hundreds of them died every summer. It is now known that the illness was malaria.

Though most plantations were located fairly close to the seashore, the healthy ocean breezes could not reach them. Many rice-growing families sought safety and relief from summertime illness by spending the months of May through November at the beaches. Pawleys Island was one of the places to which they flocked. In *Chronicles of "Chicora Wood,"* Elizabeth Allston Pringle described her yearly visits to the seashore. Pawleys Island was a mere 4 miles east of her family's plantation as the crow flies, but it could be reached only by traveling 7 miles by boat and 4 miles by land. The author recounted the long procession of flatboats that carried the entire household, including its vehicles, horses, cows, furniture, bedding, and provisions.

As you drive, you will notice that houses are situated on the left of Pawleys Island's one road, while the creek is on the right. Most of the houses have an antebellum look about them, but the fact is that only a handful of them have endured long enough to merit that distinction. Though the others have adopted the unpainted, old-time style, they are in fact quite modern. It won't take you long to learn to distinguish the antebellum homes, the same ones the planter families lived in when they came to take the therapeutic salt water and sea air during the summer months long ago.

Notice the Pawley House, number 442, which is located just before the place where the south causeway enters the road from the right. The Pawley House has one chimney and is built of gray wood. The bricks that comprise the high pillars on which the structure rests were once used as ballast in ships coming to North America from England.

The St. John the Evangelist Chapel is the only structure on the right side of the road other than the docks and piers. It was built in the 1850s as a slave

Historic Pawleys Island house being remodeled

chapel at True Blue Plantation and was later moved to its present site. As one of only two or three old slave chapels surviving in this part of the country, it is considered historically important.

The large building that seems to protrude slightly into the street is the Pelican Inn, number 506, formerly the beach home of Plowden Weston, a wealthy and scholarly rice planter. As with most of the houses on Pawleys Island, the Pelican Inn was constructed of cypress timber cut on the mainland. A Roman numeral was cut into each individual board, and carpenters assembled the structure according to the numbers once the material was shipped from the plantation to the island.

The Pelican Inn

Like other Pawleys Island dwellings, Liberty Lodge, number 520, sat well back from the ocean during colonial days. There is only a single row of dunes separating the houses and the sea today, but there used to be several rows. Note the walkways stretching from Liberty Lodge and its neighbors to the beach.

The Calhoun Lemon House, number 544, is distinguished by its two kitchens separate from the main dwelling. Built in the mid-1800s, the Calhoun

Lemon House is the only old property on Pawleys Island that has retained any of its original outbuildings. The main house, constructed of cypress, is largely unchanged, save for the addition of bathrooms and dormers and the finishing of the upstairs.

The Norburn Cottage, number 560, is one of the oldest and best-preserved dwellings on the island. Its dormer windows are unusual in that they face northeast, the direction from which most bad weather comes. The cottage was built on what may have been the first lot sold on Pawleys Island.

The Provost House, number 566, with its wraparound porch beneath a deep, overhanging roof, served as a boys' academy before the Civil War. It has been remodeled since the death of former owner Charlotte Kaminski Provost.

The road forks beyond this point, which is approximately 1.6 miles from the entrance to Pawleys Island. Turn around, retrace your route for 0.9 mile to the south causeway, and turn left. Drive 1.2 miles to a junction with U.S. 17. Turn left, heading south.

After 6.5 miles on U.S. 17, you will reach a historic marker on the right offering information about the plantation called Prospect Hill. The marker commemorates President James Monroe's visit to Colonel Benjamin Huger at Prospect Hill in 1819. It notes that President Monroe was "lavishly entertained" by his host. That may be an understatement. One local story has it that a red carpet was laid for Monroe to walk upon all the way from the landing on the Waccamaw River to the front door of Prospect Hill, a distance of about 0.25 mile.

After Benjamin Huger's death, Prospect Hill passed through the hands of Joshua John Ward of Brookgreen Plantation before it was sold to Captain Isaac E. Emerson, the man who invented Bromo-Seltzer. Emerson actually bought a number of area plantations—Clifton, Rose Hill, Forlorn Hope, George Hill, Oak Hill, and Bannockburn, in addition to Prospect Hill—and consolidated them under the name Arcadia. When his daughter Margaret married Alfred Gwynne Vanderbilt, Emerson built the young couple a mansion on Clifton Plantation and gave it to them as a wedding present. Alfred Gwynne Vanderbilt was the son of world-renowned financier Cornelius Vanderbilt and the former Alice Claypoole Gwynne. The elder Vanderbilts were among the visitors to Arcadia in those days.

Alfred Gwynne Vanderbilt died in a historic tragedy before he had a chance to fully enjoy Clifton Plantation. World War I was raging in Europe in the spring of 1915 when he decided to go to England to offer the Red Cross a fleet of wagons and his services as a driver. He was enjoying a beautifully calm passage across the Atlantic on Friday, May 7. His ship was making about sixteen knots while he and most of the rest of the passengers enjoyed lunch. Suddenly, there was an explosion, and then another. A German torpedo had crashed into the ocean liner's bow, and a second one into its engine room. Lifeboats were promptly lowered. Alfred was prepared to board when he noticed a woman who had no life belt; he removed his and gave it to her. And so it was that Alfred Gwynne Vanderbilt lost his life on the *Lusitania*, leaving behind a wife and two sons. The sinking of the *Lusitania* was one of the events that brought the United States into the war.

Margaret Emerson Vanderbilt eventually remarried and had another child, but Captain Emerson willed Arcadia to his grandson George Vanderbilt, in whom he had noticed an abiding love of the South Carolina plantations. In turn, George Vanderbilt left the property to his only child, Lucille Vanderbilt Pate, after his death in 1961. The Pate family still lives at Arcadia today.

Continue south on U.S. 17. The entrance to Hobcaw Barony is on the left 0.4 mile past the Prospect Hill historic marker. It isn't possible to tour Hobcaw Barony without prior reservation. However, you *can* enjoy a visit to the Nature

Hobcaw House

Center, which offers a movie on the life of Belle Baruch, the daughter of Wall Street millionaire Bernard M. Baruch.

It was around 1905 that Bernard Baruch became interested in piecing together the original Hobcaw Barony, one of the largest tracts in the Carolinas granted to the Lords Proprietors. By that time, Baruch had already made his fortune and established himself as a businessman and stock-market analyst worthy of giving advice to presidents. Once he set about the task of acquiring plantations, he succeeded in purchasing even more land than was part of the king's grant, though he never could manage to gain control of Clifton, Forlorn Hope, and Rose Hill plantations, which were all part of Arcadia. To give visitors a better idea of the scope of the Hobcaw Barony reestablished by Baruch, it might be noted that the property totals about 17,000 acres, some of which juts into Winyah Bay at Georgetown. There are 80 miles of roadways beyond the gates on U.S. 17. Two beautifully landscaped and furnished mansions—Hobcaw House and Bellefield—are on the property.

A view of the neighboring marsh at Hobcaw Barony

At first, Baruch and his family spent their winters in a large Victorian home at Hobcaw Barony called Friendfield House. The Baruch children loved Friendfield House for its hominess, something they said their New York residence lacked. However, those days came to an end during Christmas dinner in 1929, when the mansion was engulfed in flames. The family and its guests escaped to the lawn and looked on as Friendfield House burned to the ground. Baruch then proceeded to build a new mansion overlooking Winyah Bay. Hobcaw House, as he called it, was constructed of brick, steel, and concrete in an effort to make it as fireproof as possible. It was at Hobcaw House that Baruch entertained the likes of Winston Churchill and Franklin Roosevelt.

Among the family's three children, it was Belle Baruch who developed the deepest love for, and commitment to, the natural resources at Hobcaw Barony. In 1936, she purchased a portion of the property from her father and built a home she called Bellefield—not after herself, but after an old rice plantation once located in the area. She bought the rest of the estate in 1956. Belle Baruch died in 1964, but the legacy she left will continue to benefit the people of South Carolina for many years to come.

Hobcaw Barony remains privately owned by the Belle W. Baruch Foundation, but thanks to a trust Belle established in her will, schools like Clemson University and the University of South Carolina use the estate for research in forestry, marine biology, and the care and propagation of Low Country flora and fauna. The knowledge gained has already contributed to our understanding of coastal ecosystems.

First-time visitors to the South Carolina coast often wonder what has happened to all the beautiful beaches once they reach the area just north of Georgetown. The answer is that fine beaches exist all along that portion of the coast, but that few of them are accessible to the public. Beginning at Hobcaw Barony and extending 60 miles south toward Charleston is the longest stretch of protected shoreline on the east coast. It includes the beach at the Tom Yawkey Wildlife Center, the Santee Coastal Reserve, and federal lands at Cape Romain, Bulls Island, and Capers Island. Not until you reach the Isle of Palms, just outside Charleston, are the beaches once again residential in nature.

The tour ends at Hobcaw Barony. Georgetown is approximately 2.4 miles south on U.S. 17. If you care to head in that direction, you will pass a historical marker on the right commemorating George Washington's visit to Captain William Alston at Clifton Plantation in 1791. Alston was so rich and powerful that he was known as "King Billy." Indeed, with Hobcaw Barony to the left of U.S. 17 and the collection of plantations called Arcadia to the right, it is easy to see what a heavy concentration of small "kingdoms" this part of the South Carolina coast supported in days gone by.

The barn built by
Belle Baruch at Hobcaw Barony

The slave church at Hobcaw Barony

Slave homes on Hobcaw Barony

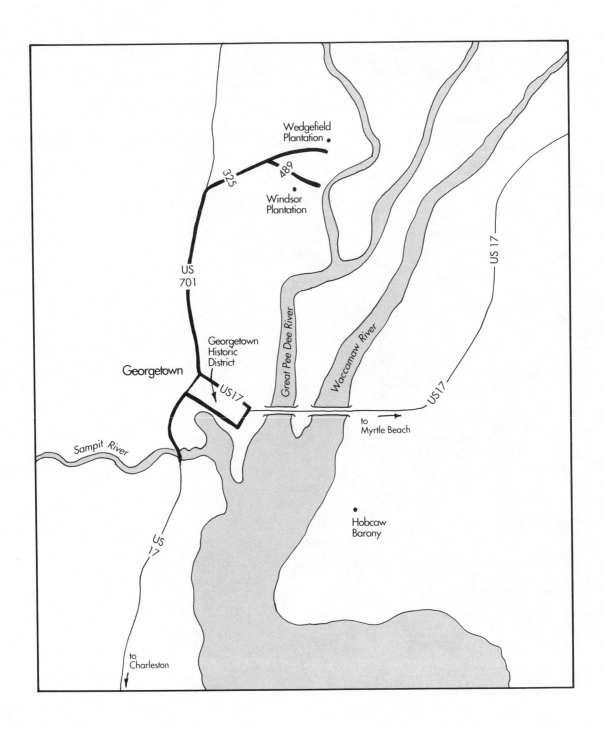

Wedgefield
Plantation

325

489

Windsor
Plantation

US
701

Georgetown
Historic
District

Georgetown

US17

Great Pee Dee River

Waccamaw River

US 17

US17

to
Myrtle Beach

Sampit River

Hobcaw
Barony

US
17

to
Charleston

The Georgetown Tour

This tour combines a driving tour of the Georgetown area with a 10-block walking tour of Georgetown's historic district. It begins north of town at Wedgefield and Windsor plantations, then heads into Georgetown to the Winyah Indigo Society Hall, the Red Store–Tarbox Warehouse, and the Old Slave Market, which houses the Rice Museum. Next comes the walking tour, which features Prince George Winyah Episcopal Church, the Georgetown County Courthouse, and a number of historic homes. The driving tour then resumes, traveling to the Harold Kaminski House before ending at the International Paper Company, just south of town.

Total mileage: approximately 11 miles.

The tour begins approximately 3 miles north of the center of Georgetown at the junction of U.S. 701 and S.C. 325, a secondary state highway that leads to Wedgefield Plantation. Drive down S.C. 325, following the plantation signs. Wedgefield and Windsor plantations, the first two stops on this tour, were once counted among the many Low Country rice plantations.

Georgetown County has had a rich history of rice growing. In fact, Winyah Bay, the body of water on whose banks the city of Georgetown was built, was once the center of the greatest rice-producing area in the world. The Waccamaw, Black, Pee Dee, and Sampit rivers empty into Winyah Bay. In days gone by, rice was grown on every inch of land along the four rivers as far inland as 30 miles.

Low Country rice production began in the eighteenth century and reached its crest around 1860. That was the golden era of Georgetown County, a time when great fortunes were made and flaunted. High rice prices in England made millionaires of the American planters. Traces of their charmed lives remain in the area even today.

There were a couple of major factors that brought about the demise of Low Country rice production. One was the Civil War, which disbanded the huge labor force necessary in rice growing. The other was an unfortunate series of hurricanes that caused sudden rises in the water level of rivers and streams. The sudden increases in water level were called "freshets" by the planters, and they were devastating. They drove salt water into the fields and washed away rice trunk docks, which were the doors that controlled the flow of water from the rivers to the fields. Rice trunk docks were situated on canals by the rivers. Young boys were assigned to sit on them and open the doors on the rising tide to allow water to flow over the fields; they then closed the doors when the fields were covered. When no more water was needed, the boys opened the doors to allow the water to reenter the river on the outgoing tide. But when the hurricanes struck and the means for controlling water flow was destroyed, the fields were quickly ruined.

It is approximately 2 miles on S.C. 325 to the gate for Wedgefield Plantation. Bear left through the gate and continue along the oak-lined avenue that leads to the manor house. The house is hidden by the trees, but when you finally lay your eyes on it, you'll understand why Michael Greer, the interior decorator of the White House during the Kennedy administration, called it one of the most beautifully designed and detailed Georgian homes in the United States.

Wedgefield Plantation dates from 1762, when a man named Samuel Wragg purchased 610 acres in the area. The bedroom in the manor house reserved for the lady of the house was said to be the most expensive woman's bedroom in the entire South. The original manor house burned about twenty years ago, but it has since been rebuilt to closely resemble the old structure. Today, Wedgefield Plantation serves as a prestigious residential development and golf-course community, with the manor house used as a clubhouse.

After you have seen Wedgefield Plantation, start to retrace your route along S.C. 325. Approximately 1 mile from the Wedgefield Plantation gate, you will reach a junction with S.C. 489, a secondary state road leading to Windsor Plantation. Turn left onto S.C. 489. You will reach Windsor Plantation after 0.9 mile. The manor house on the property is called Windsor House. It is a private residence not open to the public, but it is visible from the road. Windsor House overlooks the Black River, and like the manor house at Wedgefield Plantation, it gives visitors a peek at a replica of one of the finest homes the Old South had to offer.

Georgetown merchant and political figure Paul Trapier organized Windsor Plantation around the middle of the eighteenth century. It was his grandson, also named Paul Trapier, who built Windsor House. A popular local story concerns Hannah Trapier, sister-in-law of grandson Paul, and how she is supposed to have saved Windsor House during the Civil War. Hannah was a frail woman in her eighties when a company of Yankees came one day to burn the manor house. Some officers entered her room, where she was resting in bed. The spunky Hannah looked one of them in the eye and asked him how he would feel, and what he would do, if the old woman he saw in bed were *his* mother. It is said that the man's face turned red with shame, and that he and the entire company left rather hastily without lighting a match. However, Hannah's efforts were ultimately in vain, as the manor house burned during refurbishing in 1931. The architecture of the present Windsor House is slightly

*Wedgefield
Plantation*

*Windsor
House*

different from that of the original, but it is still a lovely plantation home by any standard.

Retrace your route off the Windsor Plantation grounds, then turn left onto S.C. 325 and follow it back to U.S. 701. Turn left onto U.S. 701, which becomes known as North Fraser Street entering Georgetown. After approximately 2 miles on U.S. 701/North Fraser Street, you will reach a junction with Black River Road. Bear left on Black River Road and follow it for 0.7 mile to U.S. 17. Turn left onto U.S. 17 and drive 0.3 mile to Broad Street. Turn right onto Broad Street and follow it for 3 blocks, then turn left onto Prince Street. After 3 blocks on Prince Street, you will reach the Winyah Indigo Society Hall, on the right at the corner of Cannon Street.

Winyah Indigo Society Hall

Broad Street marks the beginning of Georgetown's historic district. Indeed, the entire area has had a long and rich history. Way back in 1526, a group of Spaniards landed in the Winyah Bay area. They found it occupied by three distinct Indian stocks, which we now know belonged to the Iroquoian, Muskogean, and Eastern Siouan linguistic groups. The Eastern Siouan group included the Winyaw—since corrupted to *Winyah*—tribe. Some people believe that the Spaniards settled on land that is now part of nearby Hobcaw Barony, though it cannot be proven. (For information on Hobcaw Barony, see The Southern Grand Strand Tour.)

The arrival of the British *can* be proven, since there are records of land grants along Winyah Bay in 1705. The British believed that the lands bordering the Ashley, Cooper, Edisto, and Santee rivers had already been claimed, so they were looking to establish a settlement farther north. They chose this area because they were impressed by the excellent rivers emptying into Winyah Bay.

The Anglican church gained a foothold in the Carolina colony by the following year, establishing a system of ten parishes covering the entire colony. Prince George Winyah Parish was created to serve the area that included Winyah Bay. It was named for George, Prince of Wales, who was later to become King George II. Within fifteen years, church members throughout the colony were beginning to feel that the parishes were too large to serve their needs. So it was that Prince Frederick Parish and All Saints Parish were carved from the original Prince George Winyah Parish.

A man named William Swinton was commissioned to lay out the town of Georgetown in 1729. Today, Georgetown's historic district comprises the area of the original town plan. The street names are the same, the lot numbers are the same, and many of the houses are the original structures on their sites. Several of the homes and buildings in the historic district are listed on the National Register of Historic Places.

As early as 1723, the people of Georgetown were petitioning to have their town declared a port of entry. They believed that the local economy would benefit if products could be shipped directly to foreign destinations without incurring burdensome freight charges in Charleston. Royal Governor Robert Johnson made the issue a priority, and in 1731 Georgetown officially became a port of entry, with a naval officer assigned to collect fees and keep a register of all vessels arriving and departing. The early years saw vessels carrying products like rice, fruit, and naval stores to places like Charleston, Philadelphia, Boston, Bermuda, London, Liverpool, and Bristol. Traffic through the port has increased steadily from the heyday of the rice plantations right up to the present, with more than two thousand pleasure boats serviced each year at the Georgetown dock. Numerous charter boats also leave the harbor to take fishing parties to offshore fishing sites.

The Winyah Indigo Society has also played an important role in Georgetown history. Indigo is not the easiest of plants to raise, a fact proven in the American colonies and elsewhere. Indigo was first produced in India. Portuguese explorers later brought bricks of indigo dye back to Europe, where the rich purple-blue color was considered a royal hue almost from the moment of its arrival. However, all efforts to grow the indigo plant in Europe were destined for failure, as the climate is unsuitable.

Antigua and its neighboring islands proved the perfect place to produce the dye. Colonel George Lucas, the governor of Antigua, sent his daughter, Eliza, some indigo plants to test in the soil of the plantation she ran for him in the Charleston area. Eliza Lucas's seedlings were killed by frost the first year and by insects the second, but she persevered. The third year, 1743, her indigo flourished in the Low Country soil, and her father sent a horticulturist to help her in raising the plants and extracting the dye. Soon thereafter, Eliza married the dynamic, attractive civic leader Charles Pinckney, and the popular couple visited everyone who was anyone on the Charleston plantations and brought indigo plants as gifts. It is Eliza Lucas Pinckney who deserves most of the credit for the growth of the industry.

It didn't take long for indigo to assume a prominent place in the South Carolina economy and for production to spread northward to the area around Winyah Bay. The planters saw indigo as a symbol of success, and each tried to raise a better strain than his neighbors. South Carolina became known as the source of the finest indigo dye in the world. Vast fortunes resulted. Slaves on the plantations were allowed to have the skimmings that rose to the top of the indigo vats. It was a belief among the slave community that doorframes and window frames painted with the blue dye would prevent evil spirits from entering a household. Some Low Country cabins still have their doorframes and window frames painted blue.

The Winyah Indigo Society began as an informal convivial club in 1740 and was incorporated by an act of Parliament for the purpose of educating children in 1757. Thomas Lynch, whose son signed the Declaration of Independence, was the organization's first president. The society's school instructed students in letters and religion. In 1775, it began a mission of educating poor children; contributions were raised and a schoolmaster was hired. The school prospered until the Civil War, when the occupation of the building by Federal troops and the destruction of the library left it in complete disarray. Instruction began again in 1872. By that time, few indigo planters were retaining tutors for their children, opting instead to send them for the excellent education at the Winyah Indigo Society School. Some of the institution's graduates went on to the nation's finest universities. The school merged with the state system in 1887, but in 1965 its original building gave birth to Winyah Academy, a private institution that continues to grow rapidly.

Low Country indigo production began to suffer shortly after the Revolutionary War, when it was discovered that the plant could be raised successfully elsewhere. But the effects of indigo on the Georgetown area are still felt strongly today, a fact evidenced by the Winyah Indigo Society Hall, built around 1857, and the active society that inhabits it. The red brick hall with white pillars is not open to the public. It was designed by Edward Brickell White, who also designed the French Huguenot Church in Charleston and Trinity Episcopal Church in Columbia.

After you have seen the Winyah Indigo Society Hall, turn right off Prince Street onto Cannon Street. Drive across Front Street to the old brick building near the harbor, the Red Store–Tarbox Warehouse, at 16 Cannon Street.

The Red Store–Tarbox Warehouse was built during colonial days. Its purpose was to store indigo awaiting export, along with such commodities as imported wines and silk. The warehouse once boasted a wharf that could accommodate five ships. The French Tavern, also known as the Oak Tavern, was later added to the structure; only its foundation can be seen today, but the tavern was once the most fashionable watering hole in Georgetown.

The warehouse's lasting claim to fame is that it served as Theodosia Burr Alston's resting place before she set sail on her fateful voyage on the *Patriot*. The story of Theodosia Burr Alston must surely be one of the saddest ever told.

The Red Store–Tarbox Warehouse

Her early years showed great promise. She was the daughter of Aaron Burr. Her husband, Joseph Alston, finished college before he reached the age of seventeen and was admitted to the bar at twenty. The couple's 1801 honeymoon included a stop in Washington, where they witnessed the inauguration of Thomas Jefferson and Aaron Burr as president and vice president of the United States. They then made their home in the South Carolina Low Country, where Joseph had inherited the plantation called The Oaks from his grandfather. But the happiest times of their lives began in 1802, when Theodosia gave birth to a son, named Aaron Burr Alston after his illustrious grandfather. The vice president was so thrilled with his new grandson that he eagerly devoured the letters Theodosia wrote him about the child.

Things began to take a turn for the worse not long after the birth of Aaron Burr Alston. Before her marriage, Theodosia's friends had worried that, as a native Northerner, she would have trouble adjusting to the humidity of the South Carolina Low Country. Their fears proved to be on the mark. For the sake of Theodosia's health, the couple soon had to buy a home farther inland, near Greenville. Theodosia was still ailing around the time of her father's famous duel with Alexander Hamilton in 1804. Aaron Burr was eventually absolved of any wrongdoing in Hamilton's death, but the incident placed a formidable strain on the family. Young Aaron Burr Alston remained a bright light. His parents believed he had an illustrious future ahead of him.

Tragedy struck in June 1812. The family was staying at the home of Joseph's father when ten-year-old Aaron contracted malaria and died. Theodosia was not in the best of health herself, and the blow of her son's death nearly killed her. Her spirits were no better six months later. It was finally decided that a trip to New York to visit her father might be the only thing that could perk her up. Joseph had been elected governor of South Carolina earlier that year, and he was prohibited by law from leaving the state. Thus, he did not accompany Theodosia and her maid when they sailed from Brookgreen Plantation on December 30, rested at the Red Store–Tarbox Warehouse in Georgetown, and boarded the *Patriot* for New York. The *Patriot* was lost off the North Carolina coast, whether the victim of a violent storm or of mischief by privateers.

The story did not end there. Newspaper accounts appeared with deathbed confessions from pirates who said they had overtaken the *Patriot* and made Theodosia, and presumably the other passengers, walk the plank.

Another version agreed that the *Patriot* had fallen prey to pirates, but it differed in claiming that Theodosia's life was spared and that she lived for years on North Carolina's Outer Banks. The centerpiece of this version was what *may* have been a self-portrait painted by Theodosia, which she *may* have taken aboard the *Patriot*. The painting came to light when it was acquired by a North Carolina physician. The physician claimed to have taken it in payment for services rendered to a young woman meeting Theodosia's description. And indeed, others who saw the painting agreed that its subject was none other than Theodosia. It will probably never be known exactly what happened to Theodosia Burr Alston, but some people believe there is at least a grain of truth in the physician's account. The painting was later put on display in the Macbeth Art Gallery in New York.

Joseph Alston left the South Carolina governorship in 1814 and died prematurely, at the age of thirty-seven, in September 1816, less than four years after his wife. His remains, along with those of his father and young Aaron Burr Alston, are located in a family cemetery at The Oaks.

Across the street from the Red Store–Tarbox Warehouse is the Heriot-Tarbox House, at 15 Cannon Street. Built around 1740, it is a clapboard structure on an arched foundation. The windows in the upper story are set high to the cornice line, an indication of pre–Revolutionary War construction.

The Heriot-Tarbox House

The Old Slave Market now houses the Rice Museum.

TOURING THE COASTAL SOUTH CAROLINA BACKROADS

The chair rail, wainscoting, floor, and a door to the porch are all original and in good condition. However, few details of the Heriot-Tarbox House's history are known, as is the case with many other Georgetown homes, since the town's records were destroyed by Sherman's troops while they were being moved to Columbia during the Civil War.

Once you have seen the Heriot-Tarbox House, retrace Cannon Street to Front Street, turn left, and proceed 2 blocks. On the left at the corner of Front and Screven streets is a tower containing a clock. This is the site of the building called the Old Slave Market, so named because it served as Georgetown's slave market in its darkest days. It has also been used as a jail, a print shop, and the police headquarters. The structure was patterned after a town hall and clock building in Keswick, England. It now houses the Rice Museum on its second floor. When plans were being formulated to transform part of the building into a museum commemorating the rice culture, an internationally famous design firm was brought in from Wilmington, Delaware, to oversee plans for the exhibits. Today, dioramas depict scenes from all aspects of rice production.

The Rice Museum outlines the conditions necessary for the growing of rice. A large labor force was the most basic ingredient, and slaves were made to play that role. The late Dr. Archibald Rutledge, poet laureate of South Carolina, compared the slaves' arduous task of clearing rice fields to the building of the pyramids. Another factor was what the planters called "the proper pitch of the tide," meaning that the tides rose and fell by desirable, predictable levels and that water could be easily channeled from the rivers to flood the fields. The third crucial ingredient was soil quality, and the rich deposits left by the local rivers over the course of hundreds of years provided an ideal level of nutrients.

The fields were prepared during the month of March, and seeds were planted in April. Then the rice trunk docks were opened, and what the planters called "the sprout flow" covered the fields for up to six days, until the plants sprouted. After that, the water was drained and the seedlings were allowed to grow in the sun. The next flooding was called "the long flow." It completely covered the young plants, ridding them of insects. The plants were then allowed to bask in the sun again until it was time for "the lay-by flow." And so it went until the harvest in late summer.

Slave women cut the rice three rows at a time with reaper hooks, grasping the stalks in their left hand and using the hooks with their right. Each woman was expected to cut half an acre a day, a task a good worker could complete in about two hours. The stalks were left to dry in the sun, after which they were tied in sheaves and carried to the barnyard.

222 Broad Street

Almost all plantations had a rice mill with storage facilities. The mills were capable of threshing from six hundred to twelve hundred bushels per day. The grain was first removed from the straw, with fans helping the process along by blowing away the refuse and leaving only the rice grains encased in their hulls. The rice was then taken to the second story of the mill, where it was passed through a sieve that removed any chaff, sand, and weed seeds that remained. Next, the grain was passed between two heavy shelling stones that moved in opposite directions and cracked the hulls. The hulls were finally removed with mortar and pestle, after which the rice was packed in barrels and sent to a "factor," or agent, for sale. The Rice Museum captures this whole production process visually. A tour is highly recommended.

Continue 1 block on Front Street to Broad Street. The waterfront park at Front and Broad is an excellent place from which to watch the boats passing through Georgetown. Your 10-block walking tour of Georgetown's historic district begins at the waterfront park. Parking is available nearby.

Walk 2 blocks down Broad Street to the last two homes on the right before Highmarket Street. The house at 222 Broad Street has been modified, as have many of the homes on this tour. Some of the interior floors are original, and the Chippendale porch railing is an addition that seems to have followed the construction of the house by only a few years. The house dates from 1760. Mary Dealy was the original owner. In the Revolutionary War, during the occupation of Georgetown in 1780 and 1781, the commanding officer of the British forces lived here.

Old homes in Georgetown have a distinctive look about them, known locally as "Georgetown style." If you take the walking tour of Charleston later in this book, you will notice a style that is much the same, though such homes there are referred to as "Charleston single houses" or "Charleston double houses." A double house is square, with a front door at the center of the building that opens into a hall running back to a staircase at the far end. There are two rooms on either side of the hall, and the chimneys stand between the rooms. Single houses are not square but narrow and rectangular. They are entered from the street onto a wide piazza, with another piazza upstairs, the two of them serving to catch the prevailing breezes. On extremely narrow lots, single

234 Broad Street

Prince George
Winyah Episcopal Church

houses may be no more than one room in width, though the single-house concept has been modified over the years to accommodate homes more than one or two rooms wide.

Just beyond 222 Broad Street is 234 Broad Street. Built around 1825 by Benjamin King, the owner of a Georgetown rice mill, the house was enlarged in 1855 by Major Samuel Atkinson, a signer of the Ordinance of Secession. Ironically, the commander of Union troops in the area lived here during and after the Civil War. For many years, the house served as office space for Prince George Winyah Episcopal Church, but it is now used as a private residence.

By this time, you may have noticed that Georgetown is laid out with streets running parallel to and perpendicular to the Sampit River. The corner of Broad and Highmarket streets is the geographical center of town. Continue on Broad Street across Highmarket Street for a tour of Prince George Winyah Episcopal Church.

When the Anglican church established Prince George Winyah Parish early in the eighteenth century, it defined the parish's boundaries as extending "to the southwest on the Santee River, and to the northeast on the Cape Fear River, to the eastward on the ocean, and to the westward as far as it shall be inhabited by his Majesty's subjects."

Not long after the parish was established, the building of a church at the corner of Broad and Highmarket streets in Georgetown was commissioned by the Anglican church. Construction began in 1737 and was completed in 1750. However, the church was desecrated by British forces during the Revolutionary War. As a Georgetown resident wrote to his son in England in 1788, "The Town was almost all Burnt by the British Troops. . . . The Church they made a Stable and then Burnt it, they have since got a Roof upon it and a Few Temperary Seats, but not half Finish'd." If you look closely at the tile floor inside Prince George Winyah Episcopal Church, you can still see the marks left by horses' hooves in the days when the church was made to serve as a stable.

The Anglican church in the United States fell into decline after the Revolutionary War, as most of its clergy had been Loyalists. Anglican congregations were allowed to incorporate and keep their church property as they reorganized under the aegis of the Episcopal church, but the members at Prince George failed to take advantage of that law for a full decade. It wasn't until the arrival of clergyman Maurice Harvey Lance in 1815 that the church was renovated. The tower was added in 1824.

As you tour the church, note the marble baptismal font on the right side of the sanctuary near the entrance. The font was stolen from the church at one point. During the Civil War, it was found in a local cabin, where it was being used to pound rice. The font was restored and returned by 1866.

Following the Civil War, a new roof was added to the church, and new wooden pews were installed. Those box pews are still in use. On cold Sundays in years gone by, families would bring their own heaters to add warmth to their pews. There are still some reminders of slave days at Prince George Winyah Episcopal Church. For example, the window behind the altar, made of English stained glass, was originally part of Saint Mary's Chapel, the place of worship used by slaves at Hagley Plantation.

Visitors to Prince George Winyah Episcopal Church usually enjoy a tour of the churchyard, with its huge, aged live oak tree that has tilted some of the gravestones. The earliest inscription on the premises dates from 1767; many others from the eighteenth century are also in good condition. Behind the church and just to the left is a monument erected to Robert Francis Withers

The Farrow-Porter House

The 1790 House

The Masonic Lodge

Allston, a South Carolina governor and a wealthy Georgetown County planter who lost everything in the Civil War. The headstones in the wall of the church are of particular interest; when additions were made at the rear of the sanctuary, it was decided that the displaced markers should be incorporated right into the building. Both the church and its graveyard are listed on the National Register of Historic Places.

Once you have seen Prince George Winyah Episcopal Church, retrace your steps to Highmarket Street and turn left. Walk 1 block and turn left onto Screven Street. The Farrow-Porter House, built around 1740, is located on the right at 316 Screven Street. Its interior includes several touches that are characteristic of New England–style construction, a fact that has led to suggestions that the home is the product of a builder from the North. For example, the fireplace wall in the drawing room consists of wide boards that run vertically from floor to ceiling, with three rectangular panels set over a high mantelpiece—that style is common among New England homes but not those of the Low Country. The same can be said of the house's floor plan, with its front door opening into a small, square entry featuring a large, central chimney that serves the fireplaces of both the drawing and dining rooms.

Continue on Screven Street to Duke Street and turn right. After 1 block on Duke Street, turn right onto Queen Street. The Marsh-Wright House, at 315 Queen Street, is on the right. This single house boasts handmade nails and wooden pegs. Among the features surviving from the original construction are three mantels, a staircase, several handmade doors, heart-pine flooring, and some windows with handblown panes. The Marsh-Wright House has been owned by the same family for six generations.

From Queen Street, turn right onto Highmarket Street. The Waterman-Kaminski House is on the right at 620 Highmarket Street. Originally, the home's side porch extended along the front, with what is now the center window serving as the front door. Eleazer Waterman, mayor of Georgetown in 1829, 1840, and 1846, owned the home during the 1850s. A transplanted Connecticut Yankee, the well-to-do Waterman was one of the men responsible for incorporating the Methodist Episcopal Church of Georgetown in 1817.

Next door at 630 Highmarket Street is the 1790 House. It is the only home in Georgetown with Bermuda stone in its foundation. Bermuda stone was used as ballast in eighteenth-century sailing ships. Another feature that gives a clue to the house's age is the English Bond pattern of bricklaying in the foundation and supporting pillars; the English Bond pattern fell into disuse by 1800. The first floor of the 1790 House is raised above a full basement story, as

was the Low Country practice around the time of the Revolutionary War. The kitchen wing was added around 1920, but the heart-pine flooring, the wood-work, and some of the windowpanes in the rest of the house are original.

Continue on Highmarket Street to Screven Street and turn left. The last building on the left before Prince Street is the Masonic Lodge. The building's records were destroyed during the Civil War, but it is believed that the structure served as a bank beginning around 1833; it must have enjoyed a brisk business when the Bank of Georgetown went into receivership in 1870. The building has also seen service as an inn.

Turn right onto Prince Street to see the Georgetown County Courthouse, on the left. This handsome structure dates from around 1824 and holds the distinction of being the second fireproof building constructed in the United States. The architect and builder was Major Russell Warren. He designed the courthouse after the style of Robert Mills, the noted South Carolina architect of the early nineteenth century and the man who designed the Washington Monument. Mills showed that he appreciated the compliment when he wrote,

"The court-house has been lately erected of brick, and is a great ornament to the town." The Georgetown County Courthouse is still a great ornament. Its elegant combination of styles features Roman columns, elements of a Greek temple, and a Renaissance doorway to its second-floor courtroom.

Adjacent to the courthouse and sitting close to the street is the Henning-Stearns House, at 719 Prince Street. It is the only house in Georgetown with its double piazzas intact. Its original floorboards were cut from full-width trees, and some of them remain. Dating from around 1739, the Henning-Stearns House is one of the oldest homes in town.

The Henning-Stearns House

Turn left off Prince Street onto Broad Street and return to the waterfront park at Front and Broad to conclude the walking tour. You have seen only a portion of Georgetown's historic homes. At least two others should be a mandatory part of any Georgetown tour.

Leaving the waterfront park area, head south on Front Street. You will know you are heading south if the Sampit River, visible from the waterfront park, is on your left. After 0.3 mile, you will see a sign on the left for the Harold Kaminski House, at 1003 Front Street. The house is situated perpendicular to the street, so that the wide piazza extending its entire length is barely visible from the road.

The early history of the Harold Kaminski House is sketchy. It was built overlooking the Sampit River around 1760. A family named Congdon occupied the house before the Civil War. Sometime later, Confederate Captain T. W. Daggett lived here with his family. Daggett is best remembered for making the mine that sank the Union flagship *Harvest Moon* in Winyah Bay. (For more information on the sinking of the *Harvest Moon*, see The Santee Plantations Tour.) The house then passed through several owners before it came into the hands of the Kaminski family.

The Harold Kaminski House

Heiman Kaminski was born in Prussia in 1839 and came to Charleston to live in 1854. Two years later, he moved to Georgetown. He fought with the 10th South Carolina Regiment during the Civil War, after which he returned to Georgetown with the grand sum of $2 to his name. With that capital and the help of a pair of partners, Sol Emanuel and W. W. Taylor, he started the Kaminski Hardware Company, which proved to be a great success. Kaminski's second marriage brought him three sons, one of whom was named Harold. Harold Kaminski went on to marry the well-born Julia Pyatt, and the couple purchased the structure now known as the Harold Kaminski House during the Depression.

Julia Pyatt Kaminski's charm, beauty, wit, and gift for entertaining are legendary. Dr. Chalmers G. Davidson, archivist of the E. H. Little Library at Davidson College, fondly remembered a visit to the house. "Dinner at Julia Kaminski's was a never-to-be-forgotten experience," he claimed. Davidson wrote glowingly of his sumptuous meal, which began with soup and then moved on to salad, fish prepared according to the local style, meat, vegetables, dessert, fruit, and nuts. "Then we could smoke," he noted. "No one would have had the bad taste to do it before or during a Kaminski dinner."

Harold and Julia Kaminski are now deceased, but their home is open to the public, and a tour is highly recommended. The dining room at the Harold Kaminski House still boasts a mahogany Chippendale banquet table that runs the length of the room, with sixteen matched Duncan Phyfe chairs standing in readiness. An exceptionally beautiful china set bearing the Pyatt coat of arms is arranged on the table as if guests are expected at any minute. Additional china is stored in an American Empire sideboard, an American Empire china cupboard, and an antique mahogany Chippendale corner cabinet with original brass pulls. And those are only the riches to be discovered in the dining room!

The Pawley House, where Julia Pyatt lived before she married Harold Kaminski

Next door to the Kaminski House is the 1760-vintage Pawley House, number 1019, where Julia Pyatt lived before she married Harold Kaminski. George Washington visited this house when he toured coastal South Carolina in 1791, and it has since been known in local conversation as "the house where Washington stayed." The Pawley House is now owned by First Federal Savings and Loan. During its days as a residence, it was handsomely furnished with heirlooms representing nearly three centuries of culture and a collection of priceless family portraits, some of them by famous Charleston portraitist Thomas Sully.

After you have seen the Kaminski House and the Pawley House and completed your introduction to Georgetown's old money, continue 2 blocks on Front Street to Georgetown Steel Corporation, on the left. Georgetown Steel's two electric arc furnaces went into operation in July 1969. The mill has an annual capacity of approximately six hundred thousand tons. It produces such things as small-diameter, close-tolerance wire rods and coiled, small-diameter reinforcing bars. The forty-acre plant on the Sampit River has proven vital to the local economy.

To complete the tour, turn left onto U.S. 17 at Georgetown Steel Corporation and drive 0.5 mile to the International Paper Company, on the right at the bridge over the Sampit River.

During the nineteenth century, Georgetown was the site of the largest

*The Georgetown Steel
Corporation*
Courtesy of Georgetown Steel Corp.

sawmill in the world. The mill was operated by the Atlantic Coast Lumber
Company. It produced more than a half-million board feet of lumber per day,
and for a time the majority of Georgetown County residents depended upon
it for their living. But the Depression brought the Atlantic Coast Lumber
Company to its knees by 1932. It just so happened that the International Paper
Company was expanding its operations farther south at that time, and the two
companies merged. In the first month of business after the merger, the
population of Georgetown increased by more than 3,000 souls. An article in the
Georgetown Times in 1936 reported the construction of a massive, $8-million
paper mill at the old site of the Atlantic Coast Lumber Company. By the
following year, when papermaking operations began, there were 1,215 people
working in the mill. Some 593 cords of wood were consumed daily in the
production of 263 tons of paper.

Today, International Paper remains a massive forest-products business
with operations in many states. The scent of a pulp mill generally follows

water, and visitors to Georgetown frequently ask where the odor floating on the moist air comes from. If the question is posed to an International Paper employee, chances are he or she will answer proudly. To those workers, and to many Georgetown County residents, that smell is the smell of new money.

If you are heading south, U.S. 17 leads farther into plantation country. If you are heading north, it will take you back through Georgetown toward the Grand Strand.

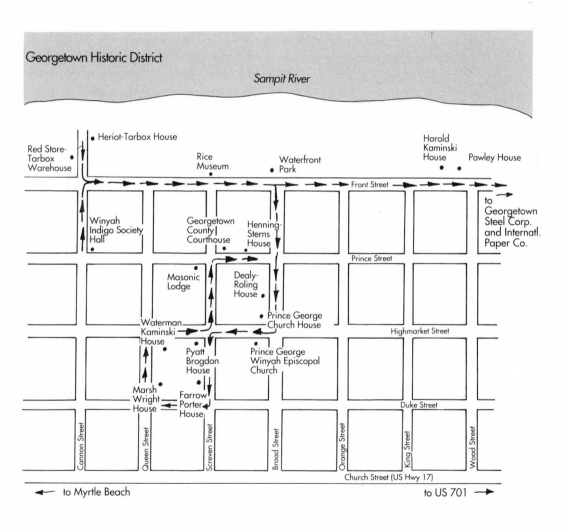

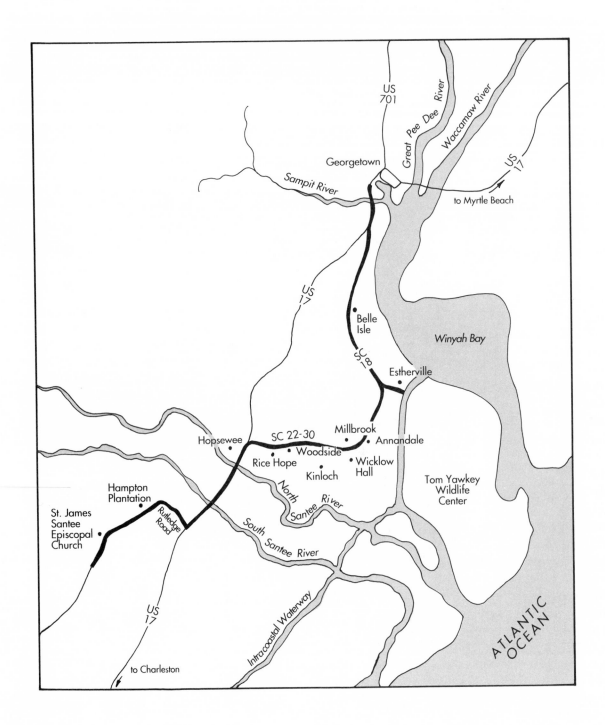

The Santee Plantations Tour

This tour explores the plantation-rich area south of Georgetown. It begins at Belle Isle Plantation and Battery White and travels past the Tom Yawkey Wildlife Center. Next, it visits Annandale Plantation, the former site of Daisy Bank Plantation, Kinloch Plantation, Rice Hope Plantation, and Hopsewee Plantation. The tour then heads south into Charleston County to Hampton Plantation before it ends at St. James Santee Episcopal Church.

Total mileage:
approximately 25 miles.

This tour begins just south of the Sampit River at the junction of U.S. 17 and South Island Road, otherwise known as S.C. 18. In its glory days, the area south of Georgetown was rice-producing country. The first stop on this tour is one of the old rice plantations, Belle Isle Plantation.

Follow South Island Road for approximately 3 miles to the plantation entrance. Turn left into the plantation and drive 0.7 mile to Egret Circle, then continue across Egret Circle into Belle Isle Villas and Yacht Club. Stop at the gate to obtain a pass, then proceed down the picturesque roadway with huge oaks on one side and Winyah Bay on the other. You will see the embankments of Battery White on the left approximately 0.4 mile from the gate.

Early in the Civil War, the Union navy began making life miserable for local planters by destroying saltworks on the ocean and then steaming their vessels as far as 30 miles up the coastal rivers. The planters along Winyah Bay had little choice but to flee farther inland and build forts to stall the Federals' advance. Battery White, originally called Mayrant's Bluff, was constructed for that purpose. It was expected to be an important fortification, thanks to its location atop a small bluff at a place where the channel narrowed to fourteen hundred yards. It boasted formidable guns and seventeen earthen breastworks. However, the siege of Battery White proved to be decidedly anticlimactic. During Sherman's march from Atlanta to the sea, Confederate soldiers withdrew from Battery White to try to help intercept Union forces. Three Federal warships steaming into Winyah Bay shortly thereafter, in February 1865, were delighted to find Battery White unmanned.

The action grew more interesting after Federal forces controlled the area. Union Rear Admiral John A. Dahlgren arrived at Georgetown aboard his flagship, the *Harvest Moon*, on February 26 and formally announced the end of slavery. Then Dahlgren went on to proclaim that since the freedmen did not have the means to provide for themselves at that stage, their former owners had to continue furnishing them food "of the usual description" for a period of sixty days. That created an uproar, and martial law had to be declared. Dahlgren appointed a temporary commander to keep the peace in Georgetown until a permanent replacement, Colonel P. P. Brown of the 157th New York Volunteers, arrived.

On February 28, the *Harvest Moon* headed to Battery White. At 7:45 A.M. on March 1, Dahlgren was having breakfast while the *Harvest Moon* steamed down Winyah Bay when an explosion rocked the ship. It was immediately evident that the vessel was sinking. Within five minutes, the admiral and his staff were safely relocated aboard the tug *Clover*. To that point, Confederate "torpedoes," or mines, had proven such a subject of ridicule that Union vessels had stopped concerning themselves with them. But Federal forces had to change their thinking after Confederate Captain T. W. Daggett's powder-keg mine claimed the *Harvest Moon*. Thus, the only sinking of a Union flagship in Winyah Bay took place after local fighting had ceased. Battery White is listed on the National Register of Historic Places. Two of its 10-inch Columbiad cannons are still in place.

The Belle Isle Museum is located just beyond Battery White. A parking area is adjacent to the museum, and a sign there indicates the site of the Marquis de Lafayette's first landing in America.

This entire area was owned by Elias Horry from 1755 to 1825, and later by his grandson Peter Horry, the man for whom Horry County was named. There is evidence that the parents of Francis Marion, the Swamp Fox of Revolutionary War fame, lived on a portion of the Horry estate and were the ones responsible for naming Belle Isle Plantation. Francis Marion spent many boyhood hours exploring the forests and fishing in the waters at Belle Isle Plantation, though it is difficult to gauge just how much influence the place had on the development of his ideas concerning guerrilla warfare. (For more information of Francis Marion, see The Swamp Fox Tour.)

More than a century later, the plantation passed into the hands of the Johnstone family. The Johnstones constructed an eighteen-room house in the vicinity of the current museum. However, fire destroyed the home in the early 1940s, taking with it an excellent collection of *objects d'art* from around the world. The plantation land was sold in 1974, after which it was developed as Belle Isle Villas and Yacht Club.

Retrace your route to South Island Road and turn left. As you drive the 4.6 miles to the Intracoastal Waterway, you will pass signs on the left for Dover

A 10-inch Columbiad cannon located at Battery White

and Estherville plantations, which are only open to the public during the two days each spring when the Georgetown Plantation Tours are held. Dover and Estherville plantations were prominent during the rice-growing years, with Estherville Plantation producing three hundred thousand pounds of rice during 1850 alone.

South Island Road ends at the Intracoastal Waterway. Across the water are three islands—North, South, and Cat islands—featuring marshland and hardwood forests. For more than fifty years, the three islands and their twenty thousand acres were the property of Tom Yawkey, the owner of the Boston Red Sox baseball team. In his 1976 will, Yawkey left the islands to the South Carolina Wildlife and Marine Resources Department. He also set up a $10-million trust fund for the operation of the Tom Yawkey Wildlife Center. Together, the property and the trust fund comprised one of the most outstanding gifts ever given to wildlife conservation in North America.

The gifts reflected the man. Those who remember Tom Yawkey like to recount tales of his generosity. For example, when his spacious house on South Island was lost to fire, Yawkey had two small mobile homes moved to the

A herd of deer grazing at the Tom Yawkey Wildlife Center
Courtesy of Robert L. Joyner

island. He and his wife lived in the trailers while the superintendent of the three islands continued to reside in a graceful two-story home in a grove of trees. Yawkey was once asked why he didn't tell the superintendent to move so that he and his wife might enjoy the comforts of the two-story house. "Why, I can't do that!" he exclaimed. "That's the superintendent's house!" The Yawkeys remained in the trailers for the rest of the years they vacationed at their island retreat. To this day, the superintendent continues to reside in the two-story house.

The Tom Yawkey Wildlife Center is still operated in accordance with Yawkey's belief that people and wildlife do not mix. Wildlife has always come first on his property. It is possible to tour the preserve, but reservations must be made about three months in advance. If you are unable to make reservations, call to find out the dates and times of the next scheduled tours, then make your way to the ferry slip on a tour day and inquire about cancellations. There are no guarantees, but many visitors have had the good fortune to get a seat at the last minute. There is no charge for the tour, which generally lasts about three hours.

Backtrack 0.5 mile on South Island Road to S.C. 22-30 and turn left. You are now leaving Winyah Bay and entering the area of the North Santee and South

A rare white pelican at the Tom Yawkey Wildlife Center
Courtesy of Robert L. Joyner

Santee rivers. The North Santee River is to your left, though it is not in sight. All of the properties mentioned in the following pages up through Hopsewee Plantation were considered North Santee River plantations. There were more than two hundred plantations in Georgetown County during colonial days, most of them highly successful.

Annandale Plantation is on the left approximately 2.8 miles from where you turned onto S.C. 22-30. Former owner Andrew Johnstone was one of the most successful rice planters on the North Santee River. At one time, his holdings also included Millbrook and Estherville plantations. In 1863, he sold the 2,290-acre Annandale Plantation to George Alfred Trenholm, the secretary of the Confederate treasury, who was looking to invest the money he had come by during his days as a blockade runner. Annandale Plantation is privately maintained today. It continues as a working plantation, with soybeans and corn grown on the uplands and shrimp and crabs cultivated in the wetlands. It is listed on the National Register of Historic Places.

Millbrook Plantation, also privately maintained, is on the right after another 0.3 mile. The original house, built in 1833, is still standing. Millbrook and

Millbrook Plantation

Annandale plantations have shared a common history; Annandale Plantation was originally operated under the Millbrook name.

Some plantations along the North Santee River have been swallowed up by land purchases and changing property lines. Daisy Bank Plantation, once located near Annandale and Millbrook plantations, was one such victim. There is a famous story about Daisy Bank Plantation. It is said that, in days long past, a seafaring man put in at Georgetown and happened to fall in love with a local girl. They wanted to marry, but the girl's family objected to the match on the grounds that a sailor was beneath the social status of a Georgetown woman. Not to be denied, the determined young man gave up his life at sea, somehow managed to acquire the ownership of Daisy Bank Plantation, and became a rice planter. The happy couple then married with everyone's blessing.

There was a party at Daisy Bank Plantation sometime later, and the young couple announced that they were expecting an heir. Everyone toasted them. The husband was the happiest man in attendance. In fact, he was busy making plans to buy an exquisite diamond bracelet to be given to his wife after the birth of their child.

Physicians were few and far between in those days, and it was not uncommon for a woman to lose her life in childbirth. That proved to be the case at Daisy Bank Plantation. When the young wife's time came, a doctor could not be obtained, and the birth proved a difficult one. The infant lived less than a day, with the mother dying shortly afterwards. The husband nearly lost his senses. In his grief, he hired a carpenter to fashion a walnut coffin with a glass top. After the bodies of the mother and baby were laid in the satin-lined coffin, the husband slipped the new diamond bracelet onto his late wife's wrist. The glass top was then put in place and sealed with lead. For some weeks, the husband would not allow his wife and child to be buried, but friends finally persuaded him to let them be interred in Daisy Bank Plantation's cemetery, located deep in the woods. Roses were planted around the burial site, where mother and child could still be viewed through the glass.

Years later, a prominent family from the North bought a nearby plantation for use as a hunting preserve. They gave a party one day, and the son of the plantation owner convinced one of the young women in attendance to leave the festivities and go for a ride in the woods with him. The young man took along a gun, as it was not his practice to go into the woods without protection.

It just so happened that the couple's route took them to the cemetery at Daisy Bank Plantation. They slipped off their horses and stood talking among the grave markers. Suddenly, the girl noticed a large pane of glass on the ground with what appeared to be the remains of a mother and child underneath. However, it was not the mother and child that attracted her attention, but rather the magnificent bracelet on the dead woman's arm. The girl expressed her wish that she might someday own such a piece of jewelry. Feeling that his honor was at stake, the young man walked to his horse, retrieved his gun, grasped it by the barrel, and smashed the glass atop the coffin so he could get the bracelet. It was a moment before the girl fully understood the despicable act she was witnessing. She grew hysterical and demanded to be taken back to the hunting preserve. For the life of him, the young man could not understand. The girl had said she liked the bracelet, yet now she would have nothing to do with it. But being a gentleman—in his own mind, at least—he obliged her wish and returned her to the party.

For a long time after that, people who happened upon the little burial ground in the woods reported seeing the dead mother and child floating just above the violated coffin, appearing to look for something. It wasn't long before the cemetery at Daisy Bank Plantation became known as haunted ground. It was generally believed that the mother and child were lingering at their grave in search of the stolen diamond bracelet.

Toward the end of its days, Daisy Bank Plantation was owned by Charleston aristocrat Arthur Middleton. Middleton lived there with his wife, the former Julia Emma Rhett, and their five children.

It is approximately 0.5 mile on S.C. 22-30 from Millbrook Plantation to Wicklow Hall Plantation, built by Rawlins Lowndes between 1835 and 1850. Some 540,000 pounds of rice were produced here in 1850. In 1927, a project was undertaken to restore the manor house, the slave quarters, the kitchen, the stable, and other buildings. In late 1988, Wicklow Hall Plantation, listed on the National Register of Historic Places, was sold to Nancy DuPont Reynolds, one of the heirs to adjacent Kinloch Plantation.

Continue another 1 mile to Kinloch Plantation, best known as the playground of the famous DuPont family of Delaware.

Just before the weather turns cold every fall, millions of migratory waterfowl in Canada and New England begin a journey that ends on the abandoned rice fields of coastal South Carolina. Canada geese and the dozens of species of ducks that accompany them are partly responsible for creating an "age of gun clubs" from the ashes of the Civil War and the rice-planting age. From about 1893 to about 1960, it seemed that nearly every oilman, railroad baron, and Wall Street kingpin wanted a Low Country hunting preserve. Names like

Baruch, Vanderbilt, Luce, Hutton, Field, and Phelps were recorded in Georgetown County property registers.

"We hunted every day," remembered Elizabeth Navarro, Bernard Baruch's nurse. "Every single day. And one would never return home without killing the allotment for that day."

George Young of Georgetown recalled that his father "set up the stands for Mr. George Vanderbilt and other hunters. There were four or five stands, in different places, far apart so there was no danger of anyone getting shot."

Each gun club had a superintendent. Sometimes, when the hunters were relaxing at dinner after a day's hunting, the superintendent would come in and say he had seen a fox. Without a thought, everyone at the table would drop their forks to go off fox hunting. Such was the spirit of the times.

Kinloch Plantation stands on the former site of Milldam Plantation, owned at one time by the Horry family. In 1911, Eugene E. DuPont and some of his friends—among them John Philip Sousa—purchased Kinloch Plantation and other properties totaling nine thousand acres. They combined their massive holdings into the Kinloch Gun Club. The present Kinloch House, built in 1923 after an earlier structure burned, contains eight bedrooms, large living and dining rooms, offices, a kitchen, and, of course, a gun room. Eugene E. DuPont was the sole owner of the property at the time of his death in 1966, when he willed it to his four daughters. The daughters subsequently sold it to the illustrious Ted Turner, chairman of the board and president of the Atlanta-based Turner Broadcasting System. Like those before him, Turner reserves the use of the massive Kinloch Plantation acreage for hunting and wildlife conservation. Members of his family spend time here each year.

It is 0.9 mile on S.C. 22-30 from Kinloch Plantation to Woodside Plantation. A winnowing house can still be seen from the road. Winnowing houses were built high off the ground, with their floors actually functioning as sieves. As rice passed through openings in the floor, foreign particles were blown away by the wind, thus cleaning the rice and preparing it for the removal of its husks.

Winnowing house at Woodside Plantation

John Vanderhorst originally received the property that came to be known as Woodside Plantation through a king's grant in 1735. The property later came into the hands of Henry Lucas. In 1983, Mr. and Mrs. Herbert J. Butler of Charleston bought the plantation and built a new Low Country home facing the abandoned rice fields.

The entrance to Rice Hope Plantation is 0.4 mile past Woodside Plantation. In the middle part of the eighteenth century, Rice Hope Plantation was part of the considerable landholdings of indigo-rich Francis Kinloch. It came into the possession of Jonathan Lucas sometime before 1822, though the exact date is not known. Jonathan Lucas was known as a great builder of rice mills; in fact, the English government bestowed knighthood upon him for his erection of rice mills in Great Britain. He and his son, Jonathan Lucas, Jr., probably did as much as anyone to boost the Low Country rice industry. Jonathan Lucas, Jr., died in 1832, leaving estates in India and England as well as in South Carolina. Rice Hope Plantation remained in the possession of the Lucas family through the Civil War and even into the early years of this century, until a severe storm destroyed all rice crops on the North and South Santee rivers in 1908. Subsequent owners have included the International Paper Company and the Georgia-Pacific Corporation. The partners who control Rice Hope Plantation today are noted as men who take great enjoyment in hunting and other outdoor activities.

Continue past Rice Hope Plantation for 0.7 mile on S.C. 22-30 to a junction with U.S. 17. Turn left onto U.S. 17 and drive 0.3 mile to Hopsewee Plantation, on the right, the last of the North Santee River plantations included on this tour.

Rice Hope Plantation

The land on which Hopsewee Plantation is located was originally granted to Thomas Lynch by King George II. Lynch constructed a home of black cypress between 1735 and 1740; one of the oldest and best-maintained dwellings in the region, the manor house at Hopsewee Plantation is listed on the National Register of Historic Places. The plantation was controlled by the Lynch family until 1763. Thomas Lynch later became a delegate to the Continental Congress. His son, Thomas Lynch, Jr., born in 1749, proved just as influential as his father. Educated at Eton and Cambridge, he, too, was a delegate to the Continental Congress, as well as a signer of the Declaration of Independence. Thomas Lynch, Jr., died an untimely death in 1779 at the age of thirty; he was sailing to France to try to improve his poor health when his vessel was never heard from again. Difficult circumstances during and after the Civil War and again around the time of World War I forced the closing of Hopsewee Plantation, but it has since been revived. Mr. and Mrs. James T. Maynard are the current owners. The property can be toured for a fee, and it is worth every penny.

Hopsewee Plantation

Drive south on U.S. 17 for 3.3 miles from Hopsewee Plantation to Rutledge Road. En route, you will cross the North Santee and South Santee rivers; the South Santee River marks the border between Georgetown County and Charleston County. Turn right onto Rutledge Road and follow it for 2 miles to history-rich Hampton Plantation, which has played host to celebrities from George Washington to Clark Gable. If you stand on the veranda of Hampton House alongside the two-story columns of solid pine, you might imagine for a moment that the Old South is really not gone with the wind.

Hampton House was built by Huguenots who settled in the Santee River area. Huguenots were followers of the teachings of John Calvin. They were also the center of religious and political quarreling in France during the sixteenth and seventeenth centuries. When Louis XIV repealed the Edict of Nantes in 1685, the Huguenots lost their freedom of worship. Many of them fled their homeland, some boarding ships headed to South Carolina, where they prospered after beginning new lives as planters along the Santee rivers.

Two of the most successful Huguenot settlers in the Low Country were Noe Serre and Elias Horry. Serre came to Charleston in 1690, and Elias Horry arrived in South Carolina the following year. In 1757, a granddaughter of Serre's married a grandson of Horry's; the young couple, Daniel and Judith Horry, lived at Hampton Plantation in the same house that is there today. The planters were very fond of associating with their own kind, so marriages between children of planters were common. It was almost unheard of for a

member of a planter family to marry below their station. On occasion, cousins married cousins.

Daniel Horry outlived his first wife and their two children. In 1768, he married Harriott Pinckney, the daughter of Charles Pinckney and Eliza Lucas Pinckney, the woman who pioneered indigo planting in the United States. (For more information on Eliza Lucas Pinckney and Low Country indigo production, see The Georgetown Tour.) Harriott Pinckney Horry entertained the likes of George Washington and Francis Marion at Hampton Plantation, as well as hosting glittering balls at a larger home she owned in Charleston. Daniel and Harriott had two children before Daniel died of bilious fever in 1785.

As the executrix of her husband's estate, Harriott decided to enlarge Hampton House. She had the entrance facing the South Santee River moved to the inland side. Matching wings were then added to both sides of the house. The west wing housed a spectacular master bedroom with a ceiling two stories high. The east wing was a ballroom forty-two feet long with a twenty-eight-foot ceiling. The floorboards in the ballroom were believed to be the longest in America. The ballroom also had cypress panels and a seven-foot-wide fireplace outlined by tiles picturing such things as Biblical scenes, trees, and seascapes.

Harriott's son married a niece of the Marquis de Lafayette and lived in France. On the other hand, her daughter, also named Harriott, showed signs of becoming an old maid. Concerned that her aging daughter didn't possess any property of her own, the elder Harriott built and decorated Harrietta Plantation on the South Santee River and prepared to give it as a present. However, it turned out that the younger Harriott was not destined for spinsterhood, for she eloped with Frederick Rutledge just before she was scheduled to move into her new plantation home. Frederick Rutledge was a son of John Rutledge, who served at various times as governor of South Carolina, associate justice and chief justice of the United States Supreme Court, chief justice of South Carolina, and congressman. Harriott Horry Rutledge inherited Hampton Plantation in 1830, and the property remained in the Rutledge family until 1971.

One of the most distinguished members of the family to own Hampton Plantation was Archibald Rutledge, a nationally recognized poet and author who was named poet laureate of South Carolina in 1934. On one occasion, Rutledge wrote an article for the *Saturday Evening Post* entitled "The Return of the Native." The article brought such national attention to Hampton Plantation that Rutledge was inspired to use it as the basis for a book, which he called *Home by the River*. In that book, he described the Santee River system—which he called the largest in the eastern United States—from its origins in the mountains of North Carolina as the Wateree and Congaree rivers through its entire course to the Atlantic Ocean. *Home by the River* also tells of the people who have owned Hampton House through the years, describes Christmas on the plantation, and recounts the author's return after a forty-four-year absence. One of the most poetic portions of the book is the ending of the first chapter, where Rutledge describes his beloved Low Country in rich detail—its immense tracts of woods, its forbidding swamps, its wild animals, its difficult rivers, its vast deltas as rich as those of Egypt. It was Archibald Rutledge's opinion that nowhere else in the world had nature been kinder to her children than in coastal South Carolina.

Hampton House had been empty for nearly two decades when Archibald Rutledge came home to live, so the task he undertook in restoring the house was an arduous one. His favorite room may have been the library. It had long been Rutledge's contention that the best indication of a people's culture is their reading matter. The books he found in the library at Hampton House seemed to place the inhabitants of the Low Country in good standing. The oldest book on the premises was Sir Edward Coke's *Laws of England*, printed in 1590.

Seventeenth- and eighteenth-century classics included the works of Voltaire, Racine, Corneille, and Montesquieu, along with a magnificent edition of Shakespeare. Some of the books had been in the library since the days of Daniel and Judith Horry, and they still had the signatures of their original owners on the covers.

Toward the end of his life, Archibald Rutledge decided to convey Hampton Plantation to the state of South Carolina. For a mere $150,000, the state assumed ownership of three hundred acres and the historic plantation home. In the fall of 1971, the property became the thirty-eighth park in South Carolina's state parks system.

Hampton House, listed on the National Register of Historic Places, is being restored to the way it was around 1791, when George Washington paid an early-morning call and stayed for breakfast. The plaster on some of the interior walls has been removed for what restoration officials call "interpretive and historical reasons"; visitors may look behind the walls to see the massive broadax-hewn studs used in the house's construction. Admission to the park grounds is free, but a small fee is charged to tour the manor house.

After you have enjoyed Hampton House, start to retrace your route toward

St. James Santee Episcopal Church

U.S. 17, but turn right onto the dirt road located 0.5 mile from the plantation. Follow the dirt road for 1.5 miles to St. James Santee Episcopal Church.

Built in 1768, St. James Santee Church has had a unique history. It was designed to accommodate a combined congregation of Huguenots and Anglicans. There were two distinct areas on the Santee in the eighteenth century. The region called the French Santee was inhabited by Huguenots, while farther north, the region called the English Santee was populated by British settlers. Each group was close-knit, but relations between the two were always cordial. When Anglicanism became the official religion of the colony by decree, the two congregations decided to merge. In order to keep everyone happy, St. James Santee Church was built with two porticos—one facing the French Santee area and one facing the English Santee area.

The church's building committee reads like a who's who of colonial South Carolina, beginning with Thomas Lynch and Daniel Horry. The original cypress benches, one of which has Thomas Lynch's name carved in it, may still be seen today, along with the original communion rail and the original pulpit, made of mahogany from Santo Domingo.

In 1773, a prominent Charleston matron gave the church three cherished items: a large folio Bible and two prayer books. When the Bible and prayer books were stolen during the Revolutionary War—some believe by Colonel Banastre Tarleton—the congregation was highly angered. In an incredible coincidence after the war, a man from the parish saw the books on sale in a London bookstall. He promptly purchased them and returned them intact to St. James Santee Church.

Services were conducted at the church every Sunday until 1865. Operations were suspended when the rector died in August of that year. There were other changes as well. At some point, the interior seating plan was altered, relocating the chancel, and the rear portico was walled in; the front portico remains as it was originally styled. And new roads were built over the years, leaving the church off the main thoroughfare. But even at this late date, the church still retains what Archibald Rutledge once called "its indefinable air of austere sanctity."

The tour ends at St. James Santee Episcopal Church. You can return to civilization by retracing the dirt road to Rutledge Road, then turning right onto Rutledge Road and following it to where it intersects U.S. 17. Georgetown is to the north and Charleston to the south. If you would like to combine this tour with the following one, turn right onto U.S. 17 and drive to McClellanville, approximately 6 miles south.

Sunset at the
Tom Yawkey Wildlife Center
Courtesy of Robert L. Joyner

Waterfowl thrive at the
Tom Yawkey Wildlife Center.
Courtesy of Robert L. Joyner

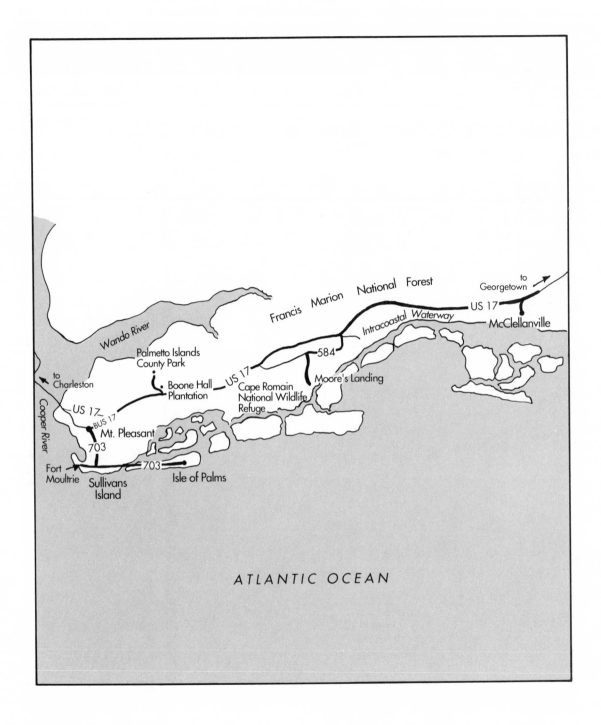

to Georgetown

Francis Marion National Forest

US 17

McClellanville

Intracoastal Waterway

Wando River

Palmetto Islands
County Park

584

to
Charleston

US 17

Boone Hall
Plantation

Moore's Landing

Cape Romain
National Wildlife
Refuge

Cooper River

US 17
BUS 17

Mt. Pleasant

703

Fort
Moultrie

703

Isle of Palms

Sullivans
Island

ATLANTIC OCEAN

The Swamp Fox Tour

This [...] McC [...] sout [...] throu [...] tiona [...] outs [...] traverses the 4-mile stretch of highway made famous by the Low Country basketmakers, who still sell their wares by the side of the road. The tour then proceeds to Boone Hall Plantation and Mount Pleasant. It explores Sullivan's Island and its Revolutionary War site, Fort Moultrie, before ending at the Isle of Palms.

Total mileage: approximately 56 miles.

The tour begins on U.S. 17 approximately midway between Georgetown and Charleston, where a sign for McClellanville directs travelers to turn east onto Pinckney Street. Follow Pinckney Street toward McClellanville.

McClellanville is a small village on the banks of Jeremy Creek. It is bordered on the north by the Tom Yawkey Wildlife Center, on the west by Franci Marion National Forest, and on the south and east by the Cape Romai National Wildlife Refuge. Since Jeremy Creek comes in from the ocean and ha tides, the atmosphere in McClellanville is definitely that of an ocean community, rather than that of a river village.

A man named Gerald McClellan sold the first lots in this area to inlanders trying to find relief from the mosquitoes and the malarial fever that once made Low Country summers miserable. Changes have always been slow in coming to McClellanville. Most changes have been imposed by outside agencies, like the paving of U.S. 17 from Charleston to Georgetown in 1929 and the digging of the Intracoastal Waterway from the Cooper River to Jeremy Creek and the Santee River in the 1930s. Left to its own devices, McClellanville is as peaceful as any community you are likely to find. Its beaches are usually deserted. "I get out on the Fourth of July, the busiest day of the year," one resident said, "and if you see one other boat, it's crowded." As the town matured, it didn't grow into the kind of place where speculators buy and develop land in the hope that they will be able to sell it for a higher price. Rather, it matured into the kind of place loved by people who want to raise their families in peace and quiet.

That peace and quiet came to an abrupt end as Hurricane Hugo approached the coast on Thursday, September 21, 1989. Early that morning, Governor Carroll Campbell called for the mandatory evacuation of South Carolina beaches by 3:00 P.M. At 5:40 P.M., Hugo was upgraded to a Category 4 storm, the second highest possible level. Experts predicted that a nineteen-foot storm surge might occur. A hurricane's winds may cause serious damage, but the greatest risk to life and property comes from the accompanying storm surge, the flood of seawater that the storm drives onto the coast. Storm surges cause 90 percent of all hurricane deaths; the danger is particularly grave if the storm hits land at high tide. By 7:50 P.M., hurricane-force winds were being recorded at Georgetown. At 8:30, Bob Sheets, the director of the National Hurricane Center, predicted that the most likely site for landfall was just north of Charleston. CBS's "48 Hours" program canceled a live report from Myrtle Beach that evening because the entire city had been evacuated.

Some observers have called Hurricane Hugo the storm of the century. It hit the coast between midnight and 1:00 A.M. on September 22, ultimately causing some $3 billion in damage. McClellanville bore more than its fair share of the destruction. Hugo's storm surge is already the stuff of legend, as it left watermarks six feet up on buildings 0.25 mile from the marsh.

In many cases, it took heroic efforts to survive the storm. McClellanville resident Mary Linen and her two children, twelve-year-old Lisa Marie and seven-year-old Christopher, were swept out of their house and onto their porch by the storm surge. Pushed by the water funneled through narrow Jeremy Creek, the porch began to tilt, then to move. It didn't stop until it hit a tree. Thinking quickly, Mary Linen grabbed an extension cord and tied herself and her children to the tree so they wouldn't be swept away into the darkness. There, the three rode out the storm. They didn't untie themselves until daybreak.

It seemed that the whole country had witnessed televised images of Hugo's rampage through the Charleston area. Help was not long in arriving in places like McClellanville. That help was certainly appreciated, but even those people most intent on coming to the aid of victims did not fully understand the scope of the damage. As Debbie Thomas of McClellanville put it, "They sent us barbecue grills, and that seems like a very nice gesture, but there's no food to cook, and there are no backyards to cook in." In an article on McClellanville published in the *Charlotte Observer*, Elizabeth Leland noted that "some residents lost their homes. All lost their hometown."

But Low Country residents are resilient, and the people of McClellanville began rebuilding their town as soon as the shock of its destruction wore off. Their efforts are an ongoing success, as a look around the village will reveal.

It is approximately 1 mile on Pinckney Street to Church Street. Turn right onto Church Street, and the St. James Santee Chapel of Ease will immediately

St. James Santee Chapel of Ease, a Gothic structure with gingerbread filigree

catch your attention. Chapels of ease were small churches constructed for those members of a congregation who lived too far away from the main church to attend services regularly. Some of the Santee River planters kept residences in McClellanville, and it was for their convenience that the St. James Santee Chapel of Ease was inaugurated. The Gothic structure was built of wood shingles and decorated with gingerbread filigree; it features high windows on the sides and front. The chapel has weathered and mellowed through the years, but it still holds the same kind of attraction that draws people to the beauty of old paintings.

Turn right off Church Street onto Main Street and drive 0.3 mile to Little Hampton, the Rutledge home, which is highly visible on the right. The original log structure on this site was built by Henry Rutledge, the father of the late Archibald Rutledge, poet laureate of South Carolina. The location was convenient—less than a day's carriage ride from the Rutledge family's main home at Hampton Plantation. The family would leave Hampton Plantation in early spring, spend a month in McClellanville, and then spend the balance of

Little Hampton

TOURING THE COASTAL SOUTH CAROLINA BACKROADS

the summer in Flat Rock, North Carolina, another haven for people trying to escape the malaria of the Low Country.

The original Little Hampton was destroyed by Hurricane Hugo. The current version features unpainted wood and a tin roof. The entire house sits on pilings, and a long, screened-in porch faces Jeremy Creek. The original structure may be missed, but there are some definite advantages to modern construction. "We now have heat and air conditioning," remarked the current owner, Judge Irvine Rutledge, who comes down from Maryland with his family several times a year to stay at Little Hampton. (For more information on the Rutledge family and Hampton Plantation, see The Santee Plantations Tour.)

If you care to linger awhile and explore McClellanville further, you might see the village's shrimp fleet on Jeremy Creek, or you might catch a glimpse of one of the fabulous yachts that travel the Intracoastal Waterway. Peace and quiet have returned to McClellanville, and a good many homes have been built since Hurricane Hugo in 1989, but local residents will never forget the images of houses knocked off their foundations, trees and power lines brought down, and water and seaweed covering everything.

Retrace your route to U.S. 17 and turn left. As you head down the coast, you are traveling through Francis Marion National Forest.

Referring to Francis Marion, General Peter Horry once remarked, "I have it from good authority that this great soldier, at his birth, was not larger than a New England lobster." The legendary Swamp Fox was always small of stature, it is true, but his skills on the battlefield more than made up for his diminutive size. Marion's grandparents were French Huguenots who settled in the low-lying area between McClellanville and Charleston. Around 1738, when he was about six, his parents moved to Belle Isle in an effort to find better schooling for their children. Living near the ocean gave Francis Marion a desire to sail the high seas. When he was fifteen, he requested and was granted permission to embark upon a life at sea. It was his parents' hope that he would gain strength from his work as a crewman.

Whatever romantic notions Marion had about life at sea were quickly shattered. He boarded a schooner at Georgetown and set out for the West Indies, only to have a whale attack and disable his vessel. Marion, the captain, and four other men escaped in an open boat. Holding onto their sanity under the unrelenting Caribbean sun proved difficult. They were without food and drink until a hapless puppy—presumably another victim of bad luck on the seas—found its way to their boat. The sailors promptly killed it and drank its blood. Two men were dead by the end of six days in the open boat. The beleaguered sailors reached land the following day. By the time he sailed back into Winyah Bay, Marion had recovered his health, but his enthusiasm for the sea was gone forever.

He found his calling just after his twenty-fifth birthday, when he convinced his brother Isaac to join him in the French and Indian War. In that conflict and in subsequent action against the Cherokees, Marion became a veteran militia-man skilled in fighting in woods and swamps. He then lived the life of a planter for a time, until relations between Great Britain and the colonies began to deteriorate. He was among the first group of representatives chosen when South Carolina elected its inaugural Provincial Congress. The early meetings of that body proved to be a disappointment, as the Provincial Congress adjourned without taking any decisive action. But then reports began to arrive that the Massachusetts militia had fired on the redcoats. The South Carolina group hastily called another meeting and this time agreed to adopt the Bill of Rights, as urged by the Continental Congress.

When South Carolina was called upon to raise two regiments of infantry and one of cavalry, Francis Marion's name was mentioned prominently. After being given the rank of captain, he went out to recruit soldiers among the Huguenots, the Scotch-Irish, and the English who lived along the Santee, Black, and Pee Dee rivers. Within three months, he had collected a company, whose members called themselves "Marion's Men." Marion and his soldiers went on to great fame in the Revolutionary War, most notably in the years around 1780, when they held eastern South Carolina from the British.

Francis Marion National Forest and Sumter National Forest—the only national forests in the Palmetto State—cover 696,995 acres in thirteen counties. When Francis Marion National Forest was organized in 1936, its entire 250,000 acres were bought directly from private owners. No property was condemned and taken by the state, as is sometimes the case.

When Hurricane Hugo rampaged through the area, over three-fourths of the mature timber in Francis Marion National Forest was destroyed. The efforts of the United States Forest Service in recovering the billion board feet of downed timber and reducing the loss of millions of dollars in revenue were nothing short of heroic.

Some 260 million feet of timber were removed from Francis Marion National Forest in the span of nine months. That figure represents a level of production almost seven times greater than the usual rate. Forest experts from thirteen states were brought in to accomplish the recovery. They crawled over, around,

Before Hurricane Hugo, much of the Francis Marion National Forest was covered with stands of long leaf pine.
Courtesy of Bill Craig

Sunrise after Hurricane Hugo showed over three-fourths of the mature timber in Francis Marion National Forest destroyed.
Courtesy of Bill Craig

The Swamp Fox Tour

and through timber jumbled like matchsticks in an attempt to determine its value, taking into consideration such things as the cost involved in clearing enough debris to make way for the removal. Meanwhile, law-enforcement officials made sure that no illegal logging activities took place in the national forest. At times, as many as 120 separate timber sales were conducted simultaneously. The purchasers of the salvaged lumber then utilized every timber-removal device known to man to retrieve their new stock—mules, horses, helicopters, skidders, and cables, among others. It was the largest salvage operation ever accomplished in a national forest in the United States.

There is a pull-off on the right approximately 10 miles south of McClellanville that marks the beginning of the Swamp Fox Hiking Trail. If you care to stroll through the forest where Francis Marion and his men held the redcoats at bay, or if you care to survey some of the damage still lingering from Hurricane Hugo, the trail is highly recommended.

Current efforts in the forest center around plans to build a visitor center south of the Swamp Fox Hiking Trail. It is to be a joint venture between the United States Forest Service and the United States Fish and Wildlife Service. The visitor center will serve visitors to both Francis Marion National Forest and the Cape Romain National Wildlife Refuge.

It is 3.4 miles on U.S. 17 from the Swamp Fox Hiking Trail to a sign on the right for Moore's Landing. Turn left at the sign onto Doar Road, then turn right onto Seewee Road almost immediately. After driving 3.8 miles on Seewee Road, turn left onto Bulls Island Road. Follow Bulls Island Road for 1.6 miles to the Intracoastal Waterway. The long pier jutting into the water is the place where visitors may board a boat for a trip to the Cape Romain National Wildlife Refuge. Reservations are necessary if you want passage on the boat, and a fee is charged for the ride.

The Cape Romain National Wildlife Refuge is a collection of barrier islands that stretches for 22 miles along the coast. Organized in 1932, the refuge encompasses nearly 90 million acres of land and water. If you plan to make the boat trip to the refuge, be sure to wear comfortable walking shoes and bring drinking water and food. Restrooms *are* provided. Some of the facilities at the refuge were destroyed by Hurricane Hugo; among the victims were hiking trails, the visitor center, picnic grounds, and a photo blind. On the other hand, the refuge was created for the sake of its natural beauty, and *that* remains as impressive as ever. The waterfowl and the seashells you are likely to see during your visit are well worth the effort in themselves.

Retrace your route to U.S. 17 and turn left. It is approximately 12.4 miles to

*Cape Romain National
Wildlife Refuge*
Courtesy of S. C. Dept. of
Parks, Recreation & Tourism

the first of the basket women who make, display, and sell their handicrafts by the side of the road. It seems that anyone who has ever traveled the section of U.S. 17 just north of Charleston remembers the basket women. There is perhaps no better souvenir of the South Carolina Low Country than one of their handmade baskets.

The local tradition of basket making goes back to the days of slavery. Baskets were used in rice production. One of the earliest basket designs was that of the "fanner," so named because rice that had just been cracked with the aid of mortar and pestle was placed in the basket and fanned until the husks were separated from the seeds. Both the baskets used in the fields and those used in the manor houses were coil baskets. They were made by starting a coil at the center of the bottom of the basket and then winding it outward and upward. There was some variation in design from plantation to plantation.

When rice production came to a halt around the turn of the twentieth century, basket making all but ceased. But as coastal South Carolina began to develop into a popular destination for tourists in the years that followed, the descendants of the basket makers of slave days began to recognize the opportunity of reviving the craft and selling their wares.

Basket making has carried local residents through some lean times. "When there were no jobs around, my family would sit down and make the baskets

---

A basket weaver's stand near Mount Pleasant

and then take the ferry over to Charleston and sell them in the market," remembered Jeanette Lee of Mount Pleasant. "The sweetgrass baskets are a part of our heritage. It is a tradition that we will not let die." And it is a tradition whose practitioners have great pride. "I remember when we made these baskets and if we didn't do it right, my mama would rip it up and say to do it the right way," Lee said. "She didn't want anything that looked like the cat had just played with it."

The construction of U.S. 17 brought an increase in business. In fact, basket making became such a popular art form that local practitioners formed an organization called the Mount Pleasant Basket Makers of Charleston County. Today, nearly two thousand inhabitants of Christ Church Parish, north of Mount Pleasant, are involved in the making of baskets. Traditionally, it is the men who go into the marshes to gather the sweetgrass and the women who sew the sweetgrass and palmetto palm leaves into baskets. Palmetto palm leaves are a darker shade of green than sweetgrass, and the contrast in colors lends the baskets an added beauty. There are over sixty stands in the famous 4-mile stretch along U.S. 17. Baskets are also sold in the City Market in Charleston, as well as along Charleston's streets.

Approximately 2.4 miles after the first of the basket women, you will see a sign for Boone Hall Plantation directing you to turn right onto Long Point Road. Follow Long Point Road for 0.8 mile to the plantation gate. An admission fee must be paid at the gatekeeper's house, but a tour is well worth the price of a ticket.

Boone Hall Plantation

Once you pass the plantation gate, your introduction to the property is the 0.8-mile-long avenue of oaks that was the inspiration for the famous plantation entrance in the movie version of *Gone With the Wind*. Like the plantations in *Gone With the Wind*, Boone Hall Plantation grew cotton, unusual for this area. The original mansion was restored by Thomas Archibald Stone in 1935, with elegant appointments in the style of Scottish architects Robert and James Adam. Some of the many elegant features are the pine floors, paneling, and beams; the imposing African mahogany doors in the entrance hall; and the brass locks. The bricks used in the two-story, fourteen-room home were salvaged from an eighteenth-century kiln. The manor house, the plantation grounds, and the restored slave quarters are open to visitors year-round except for Thanksgiving and Christmas.

If you care to take a brief side trip for a picnic or other recreation, retrace your route off the plantation grounds and turn right onto Long Point Road. After 0.4 mile, turn right onto Needlerush Parkway, then drive 1.3 miles to the entrance to Palmetto Islands County Park, one of four such parks developed by Charleston County. The foliage at the 725-acre park is so dense that you may feel you're stepping into a Tarzan movie. Palmetto Islands County Park offers a monstrous gym set and an unusual swimming pool that are sure to be hits with children. It also offers restrooms, a snack bar, picnic shelters, fishing docks, canoe and bike trails, and other amenities. A small fee is charged.

*Boardwalk at
Palmetto Islands County Park*

Observation tower at
Palmetto Islands County Park

Retrace your route to U.S. 17 and turn right, heading south. After 2.7 miles on U.S. 17, turn left onto U.S. 17 Business at the sign directing you to Mount Pleasant. A drive of 1.8 miles brings you into the northern section of town.

Property deeds in Mount Pleasant go all the way back to July 1680, when King Charles II granted 2,340 acres to an Irishman named Florentia O'Sullivan. O'Sullivan's name is commonly associated with Sullivan's Island today, but he actually made his home on land he owned in what is now Mount Pleasant.

In O'Sullivan's day, it was not unusual for the early settlers to find themselves short of rations. Island residents in the area around Charleston came to be known as "Sand Crabs," while mainlanders were called "Hungry Necks." The two groups competed over foodstuffs brought in from England as spiritedly as high-school teams embroiled in an athletic contest.

In 1770, a man named James Hibben acquired a local plantation called Mount Pleasant for the sum of $1,155. In 1808, he divided the plantation into thirty-five building lots of approximately two acres each to form a village, which he also called Mount Pleasant. Mount Pleasant and a neighboring village, Greenwich, were incorporated in 1837. A comprehensive town plan was drawn up, with streets that were to continue from Mount Pleasant right on into Greenwich. However, the plans ran into a roadblock on Pitt Street, where a Mrs. Phillips refused to let street construction interfere with a scuppernong arbor she kept on her property. In fact, she was so adamant that she stationed her husband on the site with a shotgun. The surveyors wisely capitulated, and Pitt Street remained a short street. Eventually, the communities of Greenwich, Hilliardsville, Lucasville, and the Hibbens Ferry Tract merged with Mount Pleasant and became known by that name.

While you are still in the northern section of Mount Pleasant, turn left off U.S. 17 Business onto S.C. 703 at the signs for Sullivan's Island. A drive of approximately 2 miles brings you to the Ben Sawyer Bridge onto the island. Continue another 0.5 mile on S.C. 703 to Middle Street. Turn right onto Middle Street and proceed 0.5 mile to the United States Coast Guard Station and its lighthouse, on the left.

When a Charlestonian mentions "the Island," he or she is referring to Sullivan's Island, the oldest beach resort in the area. Sullivan's Island has had a rich military history. In 1674, Florentia O'Sullivan, the island's namesake, was empowered to place a cannon on the island's southwest end and fire it when any craft crossed the bar into the harbor. It was from that cannon that a warning was issued when the French and Spanish invaded in 1706. During the Revolutionary War, American forces entrenched at what is now Fort

Moultrie on Sullivan's Island repulsed a British onslaught. And there has been military activity on Sullivan's Island in this century, too. You will notice a bunker next to the lighthouse at the United States Coast Guard Station. During World War II, many such bunkers were constructed around the island to protect a receiving station commanded by the late George Marshall, then a colonel. After the war, some Sullivan's Island residents bought the bunkers and turned them into underground homes. The northeastern portion of the island is still known as the Marshall Reservation.

Continue another 0.5 mile on Middle Street for a look at Fort Moultrie. The modern Fort Moultrie Visitor's Center is on the right.

During the first six months of 1776, the British were planning an assault on the Carolinas with a combined effort of army and navy forces. According to the battle plan, Sir Henry Clinton was to land his army on what is now the Isle of Palms. He would then cross to Sullivan's Island and attack the Americans at what is now Fort Moultrie. Meanwhile, a group of eight ships under the command of Commodore Peter Parker was to make a frontal attack on the fort. But the American forces under Colonel William Moultrie were prepared. In anticipation of an attack, they strengthened the fort with double walls of palmetto logs spaced sixteen inches apart, then filled the areas between the logs with sand.

The battle was fought on June 28, 1776. Colonel Moultrie's Second Regiment

Lighthouse on Sullivan's Island

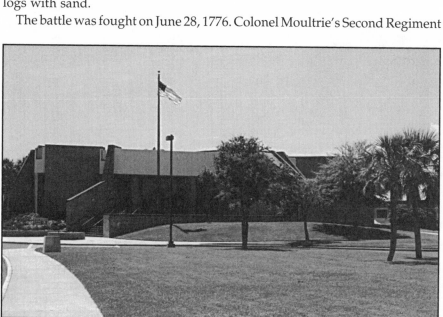

Fort Moultrie Visitor's Center

Fort Moultrie

Bunker on Sullivan's Island

kept up a strenuous barrage against Parker's ships. The British land assault was repulsed as well. The Americans were victorious, and it was a full three years before the state of South Carolina was called upon to defend itself again in the Revolutionary War. The historically correct name for the action is the Battle of Sullivan's Island, but ever since the South Carolina General Assembly honored Colonel Moultrie by naming the fort for him, the Battle of Fort Moultrie has been the more popular choice.

View from Fort Moultrie tower

Fort Moultrie has had its share of distinguished guests. For example, William Tecumseh Sherman was stationed here from 1842 to 1845. But the soldier who left the greatest mark on the island may have been a man who was fond of using aliases, among them Henri Le Rennet and Edgar A. Perry. His real name was Edgar Allan Poe. Poe arrived as a private in November 1827. His stay at Fort Moultrie lasted a year. During that time, he established a reputation as an intense young man who was fond of walking the beaches during storms. In fact, it was on one of those walks that he conceived the idea for a short story he called "The Gold Bug." Published in 1843, the story gives a perfect feel for Sullivan's Island. Among its characters are a Huguenot named Legrand and a Gullah-speaking servant called Jupiter. Today, Poe Avenue, Raven Drive, and Gold Bug Avenue memorialize Poe's days on the island.

When you are ready to leave Fort Moultrie, retrace Middle Street and continue past the junction with S.C. 703 toward the Isle of Palms.

As you head from Fort Moultrie toward the Isle of Palms, you are following the general route of a trolley line built in the early part of the twentieth century. The Isle of Palms was opened as a recreational area around the turn of the century. It was known as Long Island in those days. There was no bridge spanning the Cooper River, but ferries ran from Charleston to Sullivan's Island. Upon reaching Sullivan's Island, young ladies in long pastel dresses and their boyfriends in their straw hats would disembark to board the trolley running from Sullivan's Island to Long Island.

Their destination was usually one of the many parties held at the newly constructed beach houses. Some of the beach houses from that period are quite distinctive. You may be lucky enough to spot one before you leave Sullivan's Island. The houses were constructed in such a manner that their bedrooms could catch a breeze blowing from any direction. The bedrooms were situated at the corners of the house, with each one built almost as a separate entity, having windows on all four sides. If you can imagine a rectangular house with a tiny, square house attached at each corner, you will get the idea. Most people

Fort Moultrie

who see the houses end up wishing they owned one. They may even surprise themselves by experiencing a pang of longing for the days before air conditioning.

Approximately 2.5 miles from Fort Moultrie, you will leave Sullivan's Island and enter the Isle of Palms, where this tour ends. The street you are driving is now called Palm Boulevard. The Isle of Palms is not as rich in history as Sullivan's Island, but it remains one of the prime recreational spots for people from throughout the Charleston area. If you care to explore it at your leisure, you are sure to find something to suit your taste in entertainment.

If you will be traveling the short distance from the Isle of Palms into Charleston, retrace your route to S.C. 703. Drive back across the Ben Sawyer Bridge to Mount Pleasant, then pick up U.S. 17 Business heading south.

Houses on Sullivan's Island

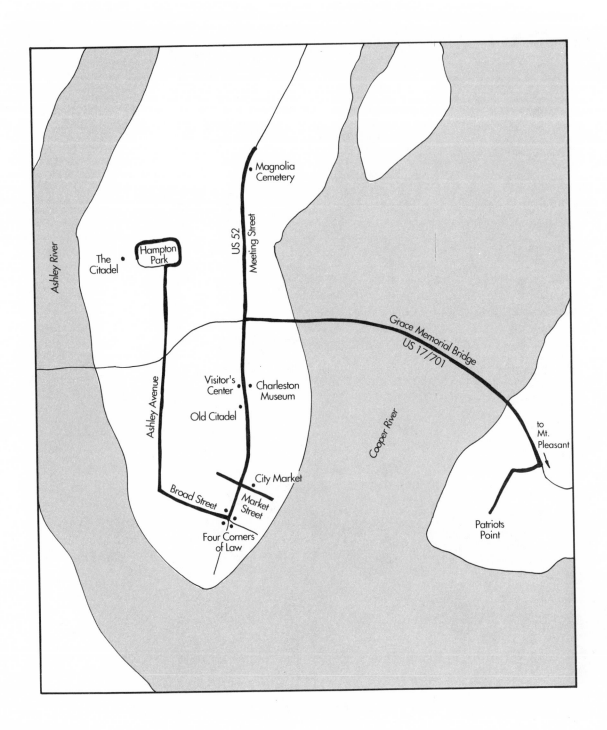

The Charleston Driving Tour

This tour explores Charleston from the Cooper River to the Ashley River. After beginning at Patriots Point, it tells the story of the well-known bridges spanning the Cooper River. In Charleston proper, the tour visits Magnolia Cemetery, then proceeds to the Charleston Visitor Center, the Charleston Museum, and the City Market before skirting much of the historic district included in The Charleston Walking Tour. The tour circles Hampton Park before ending at the Citadel, a historic liberal-arts college in a military setting.

Total mileage: approximately 9 miles.

The tour begins at Patriots Point, located off U.S. 17 at the westernmost edge of Mount Pleasant, near the northern end of the bridges over the Cooper River.

Patriots Point is a product of Charleston's celebration of our nation's bicentennial. It is said to be the world's largest naval and maritime museum. It features the aircraft carrier *Yorktown*, the nuclear-powered merchant ship *Savannah*, the World War II submarine *Clamagore*, and the destroyer *Laffey*, all of which may be toured. Each ship is a must-see, but the *Yorktown* is the focal point of the museum.

The *Yorktown* on display at Patriots Point is actually the fourth in a line of USS *Yorktown*s. Its immediate predecessor, also a carrier, met a violent death. On June 4, 1942, during the pivotal Battle of Midway, Japanese carriers closed

The aircraft carrier Yorktown

in on the third *Yorktown*. The *Yorktown* launched combat aircraft that managed to sink a Japanese carrier, but the Japanese ships sent out dive bombers of their own that knocked out the *Yorktown*'s radar. Observers on other American ships remarked upon both the grim determination of the Japanese in pursuing the *Yorktown* and the fierce resistance the American carrier offered. The *Yorktown* held out through June 7, when it finally succumbed to the damage inflicted upon it and yielded to the sea.

When the fourth *Yorktown* was to be christened, the navy asked Eleanor Roosevelt to break the traditional bottle of champagne on the ship's bow. However, Mrs. Roosevelt had already launched the ill-fated third *Yorktown*, and she was skeptical of accepting a follow-up role. "I wonder whether I should sponsor the new USS *Yorktown* inasmuch as the one I sponsored met such a sad fate?" she asked. "I know there are superstitions in the navy, and would want to be very sure that it was wise for me to do this before making any definite promise." The secretary of the navy replied that Mrs. Roosevelt's presence would indeed be welcome, so she traveled to Newport News, Virginia, in January 1943 to do the honors. The *Yorktown* was commissioned three months later and went on to earn a Presidential Unit Citation and eleven battle stars during World War II, as well as another five battle stars for service during Vietnam.

The bridges over the Cooper River

The *Yorktown* at Patriots Point is not the last of her breed. A fifth USS *Yorktown*, commissioned in 1984, is now part of the United States Navy.

Visitors to Patriots Point are sometimes treated to a glimpse of the modern navy. Before you leave, be sure to scan the lower section of the Cooper River for the low profile of a nuclear-powered attack submarine. The submarines travel right past Patriots Point as they make their way back and forth between the Atlantic Ocean and the yards where they are berthed in Charleston.

When you have completed your visit to Patriots Point, follow the signs for U.S. 17 heading into Charleston, which will take you across one of the bridges over the Cooper River. The John P. Grace Memorial Bridge, the older of the two, bears most of the southbound traffic from Mount Pleasant to Charleston. The newer Silas N. Pearman Bridge, opened in 1966, carries two northbound lanes and one southbound lane most of the time, with all three of its lanes reserved for northbound traffic during rush hour. The bridges span 2.3 miles. However, they shorten the land distance between Mount Pleasant and Charleston by a whopping 72 miles.

It is the John P. Grace Memorial Bridge, named for a former mayor of Charleston, that tends to strike terror into the hearts of visitors. The bridge seems too narrow for the traffic it must bear, and it looks a good deal more shaky than most bridges. Commonly referred to as the Cooper River Bridge, it was completed in 1929, before either the Golden Gate Bridge or the Chesapeake Bay Bridge-Tunnel. Its central span is 1,000 feet in length, and it has a clearance of 150 feet at high water. At the time of its opening, it was believed to be one of the tallest structures of its kind in the world, surpassed only by the Blackwell Island Bridge across the East River in New York and the Cauquines Strait Bridge near San Francisco.

The opening of the John P. Grace Memorial Bridge was an occasion to be remembered. People viewing it from close range for the first time thought that it resembled a roller coaster. Some prospective travelers were afraid to drive onto it, backing away at the last moment. Only a month after the opening, the sheriff of Charleston County offered the bridge for sale for delinquent taxes. The sale was prevented, but the company known as Cooper River Bridge, Inc., found itself more than $500,000 in debt, and control of the bridge had to be reorganized under bankruptcy laws.

Things have improved since then, though the bridge still seems to inspire more than its fair share of fear. For example, a New Jersey man appeared at police headquarters in 1967 and stated that he simply could not drive across the bridge. An officer had to chauffeur the visitor's car the length of the bridge

Magnolia Cemetery boasts a collection of monuments of every conceivable size and design.

Magnolia Cemetery and its ancient oak tree

while the man sat next to him holding his head between his knees. The John P. Grace Memorial Bridge has been the scene of suicides and other deaths as well. In 1946, a 10,000-ton freighter named the *Nicaraqua Victory* struck the bridge, killing six, creating damages valued at $300,000, and causing a six-month closure for repairs.

Assuming you have made it safely across the Cooper River into Charleston, watch for the sign for North Meeting Street near the end of the bridge. Two blocks after you exit the bridge, turn right onto North Meeting Street, which also serves as U.S. 52. Approximately 1.4 miles from the bridge, turn right onto Connington Street and follow it for 1 block to where it ends at Huguenin Avenue and the entrance to Magnolia Cemetery. You will see the cemetery behind the brick wall.

If you have time to explore only one of Charleston's old cemeteries, you could not make a better choice than Magnolia Cemetery. The cemetery is located on the former site of Magnolia Umbria Plantation, which thrived during colonial days. The plantation was later subdivided into farms, one of which—Magnolia Farm—came under the control of a group seeking to establish a cemetery. Under the direction of architect Edward C. Jones, roadways and paths were laid out around an ancient oak tree. Hurricane Hugo heavily damaged the tree in 1989, but it is still easily recognizable thanks to its

TOURING THE COASTAL SOUTH CAROLINA BACKROADS

age and its monumental size. At Magnolia Cemetery's dedication in November 1850, a full choir sang an ode written by two local men. Prominent Charlestonian William Gillmore Simms composed a poem for the occasion and called it "City of the Silent." Simms now lies at rest in the city of which he wrote.

The general section of the cemetery boasts a collection of monuments of every conceivable size and design. By contrast, the section reserved for Confederate veterans is arranged with traditional military precision and uniformity. It contains the graves of over seventeen hundred soldiers, known and unknown. Five Confederate generals are buried on the site, as well as some eighty-four South Carolinians who fell at Gettysburg.

Retrace Connington Street to North Meeting Street and turn left. Follow Meeting Street for 1.9 miles and park at the Charleston Visitor Center, located on the right at 306 Meeting Street, between Ann and John streets; the site is opposite the Charleston Museum. A capsule history of Charleston may give you some valuable background before you browse the Charleston Visitor Center and the Charleston Museum.

In 1629, King Charles I issued a charter to Sir Robert Heath for the New World region he called Carolana, derived from the name Charles and ultimately from the Latin word *carolus*. When a new charter was granted to the Lords Proprietors by King Charles II in 1663, the spelling was changed to Carolina. It wasn't until 1670 that the first permanent town in Carolina was established on the Ashley River. That town was Charles Town, named for King Charles II.

Charles Town and its neighboring plantations soon became the focus of the Lords Proprietors' interests. In fact, Charles Town *was* South Carolina until well after the Revolutionary War. It remained the state capital until 1786, when the city of Columbia was legislated into existence. The name was changed from Charles Town to Charleston after the city was incorporated in 1783.

The original plan for Charles Town was known as "the Grand Modell." It called for straight streets and large blocks. One old survey shows 337 town lots of varying sizes and designations, such as "low water," meaning that the land in question was exposed only at low tide; "water lots," meaning that the tracts in question extended from the low-water mark to the channel of the Cooper River; and "high land." The first grant of a town lot was issued in February 1679 for a tract at the northwest corner of what are now East Bay and Broad streets. Lot grants continued into the eighteenth century. The town was supposed to center around the intersection of Broad and Meeting streets, at what is now called "the Four Corners of Law." However, it was King Street that came to occupy the most prominent position, thanks to its location along the ridge of high ground that rides the center of the downtown Charleston peninsula.

The importance of the Charles Town waterfront was recognized at an early date. Steps were taken to protect it from both natural and man-made threats. In 1700, a brick seawall was built for the purpose of shielding the riverbank from the erosion caused by storms. The colonists also mounted large and small guns at a site called Half Moon Battery, on the Cooper River at the foot of what is now Broad Street. Sir Nathaniel Johnson, the colonial governor, directed the construction of the town's first effective walls, and by 1704 Charles Town was being depicted on maps as protected by fortifications.

Most of Charles Town's wealth came from rice and indigo. Trade with Great Britain was excellent. Wealthy Charles Town residents spent a great deal of time sailing back and forth to London, and they sent their sons there to be educated. Local sympathies were solidly with the Crown up until the time that the government of King George III instituted a large tax increase. It was at that point that the colonists began to fear their economy would be crippled.

The famous Boston Tea Party of December 16, 1773, had its counterpart in the Charles Town Tea Party of November 3, 1774. Three Charles Town tea merchants boarded a ship called the *Neptune* and dumped tea chests into the harbor. A mass meeting protesting the tea tax was held in the Exchange Building a month later. That meeting is considered the foundation of modern South Carolina government. The most significant action of the Revolutionary War in Charles Town came on June 28, 1776, when Colonel William Moultrie's American forces repulsed an attempt by Commodore Peter Parker to sail a British fleet into Charles Town Harbor. (For more information on the Battle of Fort Moultrie, see The Swamp Fox Tour.)

A fire devastated the waterfront area in 1778, and the city experienced a period of economic depression after the Revolutionary War. Prosperity returned in the 1790s, heralded by the invention of the cotton gin and the development of rice cultivation. When news reached Charleston that rail transportation was being inaugurated in Europe, it was suggested that a railroad might be the perfect prescription for forestalling bad economic times in the Low Country. Railroad construction began in 1830, and a line between Charleston and the Savannah River opened in 1833. The first locomotive was called the Best Friend of Charleston. The effect on the city's economy was immediate. In the wake of the railroad, new buildings arose and property values increased by a whopping 25 percent in the span of a year.

Nearly every planter along the coast bought or built an elegant home in Charleston during the period of antebellum prosperity. The city was the hub of activities in their lives partly because of its port facilities, from which indigo, rice, and cotton were sent across the ocean. Charleston was also a social center. The social season lasted from February until Lent, during which time the planter families raced their horses on the Washington Race Course and attended balls held by the St. Cecilia Society and the South Carolina Jockey Club. Charleston was also a haven of religious tolerance where Huguenots, Presbyterians, Congregationalists, Jews, Baptists, Anglicans, and others worshipped in harmony. In fact, it was a matter of law that no religious arguments were permitted.

In 1838, in the middle of Charleston's golden era, a great fire raged through some 145 acres of the city, consuming a thousand buildings. Many of the homes belonging to the planters were destroyed. If you happen to browse any old books on Charleston, you may notice that some of the old houses referred to are no longer standing. The fire of 1838 is most likely the reason.

Charlestonians and South Carolinians in general have always cherished their political independence. In the 1820s and 1830s, South Carolina was at the center of a conflict over state interposition—otherwise known as the Nullification controversy. The controversy centered around the checks on federal power that could be exercised at the state level. And in 1860, states' rights was the subject for discussion when the South Carolina Secession Convention met in Charleston.

The Civil War began off Charleston on April 12, 1861, when Confederate batteries on James Island began bombarding Fort Sumter, which President Lincoln had determined to hold for the Union. (For more information about the firing on Fort Sumter, see The Charleston Plantations Tour.) Since Charleston was a major seaport, and since it was considered to be "the Cradle of Secession," Union forces made it a priority objective. The Federal bombardment of Charleston began in August 1863 and lasted, off and on, until the city surrendered a year and a half later. Charleston was by then impoverished and largely in ruins.

The local economy began to revive by 1867, when businessmen perceived an opportunity in mining phosphate from the local rivers. The phosphate was baked, ground to a powder, and mixed with ammonia and sulfuric acid to make agricultural fertilizer. By 1880, twenty-one companies were engaged in that industry, and cotton mills, lumbermills, flour mills, ironworks, and other operations were expanding as well.

A mass meeting held in the Exchange Building in 1774 to protest the tea tax is considered the foundation of modern South Carolina government.

The earthquake that struck Charleston in 1886 severely damaged the United States Custom House despite its nine-foot-thick walls.

TOURING THE COASTAL SOUTH CAROLINA BACKROADS

Then disaster struck again. On August 25, 1886, a hurricane scored a direct hit on Charleston, badly damaging the seawall, flooding the city, and leaving behind $1,500,000 in damages.

As bad as the hurricane was, it proved only an appetizer for what followed less than a week later. A little before 10:00 P.M. on August 31, a major earthquake rocked the city. People poured from their homes as ceilings fell and floors collapsed beneath their feet. Many of them believed that the end of the world was at hand, and they fell on their knees praying for mercy. No section of Charleston was spared. Within the span of one minute, sixty-seven people were killed, all the clocks in the city stopped, and all but a hundred of the fourteen thousand chimneys in town were knocked down. The shock of the quake was felt as far away as Mexico, Canada, and Bermuda. The United States Custom House in Charleston was severely damaged despite its nine-foot-thick walls. The porch at St. Michael's Episcopal Church was torn away. Hibernian Hall was a pile of debris. Saint Philip's Episcopal Church was cracked, and an ugly hole gaped in its steeple. Many of the beautiful mansions on East Battery Street were wrecked. And once the earthquake was finished, overturned lamps and broken gas lines began to erupt into fire. Governor Sheppard ultimately assessed the damage in Charleston and the surrounding area at $10 million.

But Charlestonians again proved their resilience by rebuilding their city. Some feel they made it better than ever. There have been other world-class hurricanes in the intervening years—in August and October 1893 and as recently as Hurricane Hugo in 1989—but Charleston remains a city of astonishing beauty and a monument to eighteenth- and nineteenth-century design.

Today, city residents are especially proud of the $13.4-million Charleston Visitor Center. A tour is highly recommended. Besides being an interesting stop in itself, the center is also the place where countless visitors to Charleston go to make arrangements for horse-drawn carriage tours, trolley tours, boat trips to Fort Sumter, and other memorable activities.

The Charleston Visitor Center was fourteen years in the making. It is located in what was once the South Carolina Railway Freight Depot Building, constructed in 1856. It and several other nearby buildings comprise the oldest collection of railway buildings in the country. All of the old railway buildings are listed on the National Register of Historic Places. They once served the world's first scheduled railway passenger line, the Best Friend of Charleston. In fact, a replica of a wheel from the Best Friend of Charleston is built into the

Charleston Visitor Center

Charleston's blacksmith's were noted for the unusual designs they brought to their ironwork, as seen here on the John Rutledge Home.

flagstone floor on the porch where you enter the Charleston Visitor Center.

The center's attractions are many. One room contains a model of downtown Charleston; the details are so faithful that individual streets, buildings, and houses are recognizable. Near the information desk is a sample segment of Charleston ironwork. In days gone by, the city's blacksmiths were noted for the unusual designs they brought to their ironwork, much of which may still be seen in gates, fences, and other decorations around town. So special was the ironwork that the owners of some of Charleston's mansions insisted that the blacksmiths throw away their casts so that no one else could have the same design. Another attraction at the Charleston Visitor Center is an excellent multi-image slide show called "Forever Charleston," shown every thirty minutes. Its eighteen hundred slides show beautiful scenes of the city then and now, accompanied by the voices of Charleston aristocrats, speakers of Gullah, and others.

Of special interest is the room containing a replica of a Charleston single house. The single house has been the city's most notable style of dwelling since the 1730s. The style is not unique to Charleston. For example, a similar home dating from the early eighteenth century can still be found in Boston, though no one there calls it a single house. The tradition actually goes all the way back to medieval England. Some people believe that the design—having the narrow side of the house toward the street—became popular in Charleston as a means of relieving urban crowding. Others maintain that single houses were desirable because of the financial advantage they offered, since taxes were calculated according to the amount of street frontage. Another argument is that people liked them simply because of their comfort and privacy. A trademark feature of the single house is its door facing the sidewalk, which serves as a formal entrance to the piazza, though the actual front door is secluded from the street. Once you have learned the single-house style, you will have no trouble recognizing the many variations to be found throughout Charleston.

Charleston Mayor Joseph Riley, Jr., once said that it was an objective of his administration "to make this the most beautiful visitor center in America, and to convey to the visitor the sense of quality that is Charleston." Most people agree that the effort was a success.

Once you have toured the Charleston Visitor Center, walk across the street to the Charleston Museum. Founded in 1773, it holds the distinction of being the oldest city museum in North America. Before you enter, be sure to take a close look at the replica of the Confederate submarine *Hunley* on display in the yard.

A decidedly primitive vessel, the *Hunley* was made from an old iron boiler. To get some idea of the incredible courage demanded of the men aboard the submarine, try to imagine yourself as part of the *Hunley's* eight-man crew. Once the vessel was submerged, crew members had no supply of fresh oxygen until it resurfaced, and their only source of light was a single candle. Water pressure was too great for the men to lift the hatches, so there was no escaping the vessel once it was underwater. To move the *Hunley*, they had to turn hand cranks that spun the propeller, producing a top speed no faster than a person could walk on land. And worst of all, the "torpedo" with which the submarine was to attack the Union fleet was attached to a pine boom extending from the front of the vessel, so that the crew was little more than twenty feet away from the point of explosion! The *Hunley* was a deathtrap. Nonetheless, there was no shortage of Confederates willing to man her. Thirty men died in four separate training accidents before the submarine finally exploded its "torpedo" against the side of the USS *Housatonic* in Charleston Harbor in February 1864. It was the first sinking of a ship by a submarine in history, but the crew of the *Hunley* reaped no enjoyment from their success, for they perished in the blast.

Replica of the Confederate submarine **Hunley** *on display in the yard of the Charleston Museum*

You will find more Charleston sea lore in the first room inside the museum, where a forty-foot right whale hangs overhead. The right whale supposedly got its name because it was the "right" whale to hunt. It offered the advantages of being more buoyant than other whales after it was killed, of tending to stay close to land, and of having blubber and bones that were especially valuable. The specimen on display entered Charleston Harbor in January 1880. That proved to be the worst, and last, mistake of its life, as the entire fishing community came in hot pursuit. After the whale was killed, it was put on display at Pregnell's Wharf, where people could come to see it for a twenty-five-cent charge.

Before you leave the Charleston Museum, be sure to see the displays of colonial-era dolls and of infant's clothing of the late nineteenth century. Among the other attractions are exhibits detailing the steps involved in the production of rice and cotton, a display of elegant Charleston silver, and a model of the *Harriott Pinckney*, representative of American oceangoing cargo ships of the nineteenth century.

When you are ready to exit the parking lot at the Charleston Visitor Center, turn right onto Meeting Street. Follow Meeting Street for 2 blocks, where you will see a pink-colored stucco fortress on the right. The structure is known as the Old Citadel. It served as an arsenal from the time of its completion in 1830 to when South Carolina's military college was established on the site in 1842. The first corps of cadets, consisting of twenty young men, arrived the following spring. Cadets at the Old Citadel saw their first action of the Civil War in 1861, when they fired a series of warning shots at the Federal supply ship *Star of the West* to prevent it from aiding troops at Fort Sumter. Union troops occupied the Old Citadel by 1865, remaining until 1879. The military college reopened three years later. The city of Charleston gave the Citadel its present site on the banks of the Ashley River in 1918, and operations were moved there in 1922.

You may notice the statue of John C. Calhoun in the park area by the Old Citadel. It memorializes one of the leading men of antebellum Southern politics. South Carolina has never given the country a president, though Calhoun was a candidate in 1824, 1836, and 1844. He served as vice president under Andrew Jackson, secretary of war under James Monroe, and secretary of state under James Knox Polk, in addition to his tenure in the United States Senate and the House of Representatives. Calhoun was an advocate of state interposition and a believer in slavery.

Continue driving along Meeting Street for about 7 blocks until you reach

South Market Street. Turn left onto South Market Street and you will immediately come upon the City Market. Make sure you allow plenty of time to explore the premises.

Charleston's City Market encompasses three buildings that extend from Meeting Street to the United States Custom House at the Cooper River. Land was first set aside for a public market between 1788 and 1804, when Charles Cotesworth Pinckney and others ceded property to the city. Low ground and a creek were filled in by 1806. The first building on the site housed a meat market. Butchers would arrive for work around 3:00 A.M. As they trimmed their meat, they would throw the gristle and skin onto unpaved Meeting Street. By dawn, huge flocks of birds would be enjoying a feast. Subsequent buildings were designed for the sale of vegetables and fruit—much of it raised on nearby Johns Island—as well as for the sale of fish. Turtle eggs were sold at the City Market, and steaming bowls of turtle soup were a regular lunch for many working people.

Market-going remains a Charleston tradition. Today's City Market houses shops, boutiques, and restaurants, as well as an open-air flea market. The stalls offer almost anything you can imagine, from dolls, jewelry, baskets, and tiny wooden replicas of Charleston mansions to T-shirts, paintings, seashell art,

Statue of John C. Calhoun

The Charleston Driving Tour

clothing, and foodstuffs.

After you have enjoyed the City Market, return to Meeting Street and continue in your original direction for 3 blocks until you reach Broad Street. The tour now bypasses the historic district and heads toward Hampton Park and the Citadel. If you would rather take a guided walk through the historic area at this point, The Charleston Walking Tour begins at the intersection of Meeting and Broad streets, at what is known as "the Four Corners of Law."

To reach Hampton Park and the Citadel, turn right off Meeting Street onto Broad Street. Follow Broad Street for 0.6 mile, then turn right onto Ashley Avenue. Drive 1.6 miles on Ashley Avenue to where it ends just beyond Moultrie Street at Mary Murray Drive, the street that circles Hampton Park and leads to the entrance to the Citadel. Turn right onto Mary Murray Drive and follow it around the park.

What is now Hampton Park began in 1792 as the Washington Race Course, the last of three horse-racing courses owned and laid out by the South Carolina Jockey Club. The club counted among its members such luminaries as Charles

Meeting Street entrance to Charleston's City Market

TOURING THE COASTAL SOUTH CAROLINA BACKROADS

Cotesworth Pinckney, William Moultrie, and Confederate General Wade Hampton, the South Carolina governor for whom Hampton Park was named.

The thoroughbred races held at Washington Race Course were among the most dazzling of Charleston's antebellum functions. The annual race week was held in February. The men among the planter aristocracy brought their best horses, many of them from Virginia stock or imported from England. As the hour for racing drew near, courts adjourned, stores closed, and schools let out early. The wives and daughters of the planters arrived at Washington Race Course in their own carriages, decked out in dresses and jewels from Paris and accompanied by liveried outriders in buckskin breeches and top boots. It is said that lovers became more ardent during race week, and that young belles frequently chose their husbands over the course of the meet. Prizes were given to the winners of the races, but that meant little to the planters, who bred, trained, and raced their thoroughbreds as a matter of personal honor. The South Carolina Jockey Club Ball was held on the Friday night of race week. The city of Charleston has not known such lavish entertainment since those days.

Races were held at Washington Race Course until 1895, save for during the Civil War, when the Confederates pressed the facilities into service as a military prison. In 1901 and 1902, the site hosted the South Carolina Inter-State and West Indian Exposition, which counted thirty-one states and territories and several foreign countries among its participants. President Theodore Roosevelt was among the guests. Designed to show off the city's industrial potential, the exposition pumped $3 to $5 million into the local economy and convinced the American Cigar Company, the United Fruit Company, and an oyster cannery to relocate their operations in Charleston.

After you have circled Hampton Park, you will arrive at the entrance to the Citadel. The buildings comprising the college are grouped around a parade ground. Also of interest to visitors is the Citadel Memorial Military Museum, which contains relics and documents related to the college, its graduates, the Civil War, and military history in general.

The stated purpose of the Citadel is to prepare young men for positions of leadership by providing a sound education reinforced by the best features of a disciplined environment. Jim Heritage, class of 1972, once summed up the nature of a Citadel man in a prayer delivered on the campus:

> Give me a boy, O God, who is willing to learn the true value of honor, the necessity of perserverance and loyalty, and the meaningfulness of devotion to God and country. And I shall take this boy as does a

blacksmith take a crude piece of metal, and place him over a forge whose liberating flame of education is fired by the bellows of strict military discipline. Into this ingot of a man I shall temper self-respect and self-discipline, fear of God and respect for mankind, appreciation of freedom and awareness of what sacrifices must be made to preserve freedom, and above all an insatiable desire for truth and honesty. And when all these things I have done, I shall brand my finished work with a ring of gold to let all humanity know that I have given back to the world . . . a Citadel man.

Regardless of whether you favor military-style education, a visit to the Citadel is likely to leave you standing straight and thinking patriotic thoughts, particularly if you arrive around midafternoon on any Friday from October through May. It is then that the two-thousand-man corps of cadets conducts its traditional dress parade.

This tour ends at the Citadel. Charleston offers countless interesting attractions, but if you intend to leave town, turn left onto Moultrie Street upon exiting the Citadel. Follow Moultrie Street to Rutledge Avenue, then turn right onto Rutledge Avenue and watch for the signs for U.S. 17, which leads either north over the Cooper River or south over the Ashley River.

The Citadel

TOURING THE COASTAL SOUTH CAROLINA BACKROADS

Some views of Charleston's early history

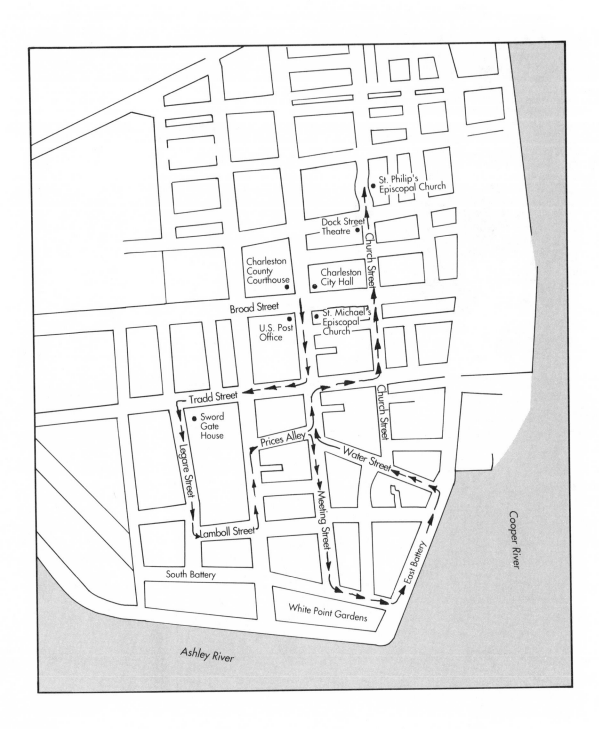

The Charleston Walking Tour

This walking tour of Charleston's historic district begins at the Four Corners of Law, at the corner of Meeting and Broad streets. It travels some of the most famous blocks in the city to visit the Sword Gate House, O'Donnell's Folly, the Miles Brewton House, the Calhoun Mansion, the Battery, the deSaussure House, the Nathaniel Russell House, the Heyward-Washington House, the French Huguenot Church, and numerous other sites before ending at St. Philip's Episcopal Church.

Total distance: approximately 25 blocks.

The intersection of Meeting and Broad streets in Charleston is known as the Four Corners of Law because the buildings on each corner stand for a different form of law. St. Michael's Episcopal Church, on the southeast corner, represents the law of God; Charleston City Hall, on the northeast corner, represents local law; the Charleston County Courthouse, on the northwest corner, represents the law of the state; and the United States Post Office, on the southwest corner, represents federal law. You may want to leave your car in one of the parking garages in the vicinity of the Four Corners of Law as you begin this walking tour of the historic district.

St. Michael's Episcopal Church stands on a site originally occupied by St. Philip's Episcopal Church in 1681; when the St. Philip's building started to show signs of disrepair, its congregation opted for a move to Church Street and a site that would allow more space for a cemetery. St. Michael's was commissioned for construction in 1751 and opened for services in 1761. It survives as Charleston's oldest church.

The steeple of St. Michael's is 186 feet high, topped by a weather vane over 7 feet long. Both the steeple and the ceiling covering the main hall, which contains no visible means of support, are considered fine examples of colonial construction. Among the highlights in the interior are the chandelier, the woodwork of mahogany and South Carolina cedar, and the wrought-iron communion rail, imported from England in 1772. The octagonal pulpit, with its massive, canopied sounding board, is original; you might notice the scars on its base, which were produced by a Union shell that struck the church in 1863. Pew number 43 was graced by George Washington in 1791 and Robert E. Lee in 1861.

The bells of St. Michael's have an interesting story behind them. They were imported from Great Britain in 1764, then captured and taken back to England as a prize during the Revolutionary War. There, they were purchased by a

St. Michael's Episcopal Church

London merchant and shipped back to Charleston. The bells were moved to Columbia for safekeeping during the Civil War, but they were burned in the great fire that consumed that city in 1865. However, all was not lost, as the surviving fragments were shipped to England to be recast and rehung before they were returned to their proper place at St. Michael's. The bells have thus crossed the Atlantic a total of five times to date.

Charleston City Hall is across Broad Street from St. Michael's Episcopal Church. Designed by a Charlestonian named Gabriel Manigault, it was purchased by the city in 1818. An elegant council chamber was constructed in 1882, but it didn't remain intact for long, as everything but its chandeliers and furniture were destroyed in a massive earthquake in 1886. (For more information on the earthquake that devastated Charleston, see The Charleston Driving Tour.)

Charleston City Hall

The Charleston County Courthouse, dating from 1791, stands across Meeting Street from Charleston City Hall. One of the most colorful moments in the history of the courthouse came during World War II, when a famous witch doctor from Beaufort, Dr. Buzzard, was put on trial. Dr. Buzzard was accused of dispensing a special potion to young men that would make their pulse race and their blood pressure soar. The potion was designed to be taken before the young men went for their medical examinations for military service, and the effect it produced in their bodies conveniently prevented them from being selected.

The Charleston County Courthouse

Those were patriotic times. Many people who attended the trial had relatives serving in areas where combat was raging, and they viewed the alleged crime with the utmost seriousness. Dr. Buzzard didn't do himself any favors when he took the witness stand and readily admitted his guilt. The observers were aghast.

When it came time for sentencing, the judge offered Dr. Buzzard the option of a five-year prison term or a $5,000 fine, even remarking on the difficulty of paying such a stiff fine during wartime. Dr. Buzzard looked the judge in the eye and casually asked, "How do you want the money?" When the judge asked what he meant, Dr. Buzzard reached into the inside pocket of his coat and pulled out a thick roll of bills held by a rubber band. Using his thumb, he peeled off fifty $100 bills, then returned the remainder of the roll to his pocket. There was pandemonium in the courtroom, with the observers either laughing, cursing, or expressing disbelief. The judge had to pound his gavel for order. Once silence was restored, Dr. Buzzard was heard to ask, "Is cash all right?" He then proceeded to hand the judge his $5,000.

The United States Post Office, a Renaissance Revival structure built in 1898, is located across Broad Street from the Charleston County Courthouse. Charleston's famous flower ladies can usually be seen selling their wares on the post-office steps; their beautiful flowers are grown on Johns Island. Basket makers also sell their handicrafts here. Local artists are fond of doing watercolor paintings of the flower ladies and the basket makers in front of the post office, and you may be lucky enough to see their work in a variety of gift shops around the city. (For more information on Charleston's basket makers, see The Swamp Fox Tour.)

When you have seen the Four Corners of Law, head south on Meeting Street; you'll know you're heading south if St. Michael's Episcopal Church is behind you to your left and the United States Post Office is behind you to your right. As you walk, you'll notice the small gardens in back of many of the houses

The United States Post Office

along the route. The owners are accustomed to having visitors peek over their fences and through their garden gates for a look.

The home on the right at 59 Meeting Street is of the variety known as a Charleston double house, which means that it is two rooms wide and two rooms deep on each floor. Lots in the city are narrow, and you will see a good many single and double houses on this tour. The drawing room in a Charleston double house is usually on the second floor, the better to catch the breezes off the Cooper and Ashley rivers. A planter named William Branford owned the

59 Meeting Street

TOURING THE COASTAL SOUTH CAROLINA BACKROADS

home at 59 Meeting Street before 1767. The front piazza, built over the sidewalk, was added in 1830 by Branford's grandson, Elias Horry.

Follow Meeting Street to Tradd Street and turn right. After 2 blocks on Tradd Street, turn left onto Legare Street. The famous Sword Gate House, on the left at 32 Legare Street, is a Charleston landmark.

The man who originally bought land at this corner was Solomon Legare, a Huguenot silversmith. The men responsible for the present house were two German merchants by the name of Steinmetz and Lorent. Andrew Talvande bought the home in 1819. His wife, Rose, operated a school for young women, and it was said for many years around Charleston that ladies trained under her tutelage were identifiable by their perfect manners alone. Madame Talvande had a love of fashion and the theater. She arrived in Charleston from Santo Domingo, where she escaped a slave uprising in 1793 that left many members of the white planter class dead. The Talvandes never became United States citizens, a fact that left Madame Talvande in difficult straits after her husband's death in 1835. Her claims to the property were disputed under citizenship and inheritance laws, and it ultimately took an act of the South Carolina legislature to confirm her right to the house.

The Sword Gate House at 32 Legare Street

There is a famous story surrounding one of Madame Talvande's students, a girl named Maria Whaley. In 1829, at the age of fifteen, Maria fell in love with George W. Morris, a Yankee who was entirely unacceptable to her parents. In fact, her father enrolled her with Madame Talvande to keep her away from her suitor. But young Morris was determined. At first, he took up residence at a nearby plantation to remain close to Maria. Maria's father contacted the plantation family and strongly suggested that they turn their young guest out, which they did. Morris saw no alternative but to set up a tent to continue his courtship. In those days, Madame Talvande's school was guarded by a wooden fence, and a portion of it was broken. One night, Maria escaped over the break in the fence. She and Morris were secretly married, after which Maria returned to the school. A week or so later, Morris came rolling up in fine style in his carriage and, to everyone's surprise, requested that his wife join him. This time, Maria left through the front door. To prevent further elopements, Madame Talvande had a higher wall constructed, topped with broken bottles. The wall still stands today.

The famous sword gates, the house's most distinctive feature and the one from which it draws its name, were actually not added until around 1849, when the property was owned by George A. Hopley, a merchant and British consul. The gates were made by Christopher Werner, the most noted iron-

The William C. Gatewood House at 21 Legare Street

The "Pineapple Gates" of the Simmons-Edwards House at 14 Legare Street

worker in Charleston. The Roman swords are a symbol of authority.

The avenue of magnolia trees at the Sword Gate House dates from 1856 and the ownership of Robert Adger. A granddaughter of Abraham Lincoln's later owned the home, though she never actually lived in it.

Continue south on Legare Street. The William C. Gatewood House, at 21 Legare Street, dates from the mid-1800s. It was constructed to catch breezes coming off the Ashley River, to the south. Note that the basement windows and doors have brownstone trim, while the upper-floor windows are trimmed in marble. The house was sold for $8,000 in 1942. It was converted into apartments at that time, but it now serves as a single-family dwelling again.

By contrast, the Simmons-Edwards House, at 14 Legare Street, sold for $2 million in 1989, which may tell you something about the way real-estate values have skyrocketed in Charleston's historic district in recent decades. That sale value is believed to have been the highest in the historic area to that date. The house was constructed around 1801. Note the set of marble live-oak acorns from Italy on the gate. The acorns bear a resemblance to pineapples, and the Simmons-Edwards House is thus informally known as "Pineapple Gates."

Turn left off Legare Street onto Lamboll Street. After 1 block on Lamboll Street, turn left onto King Street. One of Charleston's most handsome buildings is O'Donnell's Folly, at 21 King Street, built by Irish immigrant Patrick O'Donnell. The name came about because O'Donnell, in his efforts to build a special home for his ladylove, insisted on such spectacular detail that construction dragged on indefinitely, and his girl finally married someone else.

O'Donnell's Folly was designed in the Italianate style of the mid-1800s. The traditional single-house plan was modified by the addition of a slightly recessed wing on the north side containing the formal entrance hall and stairs. Each tier of the piazza has a different entablature on fluted Doric columns. The interior boasts elaborate plasterwork. An unusual feature is the face of Jenny Lind, "the Swedish Nightingale," which appears repeatedly in the ceiling medallions of the double drawing rooms. O'Donnell's Folly is truly a romantic house, and as such it proved the perfect home for novelist Josephine Pinckney, who lived here from 1907 to 1937. The house has a rich literary history. The Poetry Society of South Carolina was organized on the premises in 1920, and one-time resident Mrs. Thomas R. McGahan served as the model for Melanie in Margaret Mitchell's *Gone With the Wind*.

Continue to 27 King Street, the site of the Miles Brewton House, considered one of the best American townhouses ever built and a fine example of eighteenth-century architecture. Englishman Ezra Waite created the mansion

O'Donnell's Folly at 21 King Street

for Charleston businessman Miles Brewton. Waite's work has a strong flavor of the work of Thomas Chippendale, the famous English cabinetmaker. The house features a grand mahogany staircase and a drawing room with pedimented doors, a marble mantel, and a crystal chandelier, one of only two of its design known to have existed in colonial South Carolina.

Miles Brewton's sister, Rebecca Brewton Motte, resided in the house during the Revolutionary War, when it was made to serve as the headquarters of Sir Henry Clinton, Lord Rawdon, and Lord Cornwallis. Legend has it that Mrs. Motte locked her three young daughters securely in the attic while the British

The Miles Brewton House at 27 King Street

were in residence, and that they somehow managed to remain undetected the entire time. The daughters went on to marry well. One of them became the wife of William Alston of Waccamaw Neck, who made the Miles Brewton House his town residence for nearly fifty years. The house was also occupied during the Civil War, when Union Generals Meade and Hatch used it as a headquarters.

After you have seen the Miles Brewton House, turn right off King Street onto Price's Alley. At the end of the alley, turn right onto Meeting Street. The house at 37 Meeting Street has been nicknamed "the Bosoms" in honor of the twin bays that curve symmetrically on either side of the entrance. The house was probably constructed before 1775 and the bays added sometime between 1809 and 1848. Confederate General Pierre G. T. Beauregard, the man who directed the bombardment of Fort Sumter that began the Civil War, was headquartered here from October 1862 to August 1863 and kept his cow in the backyard. The house was purchased in 1876 by Michael P. O'Connor, who later became a member of Congress.

William Bull's House, adjacent to "the Bosoms" at 35 Meeting Street, is the oldest home in Charleston. The lot was granted to Stephen Bull of Ashley Hall and Sheldon plantations, near Beaufort, in 1696. The home was built around 1720 by his son William, who later became lieutenant governor of South Carolina. The exterior remains largely unchanged, save for the piazzas on the south and west wings added by subsequent owners. It was from the steps of William Bull's House that Governor Robert Y. Hayne dissuaded a group of nullificationists from going to the Battery, seizing a ship, and declaring war on the Union in the early 1830s.

As you walk south on Meeting Street, you'll notice that the house numbers are getting lower; it is said that the lower the house number in Charleston, the more prestigious the address.

The house at 34 Meeting Street was also built by the Bull family. It was later occupied briefly by Lord William Campbell, the state's last royal governor.

William Bull's House at 35 Meeting Street

34 Meeting Street

The "Bosoms" at 37 Meeting Street

South Carolinians were no longer bowing and scraping to royalty in the years immediately preceding the Revolutionary War. When Lord Campbell found that his distinguished presence met with a sullen silence from Charlestonians, he fled back to England after a stay of only three months. William Elliott Huger, a noted South Carolina legislator and jurist, purchased the home in 1818; it is still owned by the Huger family today. The house at 34 Meeting Street was the site of a tragedy during the earthquake of 1886, when a portion of the parapet broke loose and fell upon a young English visitor.

The homes at 27, 25, and 23 Meeting Street are good examples of the variations possible with the Charleston single house, as they all boast different shapes, heights, widths, colors, and embellishments. The houses are known as "the Three Sisters," and they are sentimental favorites among Charlestonians. Notice the earthquake rods on the sides of the houses. After the devastation of 1886, the rods had to be installed to hold the structures together.

The house at 18 Meeting Street served as the home of Thomas Heyward, a signer of the Declaration of Independence, until his death in 1809. James Adger, the man who operated the first coastal steamship line in the United States, also lived here, as did noted theologian Thomas Smyth. The house was built after the example of Scottish architect Robert Adam, whose work is characterized by its lightness and delicacy of detail. The moldings are in low

*"The Three Sisters" at
27, 25, and 23 Meeting Street*

TOURING THE COASTAL SOUTH CAROLINA BACKROADS

relief, and the panels are sunken rather than raised. The mantels and windows are decorated with such delicate ornaments as classical figures, chains of husks, and garlands of flowers. Robert Adam's designs feature some interesting touches, like oval rooms and curving staircases. It is said that there is a secret room—a wine closet—somewhere on the second floor of the house at 18 Meeting Street.

The red brick structure with the white trim at 16 Meeting Street is the magnificent Calhoun Mansion, constructed in 1876. George W. Williams, a banker and merchant, was the original owner, and William P. Russell was the architect. The mansion is often mistakenly believed to have been the residence of John C. Calhoun, the noted senator and vice president, but it was actually built after his death. However, ownership did pass through the hands of Patrick Calhoun, who was the grandson of John C. Calhoun and the son-in-law of George W. Williams.

18 Meeting Street

With its thirty-five rooms and its twenty-four thousand square feet, the Calhoun Mansion is the largest residence in Charleston. It is considered one of the most important Victorian mansions in the eastern United States. Among its many spectacular features are its fourteen-foot ceilings; its elaborate woodwork; its stairwell, which reaches to a seventy-five-foot-high domed ceiling; and its ballroom, which features a skylight forty-five feet overhead. The Calhoun Mansion was used in the television miniseries "North and South" to portray the Philadelphia home of the Hazard family. It is open to the public.

The mansion at 2 Meeting Street was constructed in the Queen Anne style. It now serves as an inn—called the Two Meeting Street Inn, appropriately enough—where guests can immerse themselves in the atmosphere of old-time Charleston. The mansion's Tiffany windows are believed to have been crafted by Louis Comfort Tiffany himself.

John Robertson, a Scotsman, built the mansion at 1 Meeting Street in 1846. It was bought by Minnie S. Carr, the same woman who owned 2 Meeting Street, in 1945; the purchase meant that she possessed the two most envied addresses in the city. The mansion at 1 Meeting Street was converted into apartments for a time, but it now serves as a single-family home again.

When you reach the end of Meeting Street, you will find yourself facing the Battery, otherwise known as White Point Gardens. Charleston's earliest records used the names White Point and Oyster Point to designate the site. The names were appropriate, as there were so many mounds of white-colored oyster shells here in the latter part of the seventeenth century that a law was passed ordering crushed shells to be spread over the city's streets and

The Calhoun Mansion at 16 Meeting Street

2 Meeting Street

1 Meeting Street

TOURING THE COASTAL SOUTH CAROLINA BACKROADS

South Battery

sidewalks.

The Battery commemorates the various fortifications that have protected the south and east shores of Charleston through the years. Broughton's Battery was located at the northeastern end of the present park in the 1730s. Guns were mounted along the seawall during the Revolutionary War and the War of 1812. And the Civil War saw earthworks thrown up in the park, with guns commanding the Ashley River and Charleston Harbor.

The seawall was built to its present height and strength after a hurricane in 1854 that breached it in several places, and it was repaired and further buttressed after other hurricanes in 1885 and 1893. It allows a view of historic Fort Sumter, which stands on a man-made island between Charleston and Sullivan's Island.

The construction of Fort Sumter began in 1829 but was not completed when the fort was occupied by Union Major Robert Anderson and his troops from Fort Moultrie in December 1860. The following spring, on April 12, 1861, Confederate forces at Fort Johnson directed the opening shots of the Civil War at Fort Sumter. Major Anderson surrendered after a thirty-four-hour bom-

The William Washington House at 8 South Battery

Villa Margherita at 4 South Battery

The deSaussure House at 1 East Battery

bardment. Confederate troops then occupied the fort. Later in the war, Fort Sumter came to be seen as one of the central symbols of Southern resistance. In one of the longest sieges in the history of warfare, Union batteries pounded the fort from 1863 to 1865; the Confederates finally evacuated on February 17, 1865. An act of Congress has since established Fort Sumter as a National Monument, to be administered by the National Park Service. Boat trips to the fort are offered from several waterfront locations. (For a more detailed account of the Civil War action at Forts Sumter and Johnson, see The Charleston Plantations Tour.)

From the end of Meeting Street, turn left onto South Battery. The William Washington House, an excellent example of a Charleston double house, stands at 8 South Battery. William Washington, a cousin of George Washington's, bought the home for his bride after the Revolutionary War.

The Villa Margherita, at 4 South Battery, was built in 1895 by Andrew Simonds, the president of First National Bank. The villa was converted into a hotel after his death, and its guests included the likes of Henry Ford and Alexander Graham Bell. In 1942, it was leased to a merchant seamen's organization; the seamen and their families were said to be especially fond of the fine swimming pool on the ground floor. The Villa Margherita was returned to its role as a family residence in 1961.

When you reach the end of South Battery, turn left onto East Battery. The deSaussure House, on the corner at 1 East Battery, commands a panoramic view of the Cooper and Ashley rivers, Charleston Harbor, and the Atlantic beyond. Had it been in existence in 1718, it would have offered the best seat in town when the pirate Stede Bonnet went to the gallows on White Point. Stede Bonnet is sometimes called "the Gentleman Pirate." He was a well-educated man and a wealthy landowner on the island of Barbados, and legend has it that he turned to piracy for no better reason than to escape a nagging wife. Bonnet came under the tutelage of the notorious Blackbeard for a time, but he never managed to learn his trade very well. He surrendered to authorities after being caught at anchor on the Cape Fear River, well to the north. Taken to Charleston, he pleaded for mercy, but Governor Robert Johnson hanged him and his men. Their bodies were left on the gallows as a warning to anyone harboring thoughts of flying the Jolly Roger.

The deSaussure House was built around 1850 by Thomas A. Coffin, a member of the well-known Beaufort clan. The mansion's namesake, Louis deSaussure, purchased it for the sum of $7,500 in 1858. It suffered damage during the Confederate evacuation of February 1865, when a large gun blew

up nearby. Additional damage was caused by the earthquake of 1886. The house has now been converted into apartments.

The adjacent mansion, at 5 East Battery, is dramatic. It boasts twenty-four rooms, six baths, four separate stairways, seven mantels of black marble, and walls that are thirty-two inches thick. Even the front door, carved in rosettes, leaves a distinct impression; it opens into a tiled foyer leading to a hallway and a semicircular staircase.

The mansion was built between 1847 and 1849 by John Ravenel, a planter and merchant of Huguenot descent who founded a shipping operation and established the Ravenel name as one of South Carolina's finest. His son, St. Julien Ravenel, was a talented physician and inventor who studied medicine in Philadelphia and France. Dr. Ravenel lived in the mansion at 5 East Battery. He also owned Stony Landing, a plantation on the Cooper River, and it was there that he built the Confederate torpedo boat *David*, a predecessor of the *Hunley*, discussed elsewhere in this book in The Charleston Driving Tour. In October 1863, the tiny *David* had the audacity to attack the heavily armored Federal ship *New Ironsides*—then the largest ironclad frigate in the world—in

---

9 East Battery

Charleston Harbor. The *New Ironsides* was damaged but not destroyed, merely whetting the South's appetite for further experimentation in early submarine warfare.

The three-story Greek Revival house with the giant Ionic columns at 9 East Battery was built around 1838 by Robert William Roper. Its attic houses an unusual relic of bygone days, a five-hundred-pound section of a cannon blown up at the corner of East Battery and South Battery by evacuating Confederates in 1865. The house has had a succession of famous owners, including Solomon R. Guggenheim, the noted mining magnate and art patron.

The next mansion, at 13 East Battery, is the William Ravenel House, dating from 1845. William Ravenel was a wealthy shipping merchant and the brother and partner of John Ravenel, the man who built the mansion at 5 East Battery. The William Ravenel House is one of the tallest waterfront structures in the city. In fact, Charlestonians gathered on its roof on April 12, 1861, to watch the start of the Civil War.

The William Ravenel House at 13 East Battery

The mansion has seen its share of disasters. For example, only the arcaded base remains of the front portico; its mighty columns were shaken down by the earthquake of 1886 and never replaced. As luck would have it, a hurricane in the 1950s uprooted a tree near the mansion, and a huge capital—the upper part of one of the fallen columns—was found underneath it. The capital had apparently been driven deep into the earth by the force of its fall more than sixty years earlier.

The Regency-style Edmondston-Alston House at 21 East Battery was built between 1817 and 1828 by Charles Edmondston, a native of the Shetland Islands who made a fortune as a merchant and wharf owner. It was purchased in 1838 by Charles Cotesworth Pinckney Alston, who added features in the Greek Revival style, such as the third level of the piazza and the roof parapet bearing his family's coat of arms. His wife, Emma Pringle Alston, was one of Charleston's finest hostesses. A brief sample from her shopping list for a ball she hosted in 1851 may give you some idea of what it was like to be a society lady in antebellum days: "18 dozn plates; 14 dozn knives—28 dozn spoons; 6 dozn Wine glasses; as many Chapaigne glasses as can be collected; 4 wild turkeys; 4 hams; 2 for sandwiches & 2 for the supper tables; 60 partridges; 6 pr Pheasants; 6 pr Canvass-back Ducks; 5 pr wild ducks . . ." And that doesn't count vegetable courses or dessert! Today, the Edmondston-Alston House is operated as a museum by the Historic Charleston Foundation.

The Edmonston-Alston House at 21 East Battery

Continue the few steps to Water Street and turn left. After 2 blocks on Water Street, turn right onto Meeting Street. The Nathaniel Russell House, at 51 Meeting Street, is half a block ahead on the left.

Nathaniel Russell arrived in the city from Rhode Island. He originally established a business on East Bay Street and lived on the floor above it, in the time-honored tradition of hard-working merchants. However, that arrangement proved less than acceptable to Charleston society. No matter how much wealth Russell accumulated, he found he was not accepted on the same level as planters, clergymen, physicians, and attorneys—and that was his ambition. Russell's solution was to build the elegant, graceful mansion at 51 Meeting Street so that his daughters might be presented into the city's highest social circles. His plan worked, as one daughter married a member of the Middleton family and another an Episcopal priest.

After Russell's death, the house was acquired by Robert Francis Withers Allston, who lived here while he served as governor of South Carolina. At Allston's death in 1870, his executors sold it to the Sisters of Our Lady of Mercy. In 1955, the Historic Charleston Foundation bought it, made it their

The Nathaniel Russell House at 51 Meeting Street
Photograph by Louis Schwartz

First Scots Presbyterian Church at 57 Meeting Street

headquarters, and restored it as a house museum open to the public. The design of the Nathaniel Russell House is considered outstanding. A rectangular, three-story brick structure, it has an octagonal wing on the south side. The focal point of the mansion is a free-flying staircase that rises three stories without visible support. If you tour the premises, be sure to visit the second-floor drawing room, where mirrors arranged on opposite sides of the room lend the illusion that you are looking through a window into a separate room.

Just beyond the Nathaniel Russell House is the First Scots Presbyterian Church, at 57 Meeting Street, constructed in 1814 to replace an earlier church. The seal of the Church of Scotland is in a window over the main entrance.

Turn right off Meeting Street onto Tradd Street. After 1 block on Tradd Street, turn left onto Church Street to enjoy the Heyward-Washington House, at 87 Church Street.

The Heyward-Washington House was built by Daniel Heyward, a wealthy planter, in the eighteenth century. He left the property to his son Thomas, one of four signers of the Declaration of Independence from South Carolina. George Washington visited here in 1791. Part of the house was converted for use as a bakery during the late nineteenth century, but it has since been restored to its original condition, and it is now operated as a house museum by the Charleston Museum. The formal garden in the rear is maintained by the Garden Club of Charleston. The Heyward-Washington House boasts notable Georgian interior features and antiques. The drawing-room mantel has been attributed to Thomas Elfe, one of the city's foremost cabinetmakers during colonial days.

Note the three-story double tenement of stuccoed brick at 89–91 Church Street. In times gone by, black tenants used to put cabbages for sale on their window sills, leading to the nickname "Cabbage Row." This locale is said to have been the inspiration for DuBose Heyward's classic novel *Porgy*. Heyward changed the name from Cabbage Row to Catfish Row and moved the setting to the waterfront. In real life, Heyward's immortal Porgy was Sammy Smalls, a crippled beggar who drove a goat cart and was frequently in trouble with the law. The character Bess was inspired by a woman named Normie, who cared for Sammy Smalls and ultimately buried him on James Island. George Gershwin later adapted Heyward's novel into the folk opera *Porgy and Bess*. (For more information on Sammy Smalls, DuBose Heyward, George Gershwin, and the *Porgy and Bess* story, see The Charleston Plantations Tour.)

Continue to 135 Church Street, the site of the Dock Street Theatre. The first theater in Charleston was located here, on the southwest corner of Church

The Heyward-Washington House at 87 Church Street

Street and Dock Street—now Queen Street—in 1736. There were actually three or four different theaters on the site in colonial days. By the time of the Revolutionary War, Charleston was recognized as the theatrical center of the colonies. In 1773 and 1774, for example, a total of 118 performances were held in town, including 11 of Shakespeare's plays.

Around the year 1800, the site came to be occupied by the Planters' Hotel, the city's first hotel. Before the hotel trade began in the area, visitors had to stay in taverns, boardinghouses, or private homes. The Planters' Hotel quickly established itself as one of the centers of social life in antebellum Charleston, playing host to a wide array of wealthy landowners and businessmen. It fell into ruins after the Civil War, but a good many of its surviving features have since been incorporated into the Dock Street Theatre, including the facade and the balcony. Opened in 1937, the Dock Street Theatre is the home of the Footlight Players of Charleston. If a play happens to be running at the time of your visit, any production at the Dock Street Theatre is a real treat.

Cabbage Row

Across the street from the theater is the French Huguenot Church, organized by immigrants who arrived on the ship *Richmond* in 1680. The first church on the site was constructed in 1687, but it was deliberately blown up in 1796 in an attempt to retard the spread of a great fire that raged through the city that year. A second church was built in 1800. Legend has it that services were scheduled according to the tides, in an effort to accommodate members arriving by boat from nearby plantations. The congregation fell into decline during the early part of the nineteenth century, and the church was closed in 1823. It was revived twenty-one years later by a group of Huguenot descendants who wanted to return to the faith of their fathers.

The Dock Street Theatre at 135 Church Street

The present structure dates from 1845, as does the Henry Erben organ, which was restored during the 1970s. The church was designed in the Gothic Revival style by Edward Brickell White, the same man who designed the Winyah Indigo Society Hall in Georgetown. For many years, the church was used only for concerts and weddings, but an active congregation was revived in 1983. There is a French Huguenot church in New York City that is part of an Episcopal diocese, but Charleston's French Huguenot Church survives as the only French Calvinist congregation in the United States. (For some brief background on the Huguenots and their reasons for coming to America, see The Santee Plantations Tour.)

After you have seen the French Huguenot Church, walk 1 additional block to St. Philip's Episcopal Church, at 146 Church Street. The first St. Philip's in Charleston was built in 1681 on the present site of St. Michael's Episcopal

French Huguenot Church

St. Philip's Episcopal Church

Church, at the Four Corners of Law. The initial priest at St. Philip's, a man named Atkin Williamson, was a colorful figure. Actually, there is considerable doubt that he was a priest at all. He had been ordained a deacon in England before coming to the colonies—that much was certain—but he claimed to have lost the papers certifying him to be an ordained member of the priesthood. Williamson also had a problem with alcohol. One episode of his drinking has survived from 1682. The story goes that Williamson had a group of friends who kept a bear as a pet. Finding the "priest" drunk one day, they persuaded him to christen the unsuspecting animal. Neither Williamson nor the bear was any the wiser the next day.

A second St. Philip's was built—thanks in large measure to duties raised from the sale of rum, brandy, and slaves—on the present site between 1710 and 1723. Its tower was placed in the center of the street, after the manner of certain English churches. The second St. Philip's featured three Doric porticoes and the first documented giant-order columns in the American colonies. On one occasion, when fire was about to claim the church, an alert slave summoned help and saved the building, a deed that won him his freedom. However, his efforts bought St. Philip's only a little time, as a different fire destroyed the church in 1835.

The present building dates from the same year. The church site was moved slightly to the east, so that Church Street had to curve around St. Philip's projecting portico. The steeple, designed by Edward Brickell White and built between 1848 and 1850, follows the English Renaissance style. During the Civil War, the church's bells were donated to the Confederacy to be melted down and made into cannons. St. Philip's proved an inviting target during the Federal bombardment of Charleston. Its steeple was used for sighting, and the church was heavily damaged as a result. The earthquake of 1886 also extracted a toll, as did a fire caused by lightning in 1924. But St. Philip's has since been restored to its former grandeur. Its congregation is the city's oldest.

The tour ends at St. Philip's Episcopal Church. This is not to suggest that you have seen everything of value in Charleston, or even a sizable portion of it. In fact, continuing your walk in any direction will lead you to delightful places of historical interest, each with its own story to tell. If you left your car in the vicinity of the Four Corners of Law, you have only to turn right onto Queen Street—the street that separates St. Philip's and the French Huguenot Church— and then turn left onto Meeting Street after 1 block.

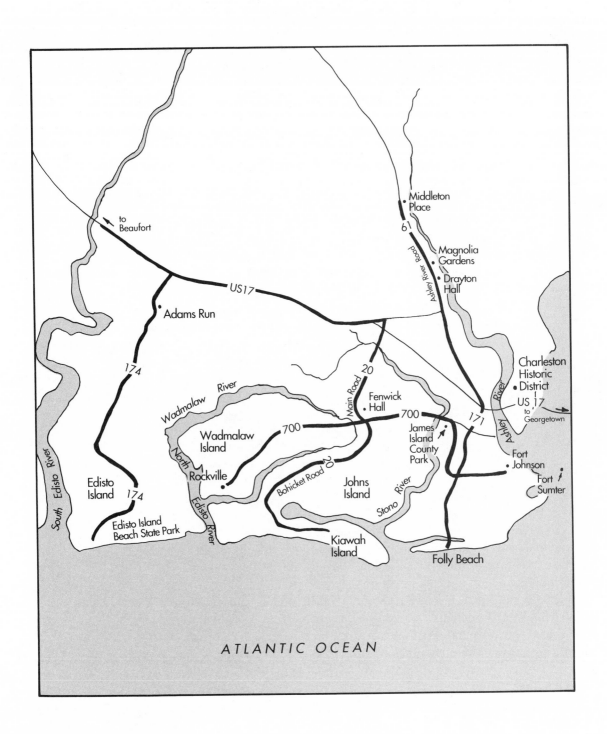

to Beaufort

US17

Adams Run

174

Wadmalaw River

20

Main Road

Fenwick Hall

700

700

James Island County Park

171

Charleston Historic District

US 17

to Georgetown

Middleton Place

61

Ashley River Road

Magnolia Gardens

Drayton Hall

Ashley River

Wadmalaw Island

North Edisto River

Rockville

Bohicket Road

20

Johns Island

Stono River

Fort Johnson

Fort Sumter

South Edisto River

Edisto Island

174

Edisto Island Beach State Park

Kiawah Island

Folly Beach

ATLANTIC OCEAN

The Charleston Plantations Tour

This tour begins at Middleton Place, Magnolia Gardens, and Drayton Hall, three plantation sites along the Ashley River. It then travels to some of South Carolina's loveliest sea islands, visiting the James Island Presbyterian Church and Fort Johnson on James Island; the street where George Gershwin lived in Folly Beach; Fenwick Hall Plantation on Johns Island; the Charleston Tea Plantation and the village of Rockville on Wadmalaw Island; and Kiawah Island. It concludes at Edisto Island.

Total mileage: approximately 140 miles.

This tour begins across the Ashley River from Charleston. The first stop is Middleton Place, located on S.C. 61, more popularly known as Ashley River Road.

It is sometimes said that the Middleton family started high society on this side of the ocean. The landholdings of the family patriarch, Henry Middleton, were among the largest in the American colonies.

Henry Middleton had a keen interest in politics. His home, Middleton Place, served as a gathering place for Southern leaders in the fight for freedom from England. In July 1774, Middleton was chosen to represent South Carolina at the Continental Congress; three months later, he was elected president of that

Middleton Place
Courtesy of Middleton Place

history-making body. His political involvement was passed down to the next generation, as his son Arthur became a signer of the Declaration of Independence. And his namesake daughter, Henrietta, married another signer of the Declaration of Independence, Edward Rutledge. It is hardly surprising that Middleton Place was considered a prime target during the Revolutionary War. British forces seized and occupied the premises and stripped the mansion of its *objets d'art*.

That loss was minor in comparison with the fate of the plantations along the Ashley River during the Civil War. All but one of them fell victim to the torches

The sweeping terraces at Middleton Place were laid out around 1741 by a gardener imported from England. Courtesy of Middleton Place

The gardens of Middleton Place encompass more than sixty acres. Courtesy of Middleton Place

TOURING THE COASTAL SOUTH CAROLINA BACKROADS

of Union raiders. The mansion at Middleton Place was gutted so badly in February 1865 that only the south wing could be restored. Further disaster struck in 1886, when an earthquake later calculated to have rated 7 or higher on the Richter scale devastated the entire Charleston area. The quake had its epicenter at Middleton Place. (For more information on the earthquake of 1886, see The Charleston Driving Tour.)

But if Henry Middleton could not bequeath us his magnificent mansion, he at least left us the enjoyment of his beautiful gardens. The gardens at Middleton Place encompass more than sixty acres. The sweeping terraces were laid out around 1741 by a gardener imported from England. The first four camellias brought to the New World were planted here by famous French botanist André Michaux in 1787. After Henry Middleton's death in 1794, succeeding generations of his family continued the project, and the gardens are more beautiful than ever today. If you happen to visit during the springtime, the dogwoods and the red and pink azaleas will give you a treat you will not soon forget. A fee is charged to tour the premises. A two-story structure built as guest quarters around 1755, now referred to as Middleton Place House, may also be explored.

Leaving Middleton Place, turn left onto Ashley River Road. After 3.5 miles, turn left into the driveway for Magnolia Gardens, formerly known as Magnolia Plantation.

The original house and gardens at Magnolia Plantation were built in the

Plantation House at
Magnolia Gardens
Courtesy of Magnolia Gardens

"Long Bridge" at Magnolia Gardens
Courtesy of Magnolia Gardens

A steamboat landing at Magnolia-on-the-Ashley in the 1870s
Courtesy of Magnolia Gardens

1680s by Thomas Drayton as a country estate. Today, the property is still operated as a working plantation by a descendant of the Drayton family. The gardens are a favorite among tourists. Every corner you turn in walking from the Biblical Garden to the Topiary Garden to the waterfowl refuge brings an unexpected sight, like a hand-carved footbridge or some form of exotic wildlife. It seems as if flowers are always hanging over your head and ground cover blooming at your feet. The green cover on the lake is composed of millions of tiny leaves that are eaten away by the ducks that visit every winter. A fee is charged to tour the premises.

Retrace your route to Ashley River Road and turn left again. Drive 0.6 mile to Drayton Hall, on the left. A fee is charged at the gateway entrance, but a tour is highly recommended.

As you come to the end of the drive beyond the gate, your first view of Drayton Hall is startling. The magnificent home sits on a wide lawn in an opening in the trees, with a small lake in the foreground and the Ashley River in the background. The house was constructed between 1738 and 1742 by John Drayton, who was born at his family's neighboring estate, Magnolia Plantation.

Drayton Hall holds the distinction of being the only antebellum mansion still standing on this side of the Ashley River. Legend has it that the Yankee sympathizers from Johns Island who burned the mansions in this area reached Drayton Hall last. Just before their arrival, Dr. Drayton, the physician who owned the mansion at that time, asked a servant girl to post yellow flags at the

Drayton Hall
Courtesy of Drayton Hall

James Island Presbyterian Church

Tombstone of Sammy Smalls

river and at the road entrance to the property. Yellow flags outside a home indicated the presence of yellow fever. The girl was just in the process of placing the roadside flag when the company of angry men arrived. She stood her ground and insisted that Dr. Drayton was indeed treating yellow fever in the mansion. The men took her at her word and left Drayton Hall intact.

The mansion is now operated in cooperation with the Historic Charleston Foundation. There is no furniture inside, but that has a way of making the house even more appealing, as it allows the walls of bald cypress decorated with carvings of foliage, fruit, and flowers to come to the front. The wainscoting in the principal rooms extends from floor to ceiling, with frames over the large mantels for pictures or coats of arms. A dogwood motif appears on much of the molding and woodwork. Note the boar's head carved in the broken pediment over the mantel in the great hall at the front of the house. If you look closely, you can see a tiny seashell in the boar's teeth. John Drayton was certainly not a man who took attention to details lightly.

The tour now leaves the river plantations and heads toward the sea islands. Return to Ashley River Road and turn left. Ashley River Road merges with S.C. 171 heading in toward Charleston. After a drive of approximately 9 miles, S.C. 171 splits off just before the bridge over the Ashley River. Continue south on S.C. 171, also known as Folly Road after this point. Another 1.4 miles brings you to the Wappoo Creek Bridge onto James Island. Drive another 3.5 miles on Folly Road, then turn left onto Fort Johnson Road. On the left as you make the turn is James Island Presbyterian Church, the burial site of Sammy Smalls.

Actually, James Island Presbyterian Church has two cemeteries begun before the Civil War, one for whites and the other for blacks. But Sammy Smalls, the black man who served as the inspiration for the character Porgy in DuBose Heyward's novel *Porgy* and George Gershwin's folk opera *Porgy and Bess*, was buried in neither of them. He was said to have been an unrepentant sinner, and as such he was not privileged to inhabit a grave in sanctified ground. According to the Low Country custom at the time of his death, Christians were buried in an east-west direction, so that they might face Christ when they arose from their graves, while "infidels" were buried in a north-south direction. Infidels were referred to as being buried "crossways of the world." Sammy Smalls was buried in a simple, handmade pine coffin crossways of the world. In the 1980s, the proceeds from a production of *Porgy and Bess* staged in Charleston went toward the erection of a tombstone for Sammy Smalls in the churchyard near the church itself. You will see it as you pull into the parking lot.

From James Island Presbyterian Church, travel 4.2 miles along Fort Johnson Road to the gate for the South Carolina Wildlife and Marine Resources Center. The impressive sign at the entrance is made of tabby, a colonial-era version of concrete composed of seawater mixed with oyster shells, sand, and lime. The practice of building with tabby originated with the Spaniards. In 1509, it was recorded that Ponce de Leon's house in Puerto Rico was made of a substance called tapia, later anglicized to tabby.

The ninety-acre Fort Johnson tract was turned over to the College of Charleston and the Medical College of South Carolina for research use in 1952. The property is now jointly owned. The College of Charleston maintains its Marine Biological Laboratory on the site, while the South Carolina Wildlife Commission operates its Marine Research Laboratory. After you pass through the gate, you will see the National Fisheries Center on the right and the marine-center buildings and Marshlands Plantation House on the left. Marshlands Plantation House was built on the Cooper River around 1810 by John Ball. It served as officers' quarters at the Charleston Naval Base until 1961, when the United States Navy decided that the site it occupied was needed for other purposes. It was then acquired by the College of Charleston and moved by water to its present location.

The ruins of Fort Johnson are behind the marine-center buildings. The first fort on the site was built in 1708 and expanded in 1737. When American forces

Marshlands Plantation House

occupied the fort in September 1775, it marked the first time that a flag of American origin was raised to replace the British flag. That was nearly a year before Betsy Ross is believed to have been approached about sewing the original Stars and Stripes. The flag at Fort Johnson was designed by Colonel William Moultrie. It featured a blue field with a white crescent in the upper right corner. A palmetto tree was subsequently added next to the crescent, and the resulting flag was adopted as South Carolina's state flag in 1865. (For more information on Revolutionary War action in the Charleston area, see The Swamp Fox Tour.)

The opening shots of the Civil War were fired from Fort Johnson. The sequence of events leading up to that momentous day began in December 1860, when South Carolina seceded from the United States and prepared to seize the Union forts in Charleston Harbor. The following March, Brigadier General Pierre G. T. Beauregard, a distinguished officer in the United States Army in days gone by, was sent by Jefferson Davis to command the Confederate troops around Charleston.

It just so happened that the officer in charge of the Union's harbor defenses was Major Robert Anderson, a former teacher of Beauregard's at West Point. The two men still counted themselves good friends. Major Anderson was originally headquartered at Fort Moultrie, on Sullivan's Island. Once he realized his position was vulnerable to Confederate attack, he moved his operation to Fort Sumter.

Abraham Lincoln was growing concerned about developments in the Charleston area, so he commissioned retired naval officer Gustavus V. Fox to go to Fort Sumter and assess Major Anderson's situation. On March 21, Governor Pickens granted Fox permission to visit the fort, having been assured that the mission was limited and peaceful. Major Anderson warned Fox that any attempt to reenforce or supply him might precipitate war.

Eight days later, President Lincoln directed his secretary of war to prepare a resupply mission to Fort Sumter. The mission fell through when the schooner *Rhoda H. Shannon* was fired upon by a battery of Citadel men on Morris Island and forced to turn back. President Lincoln retaliated with a plan that would send four ships bearing provisions to Fort Sumter. On April 8, Robert L. Chew of the State Department and Captain Theodore Talbot arrived from Washington to formally notify Governor Pickens that the garrison at Fort Sumter *would* be supplied. However, they were refused permission to visit the fort.

The situation was critical by then. Jefferson Davis passed an order through channels for General Beauregard to make a last demand for the evacuation of

Fort Sumter. On April 12, Major Anderson was advised in writing that Confederate forces intended to open fire on the fort. Anderson replied the same day that if he was not relieved or given further instructions by noon on April 15, he would surrender. The dispatches between General Beauregard and Major Anderson were marked by their courtesy. However, they were not always delivered where they were supposed to go. The aides entrusted with Major Anderson's final message of April 12 did not refer it to their superiors, but rather headed straight to Fort Johnson and ordered the bombardment to begin.

Captain George S. James commanded a company of Confederate infantry reserves at Fort Johnson, but it was Captain James Farley who pulled the lanyard to fire the first gun at Fort Sumter. In a letter he wrote some thirty years later, Farley called the attack the beginning of "the most momentous struggle in the history of the world," and he recalled his actions as follows: "The circumstances attending the firing of the first gun at Sumter are quite fresh in my memory. Captain James stood on my right, with watch in hand, and at the designated moment gave me the order to fire. I pulled the lanyard, having already carefully inserted a friction tube, and discharged a 13-inch mortar shell." So began the Civil War.

More than three thousand shells were thrown at Fort Sumter over the course of the thirty-four-hour bombardment, but not a single life was lost. Major Anderson agreed to the terms stipulated by General Beauregard and surrendered under honorable conditions. Out of respect for his friend and former teacher, General Beauregard declined to be present at the capitulation ceremony at Fort Sumter.

Additional artillery pieces were added at Fort Johnson during the next three years, but the only other major action involving the fort occurred in July 1864, when Confederates pushed back two Union regiments totaling about a thousand men.

When you have seen Fort Johnson, retrace your route to Folly Road and turn left. It is approximately 4 miles on Folly Road to a bridge over the Folly River, then another 0.7 mile to the ocean and the heart of Folly Beach itself. En route, you will see great expanses of marshland on both sides of the road. Some of the small islands in the marsh are so completely covered with palmetto trees that they look like huge baskets of palm vegetation floating on the water.

It should be pointed out that Folly Beach's name does not denote foolishness. Rather, it is taken from an Old English word used to describe areas of dense foliage. The name seems appropriate, as cherry laurel, magnolia, saltwater cedar, palmetto, and other trees thrive on the island.

This area first came under European control in 1696, when a man named William Rivers was deeded seven hundred acres of land. His tract was bordered by the Atlantic on the southeast, by a creek on the west, by a marsh on the northwest, and by James Island on the south. For most of its history, Folly Beach was considered a "hunting island," meaning that it was kept from farming and development. Development began in the 1920s. Today, there are over thirteen hundred houses at Folly Beach, nearly a thousand of them inhabited year-round. The island runs 6.2 miles along the Atlantic and is roughly 0.5 mile wide.

Folly Road ends at a stoplight at the corner of Ashley Avenue in the "downtown" section of Folly Beach. Continue straight through the intersection into the parking lot for the Holiday Inn. Look carefully to your right and you will see a small, hidden street that sits right on the ocean. That street is West Arctic Avenue. Only two blocks of West Arctic Avenue are left today, but that does little to diminish the street's significance. It was on West Arctic Avenue that George Gershwin lived when he came to Folly Beach in 1934. Gershwin came to enjoy the island lifestyle and to study the native patois before he began writing *Porgy and Bess*. Turn right onto West Arctic Avenue to explore the street where Gershwin lived.

The story of *Porgy and Bess* goes back to 1923. That year, Charleston poet DuBose Heyward took refuge on his farm in the Great Smoky Mountains of North Carolina to write a novel. His principal character was a crippled fishmonger who lived in a waterfront tenement called Catfish Row, modeled on a tenement called Cabbage Row that actually existed in Charleston. Heyward called his novel *Porgy*, and it proved to be both a critical and a popular success. "With his feet on solid South Carolina soil he [Heyward] has created a story as lovely and as imaginative as a poem, and this is no simple achievement," wrote the critic for the *Baltimore Evening Sun*. The *Chicago Tribune* stated simply that *Porgy* was the kind of book poets ought to write more often.

The Metropolitan Opera approached George Gershwin about writing a folk opera based on the novel. Once Gershwin was convinced that such an opera might attract wide attention and prove of lasting value, he was interested. He signed a contract with the Metropolitan Opera in October 1933 and traveled to Charleston to meet with Heyward. He also visited James Island to get a taste of South Carolina's sea islands. He and a cousin, Henry Botkin, took up residence in Folly Beach in 1934.

The talk between Gershwin and Heyward focused on the Gullah language that Gershwin wanted to use in his folk opera. Gullah is the Negro dialect spoken by descendants of slaves in coastal regions from Georgetown County, South Carolina, down to Florida. It represents a linguistic link among Africa, the Antilles, and the United States. Gullah has a unique way of forming plurals and possessives, and it uses a simpler system of pronouns but a more complex system of verbs than standard English.

Gershwin and his cousin took to visiting country churches in the area to soak up the language and to learn the complicated rhythmic pattern of local spirituals. One night in a tiny chapel, Gershwin began shouting with the congregation, whose members were surprised to find a white man who was their match. On another evening as he was about to enter a different chapel, he paused to take in the sounds from within. A dozen or so voices of extraordinary quality were raised in a loud, rhythmic prayer in which each person started at a different moment and petitioned a different blessing, producing an effect of terrifying intensity. That prayer meeting was Gershwin's inspiration for the invocation to God in the face of the hurricane in *Porgy and Bess*.

Many local stories are told about Gershwin. He once went to a country church and heard a woman singing in a minor key, her eyes looking heavenward and her body swaying. Her voice was lyric soprano, and she took the haunting melody through runs and trills before she was joined by another woman, and then others. They moved closer together with their bodies swaying and their voices growing stronger. From that experience came the inspiration for the classic song "Summertime." The song "Bess, You Is My Woman Now" also had its beginnings in a church meeting.

Those who knew Gershwin during the time he was writing the score for *Porgy and Bess* said he was so excited with the music that it was all he could talk about. A friend who visited on one occasion received a special treat when Gershwin sat at his piano and gave an extended preview of his work. Some of the people closest to Gershwin wondered whether he would ever recover from the delirium of his sea-island experience.

Porgy and Bess opened at the Colonial Theater in Boston on September 30, 1935. Shouts and cries went up during the performance, and the ovation afterwards lasted for a full fifteen minutes. Pandemonium broke out when Gershwin made a curtain call. Two weeks later, the folk opera was presented at the Alvin Theater in New York. The audience was a virtual roster of the city's high society, and they thoroughly enjoyed the production. Reviews of *Porgy*

James Island County Park

The Stono River, named for the Stono Indians, who once inhabited the islands in this area

and Bess were thick with words and phrases like "glorious" and "compellingly dramatic."

George Gershwin died in 1937. In the spring of the following year, a friend of his visited James Island to speak with the people there. They remembered Gershwin vividly and spoke fondly of the days when he had become one of them. DuBose Heyward died in 1940. Both *Porgy* the novel and *Porgy and Bess* the folk opera are recognized as American classics.

Retrace your route to the stoplight at the end of Folly Road. If you care to make a brief side trip for a little recreation, turn left at the stoplight onto Ashley Avenue and follow it to Folly Beach County Park, at the southern tip of the beach. Folly Beach County Park is a wide-open park with four thousand feet of ocean frontage and two thousand feet of frontage on the Folly River.

If you'd rather continue the tour without stopping at the park, retrace Folly Road for 4.7 miles to an intersection with Riverland Drive, on the left. You may recognize the intersection. Fort Johnson Road is to the right, leading past James Island Presbyterian Church to Fort Johnson itself. This time, turn left onto Riverland Drive, a pastoral country road with overhanging foliage.

It is 2.4 miles on Riverland Drive to the entrance to James Island County Park, another good place to stop for recreation. The 640-acre park is open year-

TOURING THE COASTAL SOUTH CAROLINA BACKROADS

round. It offers such things as campsites, trails for walking and bicycling, and a fishing and crabbing dock on a tidal creek. The park also hosts an open-microphone night for aspiring performers brave enough to strut their stuff before a live audience. People come from all over South Carolina to see the Christmas lights at James Island County Park, which are lit from November through January 1. If you happen to be passing through the area during that part of the year, the display is a real treat.

Continue another 1.6 miles on Riverland Drive to a traffic light at Maybank Highway, also known as S.C. 700. Turn left onto Maybank Highway. It is 0.9 mile to a bridge across the Stono River, named for one of the Indian tribes that inhabited the cluster of islands in this area around the year 1600. It was the custom of the tribes to live on the islands during summer and move inland for the winter. The Stono Indians once lived at the present site of the beautiful marina you can see as you traverse the river.

Once you've crossed the Stono River, you are on Johns Island, named for Saint John. It is 1.7 miles from the bridge to a traffic light at the corner of River Road. Turn right onto River Road and drive 0.3 mile to Fenwick Hall, on the right. Note the impressive wrought-iron gates. The manor house is at the end of the avenue of oaks. It now serves as a substance-abuse center, so it is not open to the public.

John Fenwick, the builder and owner of Fenwick Hall, was an unusual man. He was known for his friendly dealings with pirates. In fact, it is said that he actually enjoyed their company. Legend has it that there is a tunnel running from a nearby creek to Fenwick Hall. Pirates supposedly visited John Fenwick by traveling up the Stono River to the creek, and then through the tunnel to the manor house.

John Fenwick also raised thoroughbred horses and raced them on a track that ran straight for 3.5 miles. There is a sad story about the love between a groom who cared for the horses and one of Fenwick's daughters. Grooms were well beneath the social station of the Fenwicks, so the master of the house was solidly against any relationship between his daughter and one of his horse-men. One night as Fenwick was meeting with pirates in the basement of the manor house, a servant girl entered the room and whispered that his daughter and the groom had run away. Not bothering to inform his guests, Fenwick raced up the stairs to his daughter's bedroom to see for himself. He found her room empty. He and some outriders then headed at top speed for the Stono River.

The servant girl's word proved true. Fenwick and his outriders discovered

Fenwick Hall

During early summer, truckloads of green tomatoes are taken from the Johns Island fields.

the daughter and the groom riding a single horse. The master ran to his daughter and pulled her down. Outraged, he had his outriders tie the groom's hands behind his back and throw a rope over an oak limb. The horse bearing the groom was then led under the limb and a noose tightened around the young man's neck. Fenwick turned to his daughter and extended her his riding crop. She resisted, but he forced her to take it and lash the hindquarters of the groom's horse. The horse bolted, and the groom's neck was snapped. The daughter fell into a faint and was carried home. It is said that she never regained her senses. The groom was buried near the tree on which he died, known even today as John's Oak.

Leaving Fenwick Hall, retrace your route to Maybank Highway and turn right. The area you are traveling through is mostly residential, but you may notice some large fields scattered here and there. During early summer, countless truckloads of green tomatoes are taken from these fields to ripen on their way to market.

A drive of 4.8 miles on Maybank Highway brings you to the Esau Jenkins Memorial Bridge. After crossing the bridge, you are on Wadmalaw Island. Continue approximately 10 miles to the Charleston Tea Plantation, on the left.

The South Carolina Low Country was thick with rice plantations in times

Charleston Tea Plantation

gone by. And sea-island cotton was raised on Edisto Island and elsewhere in the area. But the Charleston Tea Plantation is the only tea plantation in the Low Country. In fact, it is the only tea plantation in the United States. As soon as you drive onto the grounds, you will see the vast field of tea plants, so perfectly trimmed that they look like boxwood hedges in an English garden.

The plantation was owned by the Lipton Tea Company prior to 1987, when current owners Mack Fleming and Bill Hall took over the operation. Fleming, a Clemson University alumnus, directed the plantation for ten years for the Lipton Tea Company. He is the only tea horticulturist in the country. Hall is a third-generation English-trained tea taster with twenty-three years of experience in the international tea trade. He is very picky about quality. When he tastes the tea produced on the plantation and finds it to be of less than the highest standard, the whole day's harvest is thrown out.

The original tea plants on the plantation were imported from Kenya, Brazil, and other countries. The current ownership is careful to make certain that their tea is a match for that produced by the mother plants in terms of quality, taste, and color. Tea is cut by machine every thirteen days from May to October. At each cutting, two leaves and one bud are taken from each plant. All growing, harvesting, drying, grading, and packaging are done on the site. The American Classic Tea produced at the Charleston Tea Plantation is considered gourmet fare. Unlike imported tea, it is free from insecticides and fungicides. It has been used at official and ceremonial events at the White House.

The Charleston Tea Plantation is a working plantation, but scheduled tours are conducted. If you take the tour, you will not only get to see how tea is made and packaged, but you will also get to savor a cup of hot or iced American Classic Tea. Chances are you will love it.

Continue for 1 mile on Maybank Highway from the Charleston Tea Plantation to the village of Rockville, at land's end. If you've ever been to Massachusetts and visited Nantucket or Martha's Vineyard, you may notice a basic resemblance. Whitewashed clapboard houses on tabby foundations sit high off the ground, topped by old, high-pitched tin roofs. Picket fences, huge oaks, hollyhocks, and azaleas are in abundance. Green lawns sweep down to piers and docks that await the return of shrimp boats or the arrival of boats bearing friends from such places as Seabrook, Kiawah, and Edisto islands. "Only by coming here by boat do you get the finest view," one resident remarked to me.

Grace Chapel at Rockville

The tiny Grace Chapel is located on the last side street on the left before you reach the waterfront. The first time this writer visited the village, Grace Chapel was bordered by an ancient-looking cemetery featuring unusually elaborate grave markers of wood and marble surrounded by a wall of aged bricks. On a second visit a few weeks later, a green, freshly mowed lawn stood on the site of the old cemetery. A local resident explained that the cemetery had actually been a movie set, left over from the filming of the 1991 motion picture *Paradise*, starring Don Johnson and Melanie Griffith. If all movie sets are as convincing as the one near Grace Chapel, they must leave Hollywood crews a little uncertain about where reality ends and fantasy begins.

Retrace Maybank Highway for 11.6 miles from Rockville to Bohicket Road. Turn right onto Bohicket Road. A drive of 3 miles beneath majestic oaks that meet overhead brings you to Johns Island Presbyterian Church, founded by English, Scottish, and French settlers around 1710. Johns Island Presbyterian Church has one of the oldest Presbyterian congregations in South Carolina. The original sanctuary, believed to have been built around 1719, was enlarged in 1823.

Continue 7.4 miles on Bohicket Road through an agricultural area until you reach Kiawah Island Parkway. Turn left onto the parkway. When you cross the bridge over a tiny channel, you are on Kiawah Island, named for an Indian

Waterfront house at Rockville

TOURING THE COASTAL SOUTH CAROLINA BACKROADS

tribe. After approximately 1.9 miles on Kiawah Island Parkway, you will see a sign directing you to Beachwalker Park. Turn right to enter the property and drive 0.6 mile back into the park.

Beachwalker Park at Kiawah Island

Much of Kiawah Island is privately owned, but Beachwalker Park is operated for public enjoyment by a cooperative effort of the Kiawah Island Company, the Charleston County Council, and the Charleston County Park and Recreation Commission. The popular park is located between the Bohicket River and the ocean, with Captain Sam's Inlet and the Kiawah River along its southern edge. One of the park's best features is a wide boardwalk that snakes its way among live oaks, pines, palmettos, and yucca plants before suddenly ending in an openness of beach and sky, where lines of pelicans can often be seen gliding by overhead. At one point along the boardwalk, there is a sign that reads, "Beyond this point Kiawah takes over." In this context, Kiawah is understood to mean a heavy concentration of recent development. Once the boardwalk reaches the beach, gray-colored condominiums can be seen lining the shoreline.

Opinion is divided over the efforts to develop Kiawah Island. Some believe that development has led to the destruction of natural beauty, while others point to the environmental awards that the development plan for the island

Beachwalker Park

The Straw Market

has won. The Royal family of Aiken, South Carolina, purchased Kiawah Island for the sum of $125,000 in 1951. By 1974, when a group of Kuwaiti investors bought the island, that price had skyrocketed to $17 million. Today, an acre of land on the island sells for more than $1 million, with houses going for about the same.

If you want to make a side trip to see the private part of the island, turn right onto Kiawah Island Parkway when you leave Beachwalker Park. You will have to stop at the gate for a permit. You might ask for a permit for the Straw Market, which is the island's shopping area.

The VanderHorst Mansion is located on the private part of the island, but it is not in an area where it can be viewed by visitors. The four-story mansion was built high off the ground and surrounded by palmetto and orange trees. The VanderHorst family owned Kiawah Island back in the days when it was known as Key-war. The family's original wealth came from growing indigo, but they later expanded into cotton production. Cotton was grown on the island until 1914, when the boll weevil, a beetle that feeds on the buds of cotton flowers and the silky fibers inside the seed pods, wiped out the crop.

Mr. VanderHorst, the family patriarch, had a special relationship with a servant called Squash. Two of Squash's principal duties were to scout the hunting preserves that covered the island and to build hunting blinds. He also led Mr. VanderHorst and his planter friends on two-day hunting expeditions. The planters dressed rather formally on those occasions, in suits with vests and neckties. On one hunt, Squash was preparing lunch when Mr. VanderHorst wandered away carrying his gun. A single shot was heard about thirty minutes later. When Mr. VanderHorst did not return in due time, the party went looking for him. He was found in a ditch where he had fallen and accidentally shot himself. Squash was a broken man. For as long as he lived, he sat on the porch of the VanderHorst Mansion and told stories of the old hunts. He claimed to be able to hear the voice of Mr. VanderHorst telling him to round up the dogs for a two-day outing.

Retrace Kiawah Island Parkway to Bohicket Road and turn right. Return the 10.4 miles to the junction with Maybank Highway, where Bohicket Road's name changes to Main Road. Follow Main Road for 5.7 miles to the John F. Limehouse Memorial Bridge, which takes you back to the mainland. Drive another 0.8 mile to U.S. 17 and turn left, or south, heading toward Edisto Island. Follow U.S. 17 for 15.5 miles to S.C. 174 and turn left again. It is a drive of 3.1 miles on S.C. 174 to Adams Run. The focal points of this small community are the 1835-vintage Christ Church Episcopal, with its red tin roof and its four white pillars on the porch, and the ancient building that houses the post office. It is another 10.9 miles on S.C. 174 from Adams Run to the Edisto Island Historic Preservation Society, located in a white house on the right. The Edisto Island Historic Preservation Society is a good place to obtain information about the island.

Edisto Island is one of the oldest settlements in South Carolina. Once the home of the Edistow Indians, it still bears traces of their presence. There is a shell mound of Indian origin on the beach. It may have been used as a burial ground, a ceremonial site, a refuse heap, or some combination of the three. During the hundred-plus years that the Spanish exerted their influence over the area before the arrival of the British, they called the island by the name Oristo. It was in 1674 that the earl of Shaftesbury purchased the island from the Edistow Indians. A man named Paul Grimball was issued a land grant of six hundred acres along the North Edisto River, where he built a plantation house that is in ruins today.

The early settlers tried their hand at producing rice, but the water supply at

Christ Church Episcopal at Adams Run

The post office at Adams Run

Edisto Island proved too salty. They also tried growing indigo. By 1790, local planters had turned to sea-island cotton, and it was that crop that brought them success. Sea-island cotton was distinguished by its black seeds and its silky fibers $^3/_8$ to $2^1/_2$ inches long. The cotton was carefully bred so that its fiber length increased from one year to the next. And since sea-island cotton could only be grown on the narrow islands along the coast of South Carolina and Georgia, a powerful caste of plantation nobles quickly developed.

Edisto Island cotton is said to have been the finest ever grown. Legend has it that it never went to market, as lace mills in France contracted for the entire crop before the seed was even planted.

Edisto Island may be the proudest and most self-sufficient place in South Carolina. Each of its plantations became a kind of independent principality, a kingdom by the sea. The planters treasured their particular strains of cotton and jealously guarded their secrets, handing them down from father to son. Cotton and supplies moved in and out from private wharves on the deep creeks that abound on the island. When the planter families traveled to Charleston, it was in cypress canoes rowed by slaves who chanted in rhythm with their oar strokes. The scene is difficult to imagine today.

In 1810, Edisto Island had about 250 white inhabitants and 3,000 slaves. The annual cotton crop was said to have averaged $1,360 for every white inhabitant—man, woman, and child. The planters seemed favored by fate until the arrival of the boll weevil in 1914. The insect was unlike any enemy they had ever fought. By 1921, the boll weevil had thoroughly outwitted, even destroyed, the lofty cotton planters.

Traces remain of some of the magnificent manor houses built during the heyday of the cotton plantations, but the narrow, unpaved roadways that lead from the highway back toward the plantations are not open to the public. The best time to view the manor houses is in October, when the annual Island Tour of Historic Plantations and Churches is held. Representative of the sites visited on the tour are Middleton Plantation, also called the Chisholm House, built around 1815; Oak Island Plantation, built in 1828, with its fine gardens boasting over four hundred varieties of award-winning camellias; and the ruins of Brick House, built between 1720 and 1725 and destroyed by fire in 1929. Each is recognized as a National Historic Landmark.

Continue 0.7 mile on S.C. 174 from the Edisto Island Historic Preservation Society to Edisto Island Presbyterian Church, on the left. The church was founded in 1685, though the present building dates from 1830. The graveyard at the back of the church holds the remains of some of the most prosperous of the sea-island cotton planters. You may also be interested in the Legare Mausoleum, the pink building that looks like a temple at the back of the cemetery. But don't get too close—some people swear there is a ghost inside!

In times long past, the story goes, a young woman became seriously ill while she was visiting the Legare family for the summer. She lingered near death for several days, long enough for her family to be summoned. By the time they arrived, she was in a coma. When it appeared that the end was at hand, the family moved outside the room, leaving only a physician to attend to the girl's final needs. He emerged some time later and solemnly announced that she was dead. It was the doctor's opinion that the funeral should be conducted that very day; the weather was hot, and this was in the time before embalming fluid. Edisto Island Presbyterian Church hosted the funeral, after which the remains were placed in the Legare Mausoleum.

It was fifteen years after that before a member of the Legare family died. When the mausoleum was opened, something was heard clattering to the floor behind the heavy marble door. To the horror of the mourners, it proved to be the skeleton of the young girl. She had been laid to rest prematurely! Her remains were interred again that same day, along with the corpse of the man whose funeral had just been held.

Edisto Island Presbyterian Church

Several days later, a custodian walking through the cemetery noticed that the door to the Legare Mausoleum was standing open. He notified the family. They had it closed, but it was open again within days. They had it closed again. When the door was found open a third time, the Legares ordered the largest chains and locks available at the time. They had the mausoleum sealed up tight, as they never planned to use it again. After only a few days, the locks and chains lay on the ground and the door stood open once more. This time, the Legares made no further effort to close the mausoleum. It was their belief that the spirit of the young woman would never allow the door to remain closed, lest someone else be laid to rest before their time. The door stayed open for more than a hundred years after that. Today, you may see pieces of the marble door on the ground near the ill-fated Legare Mausoleum.

It is another 1.5 miles on S.C. 174 to Edisto Island Baptist Church, on the left. The church was founded by Mrs. Hephzibah Jenkins Townsend, a well-remembered woman in this area. Hephzibah and her husband, Daniel Townsend, were renowned for their bickering, of all things. She was Baptist and he was Presbyterian, and the majority of their arguments came over religion. Some of them were quite heated. But the argument that caused the deepest rift came when Hephzibah learned that Daniel intended to leave all his property to their eldest son. She felt very strongly that all fourteen of their children should share equally in the inheritance, and when she failed to convince Daniel to change his will, she moved out. She even built a new home on property she had inherited from her brother. When Daniel finally relented and changed his will, she moved back in.

Hephzibah had a considerable interest in church activities. During the nineteenth century, she founded the first women's church group in the South, the Female Mite Society of Edisto and Wadmalaw Island. Her husband continued to nag her about joining the Presbyterian church, but she was unmoved. In 1818, when it came time for the construction of the present Edisto Island Baptist Church, she baked cookies and sold them by the side of the road to show her commitment to the fund-raising effort.

Edisto Island was rich in churches even before Hephzibah Jenkins Townsend came along. Drive 0.3 mile farther and you will see Trinity Episcopal Church on the left. The church was founded in 1774. The cornerstone of the present building, a white wood structure with a red roof and steeple, was laid in 1810. That cornerstone is visible in the brick wall by the front steps.

Continue for 5 miles on S.C. 174 to Edisto Beach State Park, on the left. With its 1,255 acres, its 1.5 miles of oceanfront, its dense live-oak forest, and its expansive salt marsh, Edisto Beach State Park is one of the most popular of South Carolina's state parks. It is an excellent place for gathering seashells. Fossils and relics of the Indians who inhabited this area as much as four thousand years ago have also been discovered in the park.

Turn right just beyond the entrance to Edisto Beach State Park, where S.C. 174 becomes known as Palmetto Boulevard. This is where the tour ends, at the start of Edisto Island's main street. Palmetto Boulevard extends south for 4 miles between rows of neat beach houses featuring well-kept yards landscaped with palmettos and oleander. It is unusually wide, uncluttered, and traffic-free for an ocean boulevard. In fact, neat, clean, peaceful, and tropical Edisto Island is wholly free of the congestion that is sometimes the bane of places like Myrtle Beach and Hilton Head Island. If you have the time and the inclination to strike out on your own, you will find it a welcome change and a place well worth exploring.

To return to the mainland, simply retrace S.C. 174 to its junction with U.S. 17, which heads north into Charleston and south toward the Beaufort area.

Edisto Island Baptist Church

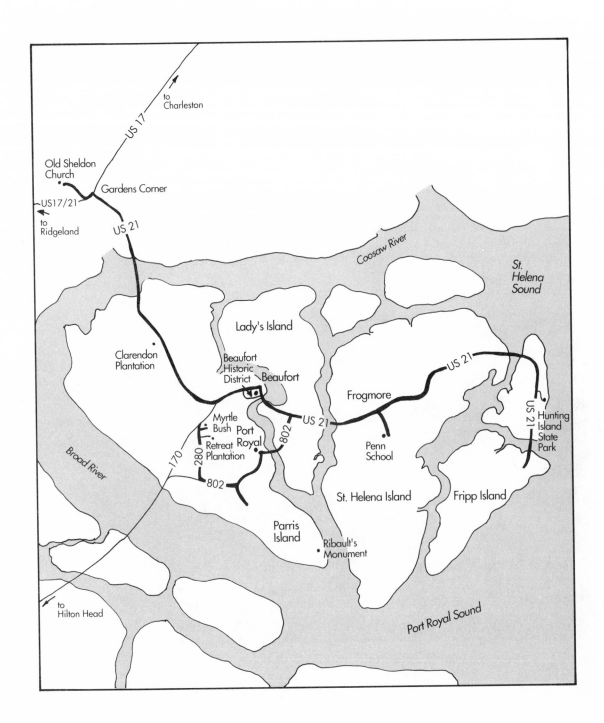

The Witch Doctor Tour

This tour concentrates on the areas northwest, east, south, and west of Beaufort, leaving a detailed treatment of the city itself to The Historic Beaufort Tour. It begins northwest of Beaufort at the ruins of Old Sheldon Church, then heads east toward St. Helena Island—the site of the Penn Center, Frogmore, and Coffin Point Plantation—Hunting Island, and Fripp Island. Next, it swings south to Parris Island and northwest to Retreat Plantation before ending at Myrtle Bush Plantation.

Total mileage: approximately 76 miles.

This tour begins at the junction of U.S. 17 and Old Sheldon Church Road northwest of Beaufort, near the area called Gardens Corner. If you have been traveling south on U.S. 17 from Charleston, turn right onto Old Sheldon Church Road; if you have been traveling north, the correct turn is left. Old Sheldon Church is located approximately 2 miles down Old Sheldon Church Road.

Some people believe that Old Sheldon Church took its name from nearby Sheldon Hall Plantation, owned by the Bull family. Others claim that the name

The ruins of Old Sheldon Church

honors Gilbert Sheldon, the seventy-eighth archbishop of Canterbury, the man under whose spiritual care the American colonies were first placed. Whichever the case, Old Sheldon Church was built sometime before 1757 on land donated by Elizabeth Bellinger of neighboring Tomotley Barony. All construction costs were fully paid by the time of its consecration. In 1766, colonial missionary Charles Woodmason compared it favorably with the finest churches in Charleston, noting that Old Sheldon Church was "beautifully pewed and ornamented."

The church has had an interesting history. A member of the aristocratic Bull family, formally known as "Stephen Bull of Sheldon" to distinguish him from his father and namesake, served as the church's patron. He took his adopted role very seriously, even to the extent of entertaining most of the congregation at Sunday dinner, when some sixty or seventy carriages would roll up to his doorstep to discharge their hungry occupants. Stephen Bull of Sheldon was buried under the church's altar.

During the Revolutionary War, General Augustine Prevost and his British troops burned Old Sheldon Church, whose brick walls stubbornly refused to fall. For a time after the burning, parishioners worshipped inside the open walls. The parish grew during the period when indigo and rice crops brought prosperity to the area, and the restored church was consecrated in 1826.

Sometime later, it was learned that a Beaufort woman had a gift for the congregation. When church officials visited her, she presented them with some heavy items wrapped in a rector's black silk robe. They threw back the covering and discovered, to their amazement, an alms plate, chalices, and the other items that constituted the parish's communion silver, which had been lost during the Revolutionary War. The generous woman hastened to explain that an English soldier had given them to her on the sly during the war years.

Late in the Civil War, when Sherman's troops were marching their way from Savannah, Georgia, to Columbia, South Carolina, Old Sheldon Church was burned again. But the original walls still stood. The church continued to experience difficult times during Reconstruction, with the planters' assets gone.

Today, every year at noon on the second Sunday after Easter, descendants of the planter congregation come to worship within the old walls that neither wars nor economic disaster nor the ravages of time have been able to lay low. Artists come to sketch the stately, vine-covered walls and columns. The church cemetery is also of interest, especially the ornate marker with the huge claw feet that commemorates the resting place of Mary Middleton.

When you have seen Old Sheldon Church, retrace Old Sheldon Church Road to U.S. 17 and turn left. A drive of 0.5 mile on U.S. 17 brings you to Gardens Corner, where U.S. 21 bears off to the right. Turn right onto U.S. 21, heading south toward Beaufort. You will pass through an area featuring old, moss-covered oaks, horse farms, vegetable farms, and marshlands. Spartina grass, or marsh grass, is the dominant and the most visible form of vegetation in the coastal marshlands. It grows in the intertidal zones, where there is no wave action. As Spartina grass decays, it provides food for the oysters, crabs, and shrimp that grow to maturity within the protective environment of the marshlands. The grass stabilizes the inlets—its most important function—and it also serves as a kind of sewage-treatment system, cleaning the marsh water of microscopic wastes and chemical agents.

After approximately 7 miles on U.S. 21, you will reach a junction with S.C. 71. If you care to take a brief side trip for a look at Clarendon Plantation—not open to the public—turn right onto S.C. 71 and drive 0.5 mile to the impressive gates of wrought iron and brick. The plantation dates back to 1780. The magnificent Georgian mansion was built in 1933 by the Corning family. In 1966, the Cox family paid slightly over $1 million for the property, said to be

Clarendon Plantation

the largest single land transaction in Beaufort County to that date. The red-brick mansion has been painted white to lend a feeling of springtime in the French countryside.

U.S. 21 becomes known as Boundary Street when it enters Beaufort. Approximately 6 miles from the junction of U.S. 21 and S.C. 71, you will pass Beaufort National Cemetery, on the left. The cemetery was established by Abraham Lincoln in 1863 for the purpose of interring Union soldiers originally buried at a variety of locations from Charleston south to Hilton Head Island and parts of Georgia. Some 3,798 graves were dug on the fifty-acre site by the close of the Civil War. Today, Beaufort National Cemetery contains more than 11,000 graves, 4,000 of them marking the resting place of unknown victims of our nation's wars.

At the end of Boundary Street, approximately 0.5 mile past Beaufort National Cemetery, U.S. 21 turns to the right and runs conjunctively with Carteret Street. The tour now passes directly through the heart of Beaufort without stopping, heading instead toward the islands east of town. Approximately 0.5 mile from the end of Boundary Street, you will reach Bay Street and the bridge across the Beaufort River. If you would like to leave the present tour and explore Beaufort's historic district, turn right onto Bay Street. The Historic Beaufort Tour begins at the John Mark Verdier House, on the right after 1 block on Bay Street.

To continue the present tour, follow U.S. 21 across the Beaufort River, which serves as the Intracoastal Waterway in this area. Once you reach the far side of the bridge, you are on Lady's Island.

Beaufort is surrounded by a total of sixty-four islands, some large and some small. In fact, first-time visitors cross so many waterways and inlets that they often have a difficult time telling when they've left one island and entered another. In days gone by, traveling from the islands to the mainland entailed several hours of rowing across the wide waters of the Broad and Beaufort rivers. Residents of the prosperous plantations on the islands were isolated and extremely close-knit. Some island planters lived year-round at their plantations, while others kept homes in Beaufort or Charleston, where they spent several months out of the year. Some Beaufort-area planters left the production of their island crops entirely in the hands of overseers, rarely visiting their plantations. One Londoner who owned an island plantation never even visited it at all.

The drive across Lady's Island is approximately 4 miles. When you cross the bridge over Cowan Creek, you are on St. Helena Island. Continue another 2.6

Penn Center

miles on U.S. 21 to a junction with Land's End Road. Turn right onto Land's End Road and travel 1 mile to the Penn Center, on the right.

Shortly after the start of the Civil War, Union forces seized nearby Hilton Head Island and used it to establish a base for the fleet blockading the east coast. In the wake of the Union occupation, the wealthy planters on St. Helena Island abandoned their property and fled inland. Their plantations were promptly confiscated by the Federal government. A group of abolitionists then established themselves in the area and inaugurated the Port Royal Experiment for the benefit of the ten thousand blacks who remained in the area after the planters fled.

The purpose of the Port Royal Experiment was to provide the newly freed slaves with opportunities for education and self-sufficiency. The abolitionists continued the cotton-growing operations on the plantations, only this time the former slaves were paid wages. Some of the land was given to former slaves or sold to them once they had accumulated money. In 1862, two female missionaries established the first local school for blacks. It was located in a ready-made school building sent all the way from Philadelphia. The school

---

The Witch Doctor Tour

was called the Penn School. Those two original teachers—Charlotte Forten of Massachusetts and Laura Towne of Philadelphia—stayed for forty years, through some of the most difficult times the South has ever seen.

At the time of its opening, the Penn School had a total of forty-seven students and teachers. The classrooms at the school were said to be comfortable. Those who could afford five cents a day for lunch generally received a large cup of soup and four slices of cornbread. Observers of educational trends came from India, Africa, and across the United States to chart the progress of the Penn School through the early part of this century.

Hard times arrived around 1948. A public high school was organized elsewhere on St. Helena Island, and the private Penn School battled falling enrollment. The problem worsened as growing numbers of black families migrated north. The school graduated its last class in 1953.

However, it wasn't long before a new mission was begun. The school was renamed the Penn Center. The Penn Center's purpose was to provide services related to health care, land preservation, and community enrichment for the benefit of islanders struggling to hold out against the threat of encroaching development. It also served as a conference site. During the early 1960s, Dr. Martin Luther King, Jr., and other black leaders met here to plan their 1963 march on Washington and their 1965 march on Selma, Alabama.

The future of the Penn Center, a National Historic Landmark, is uncertain. In June 1991, the National Trust for Historic Preservation placed the center on a list of the eleven most endangered historic places in the United States. It was the finding of the trust that the Penn Center is too poor to provide for the upkeep of its nineteen buildings, which date to the early 1900s, and that its facilities suffer from "severe coastal climate and termite infestation." Today, the only learning accomplished at the Penn Center is done by Peace Corps volunteers who tend goats and plant small gardens in preparation for their work in Africa. "I'm not accustomed to seeing it like this," lamented Evangeline Major, a 1941 graduate, on the state of her alma mater. But if the past is any indication, the Penn Center will soon find a new mission and again prove its value.

Before leaving the vicinity, walk across the road to Brick Church. In 1855, at the time of the church's construction, the local planters worshiped in pews on the ground floor, while their slaves had to climb the steep stairway to the balcony. After the Civil War, Brick Church became the spiritual home of the students at the Penn School. The church is still in use today.

Continue driving on Land's End Road for 0.3 mile to the ruins of the St. Helena Episcopal Chapel of Ease, on the left. It is not known when the chapel was built, though records indicate that it was standing in 1740. Some wealthy planter families on the island attended church here, rather than making the arduous trip to St. Helena Episcopal Church in Beaufort. If you are familiar with tabby—a building material made of ground oyster shells, lime, and sand—you will notice a good deal of it in the ruins of the St. Helena Episcopal Chapel of Ease. The chapel's tabby had a pink hue, said to be especially beautiful. The chapel's demise came in February 1886. Some local residents were burning ground nearby in an effort to clear it for planting, and the fire grew out of control.

St. Helena Episcopal Chapel of Ease

After you have seen the St. Helena Episcopal Chapel of Ease, retrace your route to U.S. 21 and turn right. You are now in Frogmore. Local residents make the claim that Frogmore is the witchcraft capital of the world, and they may well be correct. Witch doctors have practiced their irregular medicine at this place for generations.

Traditionally, residents of the area have been extremely superstitious. One local belief claims that when a couple marries, the first spouse to sit down after the ceremony will be the first to die. Another belief says that if your right hand itches in the center, money will come to that hand, but if your left hand itches, money will soon be paid out. Local custom has it that persons who die by drowning in the ocean ought to be buried near the sea, so that the high tide might reclaim their bodies. It is also said that the first person to be buried in a new cemetery will be joined by a member of his or her family within a year.

Witch doctors made charms, or amulets, which they sold to people to ward off evil spirits or remove hexes. Faith in the power of amulets still lingers. Once, when this writer was in Beaufort to interview a police detective, the detective's assistant—a sensible young woman who appeared to be the last person in the world who would believe in witchcraft—was asked if she knew anything about the charms made by witch doctors. She replied by reaching for her expensive leather handbag, unzipping it, and removing a square made of red felt. "This is mine," she said.

Frogmore's preeminent witch doctor was a black man known as Dr. Buzzard. I once had the opportunity to ask Dr. Buzzard's son, who went by the name of Root Man, how his father obtained "the power." Root Man described how Dr. Buzzard would put water in a large, black iron pot and build a fire underneath. When the water came to a rolling boil, Dr. Buzzard would toss in a live black cat. "That cat would stand up on his hind feet and talk like a man," Root Man claimed. After the cat had been boiled, its remains were placed in a cloth bag and thrown in the nearest river. "All of that cat would flow according to the flow of the tide," Root Man said. "All but one bone. And that bone floated right back to the witch doctor." Root Man declared there was no stronger force in the world than that which came from a bone of a black cat that had been boiled alive. Such was the source of Dr. Buzzard's power. (For another story about Dr. Buzzard, see The Charleston Walking Tour.)

But Frogmore is more than just the home territory of Dr. Buzzard. It is also the birthplace of Frogmore Stew, a current favorite at some of Charleston's finest restaurants and a dish that residents of South Carolina's sea islands have enjoyed for more years than anyone can trace. While people in other parts of the country celebrate special occasions with a barbecue or an oyster roast, the citizens of St. Helena Island make a pot of Frogmore Stew. This folk dish is a combination of sausage, shrimp, crabs, tomatoes, and corn on the cob, all boiled in beer. For years, visitors from as far away as Paris have come to Frogmore to get hexes removed, to hear the Gullah language, and to eat generous portions of Frogmore Stew.

It is 5.1 miles on U.S. 21 from Land's End Road to a junction with S.C. 7-77. Turn left onto S.C. 7-77 and drive 2 miles to where the road ends at Coffin Point Plantation. The striking three-story white clapboard mansion with the red tin roof commands a sweeping view of the ocean, the sky, and Edisto Island in the distance. On clear nights, the lights at Coffin Point Plantation can be seen nearly 50 miles at sea.

The mansion was built by Thomas Astin Coffin between 1780 and 1800. The Coffin family lived on the premises until shortly before the Civil War. During the war, the plantation was used by the men and women who came to St. Helena Island to teach at the Penn School. Laura Towne, one of the missionaries who founded the school, resided in the mansion.

It was after the turn of the century when United States Senator J. M. Cameron of Pennsylvania first learned of Coffin Point Plantation. As chairman of the Naval Committee, Cameron was invited to a party at the plantation, which was then being used as an officers' club by the military brass at nearby Parris Island. The senator immediately liked what he saw—the hand-carved moldings; the graceful, curving stairway; the view of Egg Island, which was said to be so covered with birds' nests in the springtime that a person couldn't take a step without crushing an egg; the view of Hunting Island and its lighthouse; and the long avenue of oaks at the back of the house. It wasn't long afterwards that Cameron bought the property. He and his family loved the place so much

Coffin Point Plantation

that they made it their home for four months out of each year. Boatloads of guests arrived nearly every weekend they were in residence.

After Senator Cameron's death in 1913, a clause in his will provided funds for the upkeep and restoration of Coffin Point Plantation. Some items from the mansion were sold at auction, but workmen continued to come to the plantation to make repairs and add new coats of paint. A man named C. S. Steinmeyer, who lived nearby with his family, attended the 800 pecan trees on the property and worked 260 acres in crops.

During the 1950s, Coffin Point Plantation was bought by local legend J. E. McTeer. At the time of the purchase, McTeer was in his eighth term as sheriff of Beaufort County. His public service dated all the way back to 1926, when he replaced his father and became, at the age of twenty-two, the youngest sheriff in the nation. "My father had died in office and the governor appointed me for one year," McTeer explained. "I was so young he wanted to test me. But I'd been raised in an atmosphere of law."

Indeed, his thirty-seven-year tenure won widespread admiration. "We're going to miss him," said Beaufort Police Chief Jesse Altman at the time of McTeer's retirement. "He was the epitome of a law-enforcement officer. He did a great job of making Beaufort a better community to live in. He goes back to the horse-and-buggy days; I think he actually rode a horse in here in the beginning."

McTeer's expertise was much broader than the law-enforcement field. He had an interest in witchcraft thanks to his grandmother, who had seen slaves employ hexes and spells back in the days before the Civil War; she had been especially impressed with the fact that no planter could make a slave refuse a witch doctor's command. McTeer understood the Gullah language, and he immersed himself in the study of witchcraft. When his interest turned to writing in later years, his book *Fifty Years as a Low Country Witch Doctor* chronicled his experiences with witchcraft, while *High Sheriff of the Low Country* told the story of his time in law enforcement. McTeer remained involved in both fields until the end of his life.

McTeer first became interested in Coffin Point Plantation as a possible site for raising livestock. However, he was initially discouraged upon being told that the area was too dry for that purpose. He decided to consult an old black employee who had been born on the plantation. The story goes that when McTeer asked the aged man where the former owners had gotten water, the man pointed to a piece of ground nearby, dug a hole several feet deep, and stood by as water began seeping into the hole. Another hole was dug, and it, too, filled with water. The underground springs at Coffin Point Plantation spouted a million gallons of water in the three weeks that followed. Satisfied, McTeer bought the property. In addition to raising livestock, he started a residential community facing the sound.

Once you have enjoyed Coffin Point Plantation, retrace your route to U.S. 21 and turn left. After 2.9 miles on U.S. 21, you will cross a bridge over the Harbor River onto Harbor Island, where you will find yourself surrounded by a maze of inlets, marshes, and tropical growth. Another 1 mile brings you to a bridge across Johnson Creek onto Hunting Island.

Hunting Island is the largest of a cluster of local islands that once served as the hunting preserves of the wealthy planter families. A group of St. Helena Island planters owned two thousand acres on Hunting Island. Their hunting parties lasted several days. Wives were welcome. The days were taken with hunting expeditions, while the nights were reserved for rather boisterous feasts of fish and wild game. Food was washed down with demijohns of wine.

North Beach Lighthouse

The 4-mile-long island now serves as a state park, but it still manages to give a feeling of the days when the planters came to hunt and celebrate. A Hunting Island State Park sign welcomes you as soon as you enter the island, but you must continue approximately 1.7 miles and turn left to reach the ocean portion of the park. Stop at the gate for a ticket, then continue past the visitor center— a gray building in the woods—to the North Beach Lighthouse. The dense growth of yucca, palmetto, pine, and wild magnolia along the way may remind you of the exotic vegetation of a Tarzan movie. The road ends at the lighthouse. If you look up to the top, you will probably see tourists who have braved the steep spiral stairway. The lighthouse was built in 1873 and boasted a beam of 120,000 candlepower before it was retired.

When you have seen the North Beach Lighthouse, follow the exit signs back to the main road running the length of the island. Turn left and continue on park property for approximately 2.3 miles to the small bridge leading to Fripp Island. Fripp Island is privately owned today, but if you happen to be arriving around mealtime, you might ask for a restaurant pass at the gate. The lovely, history-rich island is well worth a quick tour.

During the seventeenth century, as a reward for his defense of the British encampment at Beaufort, British privateer Johanne Fripp was given the land that later came to be known as Fripp Island. Actually, John Fripp of Edisto Island was the first member of the Fripp family in the New World. His son, John Fripp II, acquired holdings on St. Helena Island, and subsequent generations of the family took to using Fripp Island as a hunting preserve.

Entrance to Fripp Island

Much of the lore centered around Fripp Island has to do with a native of Bristol, England, who is said to have buried treasure chests in the local dunes. That man's name was Edward Teach, better known as Blackbeard, perhaps the most notorious pirate of all time. One popular story concerns a 1708 incident. Blackbeard's ship, flying the Jolly Roger, was anchored just off Charleston, where its crew was busy plundering and taking prisoners from the vessels entering and leaving the harbor. One morning, Blackbeard sent a messenger into Charleston bearing word that the pirates would be willing to free their prisoners in exchange for some much-needed medical supplies. A deal was struck, one of the stipulations being that Blackbeard himself had to come ashore to obtain the medicine.

Never one to turn down a challenge, the heavily armed Blackbeard came swaggering into town one May morning. He slowed down briefly at a mansion near St. Michael's Episcopal Church when a young woman waved at him. After picking up the medical supplies, he retraced his route past the young woman's home. Seeing her again, he snatched her up and carried her along with him, though she fought fiercely every step of the way. Blackbeard went

TOURING THE COASTAL SOUTH CAROLINA BACKROADS

so far as to take her to his ship and sail for North Carolina, where his friend, Governor Charles Eden, married them over the young woman's strenuous objections. From there, Blackbeard took his unhappy bride to Fripp Island, where she was left under heavy guard while he continued to roam the high seas. Blackbeard provided her a steady diet of diamonds and pearls, and legend has it that she eventually came to see him as a swashbuckling hero. Her illustrious husband later took her to the West Indies, where she presumably lived happily ever after—at least until Blackbeard's violent death in 1718. No sign of the young woman's presence remains on Fripp Island today.

On the other hand, some claim that the island does harbor traces of Count Casimir Pulaski, the Polish patriot who served as a brigadier general on the American side during the Revolutionary War. Pulaski's resting place has been a subject of speculation for more than two hundred years. Interest was revived around the middle of this century, when a grave was discovered on a high bluff on Fripp Island and preliminary reports seemed to suggest that it contained Pulaski's corpse. However, the findings were inconclusive, and the mystery continues to linger.

During the Civil War, the island was confiscated by the Union for "nonpayment of the Direct Tax," in the words of the government. After the close of the war, Julia M. Prioleau restored Fripp Island's good name by paying $4 in back taxes, a $2 penalty, $.30 in miscellaneous costs, and $.37 in interest, making the total price of redeeming the island $6.67, a terrific bargain compared with the $24 Peter Minuet paid for Manhattan way back in 1526.

When you are ready to leave Fripp Island, retrace U.S. 21 for approximately 18 miles to a junction with S.C. 802 and turn left. After approximately 3.1 miles on S.C. 802, you will cross the Beaufort River on the McTeer Memorial Bridge, named for Sheriff J. E. McTeer. You are now in the village of Port Royal. Approximately 0.4 mile after the bridge, S.C. 802 turns left, or south, and runs conjunctively with S.C. 281 and Ribaut Road. Another 2.9 miles takes you across a bridge over Battery Creek and to the entrance to the United States Marine Corps Station at Parris Island. Bear left to enter, then stop at the entrance gate to pick up a printed driving tour, which will direct you to all the important sites on the base. As you tour Parris Island, keep in mind that what began in 1891 as a small naval station for marines now turns out nearly twenty thousand trained recruits per year.

The first place of interest you will come to along the pristine, palmetto-lined avenue is the parade field, on the left. You may catch a glimpse of some of the harried recruits as they march under the stern eye of their sergeant. Also at the parade field is the famous statue that commemorates the group of five marines that raised the American flag on Iwo Jima's Mount Surabachi in 1945. The statue was made by Felix de Weldon, the same artist who later created the Iwo Jima Monument in Arlington National Cemetery, outside Washington, D.C.

The next stop along the avenue is the visitor center, the main point of contact for the hundred thousand people who tour Parris Island every year. Adjacent to the visitor center is *Iron Mike*, a statue designed and constructed by Robert Ingersoll Aiken. Erected in 1924, it is dedicated to the memory of marines trained at Parris Island who lost their lives during World War I.

The base's museum is 1 block beyond the visitor center. As you enter, you will see another statue of the marines raising the flag on Iwo Jima. The museum features marine uniforms dating back to 1859, huge photographs of marines in action during various conflicts, portraits of some well-known marines who have received high military decorations, and dioramas of Parris Island under the rule of Indians, the Spanish, and the French.

Statue commemorating the raising of the American flag on Iwo Jima's Mount Surabachi

If you care to explore further, the printed driving tour provided by the base can direct you down Tripoli, Nicaragua, and Cuba streets toward the Ribaut Monument and the Spanish settlement site. Jean Ribaut arrived in this area in 1562 and attempted to establish a permanent settlement. The monument to Ribaut and his group of French Huguenots was dedicated in 1926, after an archaeological excavation seemed to confirm the site as the location of their colony. However, more recent excavations by the South Carolina Institute of Archaeology and Anthropology have determined that the site is rather that of Fort San Marcos, used by Spanish settlers around 1580 to defend the territory *they* claimed. The exact location of Ribaut's colony remains undetermined, though it is known to have been somewhere on Parris Island. (For more information on early efforts at colonization in the Beaufort area, see The Historic Beaufort Tour.)

Retrace your route off the base and turn left on S.C. 802. After 1 mile, bear right onto S.C. 280. It is approximately 2.5 miles on S.C. 280 to the entrance to Retreat Plantation, on the right. The manor house, which sits 0.7 mile off the highway, was built before the Revolutionary War. Today, it is a private residence not open to the public, but its sad story still bears repeating.

Jean de la Gaye was a polished, well-educated, handsome Huguenot. He turned many a lady's head, but it was said he never cast a second glance at any woman after he laid eyes on the beautiful Catherine Gautier. In fact, he bought several hundred acres on Battery Creek to build her a house. Tabby was the preferred construction material in those days, and the walls of the manor house at Retreat Plantation were built twenty-two inches thick. The couple was married shortly before the completion of their home. They intended to spend the rest of their lives there.

Ribaut Monument

Jean de la Gaye had a private fortune to use as he chose. His ambition was to establish himself as a gentleman vintner. Toward that end, he set out row after row of grapevines on the plantation. Catherine came to love the place as much as did her husband.

One day, a servant hurried to Jean where he was at work in the vineyards and told him to hurry home, that Catherine had taken ill. Dangerous fevers abounded in the coastal area in those days. Jean took his wife in his arms as soon as he arrived home, but she died before a physician could be summoned. Servants dug a grave between the manor house and the water, and Catherine was laid to rest the following day.

To everyone's utter surprise, the psychological blow of his wife's death brought about a complete change in Jean's personality. Where before he had

been kind, considerate, and happy, he was now bitter, disconsolate, and reclusive. For a time, he refused to leave the plantation. He began to mistreat his servants. Hoping he would return to his senses, they at first put up with the abuse. But matters grew steadily worse. Finally, two servants decided they would tolerate the poor treatment no longer. They plotted to murder the master of Retreat Plantation.

Jean's condition did improve to the point that he would leave his property when the need arose. He did his shopping in Beaufort, which meant that he had to ride the water around the southern tip of Port Royal Island and up the Beaufort River. One evening when he was returning from town, the two servants rowed out to meet him. They climbed from their boat into Jean's, murdered him as quickly as they could, and pushed the body overboard. However, someone on shore witnessed the crime, and that person was able to identify the servants. One of the men was beheaded upon being caught. His head was impaled on a pole set in the mud along a bend in the Beaufort River. It is said that the skull remained there for two generations as a warning to others harboring murderous thoughts.

Myrtle Bush Plantation

Jean de la Gaye left no will. Retreat Plantation was sold at auction to Stephen Bull. When his daughter Sarah married John Gibbes Barnwell in 1798, Bull presented the plantation to them as a gift. Sometime before the Civil War, Retreat Plantation came into the possession of the Reverend Edward Tabb Walker, who had married into the Barnwell family. When the wealthy planters were evacuating their property during the war, the Reverend Walker hid the family Bible under the floorboards at the manor house and took his wife and nine children to a refuge near Walterboro, South Carolina. It is believed that General Sherman himself went to Retreat Plantation intending to burn it. The story goes that when the Bible was found and it was determined that the plantation's owner was a clergyman, Sherman decided to spare the manor house. The property was sold for taxes after the war, and former owner John Gibbes Barnwell bought it back for the grand sum of $8, then returned it to the Walker family. Neglect showed inside and out, but the manor house has since been restored to its former beauty.

From Retreat Plantation, continue 0.9 mile on S.C. 280 to Old Jericho Road and turn right. A drive of 0.4 mile brings you to Myrtle Bush Plantation, on the left.

From the late 1700s to the early 1900s, Myrtle Bush Plantation was owned by the Barnwell family. The original manor house was located at the end of the avenue of oaks, but it burned in the 1800s. In 1921, John W. Gray bought the property and built the present manor house in the middle of the avenue of oaks. It is a bit unusual to see a home situated midway down such an avenue, rather than at the end, but the present owners say that breezes blowing from either direction between the rows of oaks manage to keep the house cool throughout the summer months. Myrtle Bush Plantation served as a truck farm until the 1950s. It is a Christmas tree farm today.

Once you reach Myrtle Bush Plantation, you have circled almost all the way around Beaufort, and you have also completed this tour. Continuing on Old Jericho Road in your original direction will bring you to an intersection with S.C. 170. If you want to travel into Beaufort, bear right on S.C. 170 and follow it to where it intersects U.S. 21 at the outskirts of town. If you are headed south, turn left onto S.C. 170 and follow it across the Broad River toward Hilton Head Island and the Georgia border.

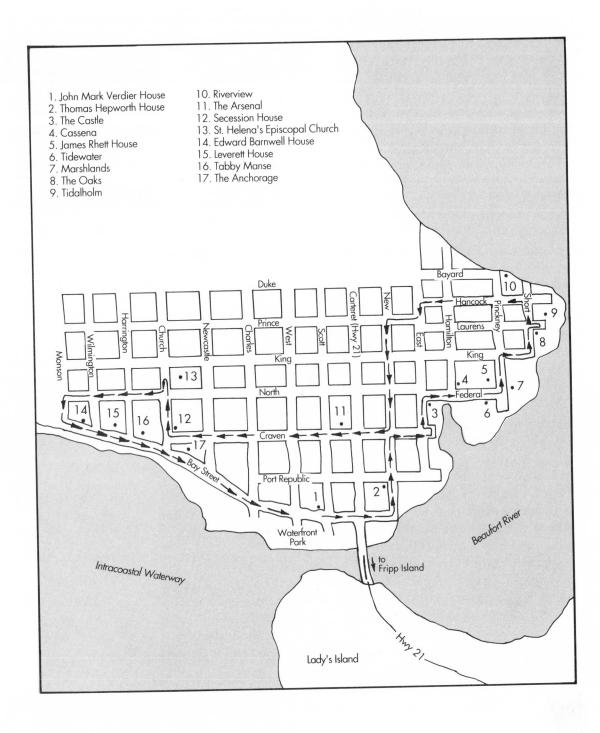

1. John Mark Verdier House
2. Thomas Hepworth House
3. The Castle
4. Cassena
5. James Rhett House
6. Tidewater
7. Marshlands
8. The Oaks
9. Tidalholm
10. Riverview
11. The Arsenal
12. Secession House
13. St. Helena's Episcopal Church
14. Edward Barnwell House
15. Leverett House
16. Tabby Manse
17. The Anchorage

Duke
Bayard
Hancock
Carteret (Hwy 21)
New
Harrington
Prince
Laurens
Church
Charles
West
King
Hamilton
Wilmington
Newcastle
Scott
East
King
Monson
13
North
Federal
12
11
3
14 15 16
Craven
17
Bay Street
Port Republic
1
2
Waterfront Park
to Fripp Island
Beaufort River
Intracoastal Waterway
Lady's Island
Hwy 21
Pinckney
Short
10
9
8
7
5
4
6

The Historic Beaufort Tour

This tour of Beaufort's historic district can be enjoyed by car, on foot, or in some combination of the two. It begins on Bay Street at the John Mark Verdier House and first explores the eastern half of town, with stops at the Castle, Tidalholm, Riverview, the Henry McKee House, and the Arsenal among other sites. The tour then heads into the western portion of the historic district, with stops at Secession House, St. Helena's Episcopal Church, and other attractions before it ends at the Anchorage.

Total distance:
approximately 36 blocks.

The tour begins in the heart of historic Beaufort at the John Mark Verdier House, at 801 Bay Street. The house is located 1 block west of the bridge over the Beaufort River to Lady's Island.

John Mark Verdier was a well-to-do merchant. His lovely, symmetrical home, built in 1790, follows the Federal style. One of the most important moments in the history of the house came in March 1825, when the Marquis de Lafayette was touring the United States. His scheduled arrival in Beaufort was eagerly anticipated by the local people. A formidable crowd of citizens

John Mark Verdier House

formed a welcoming committee at the city's wharves at the appointed hour, only to learn that Lafayette had run into a delay at Edisto Island, to the north. It was the middle of the night when he finally arrived. A messenger was sent on ahead to announce his approach to Beaufort, and the crowd reassembled in time to cheer his steamboat as it appeared around a bend in the Beaufort River. Lafayette was so far behind schedule that he couldn't really afford the time to stop, but gentleman that he was, he insisted upon disembarking, and it was from the balcony of the John Mark Verdier House that he addressed the townspeople. Since that night, the home has been informally known as "the Lafayette House."

During the Civil War, Union forces established a headquarters on the premises. The house saw a variety of uses after the war, serving as a fish market, an icehouse, law offices, a telephone-company office, and a barbershop. It fell on hard times during the Depression and was finally condemned in 1942, only to be rescued by the efforts of a preservation committee organized by Chlotilde Martin, a columnist for the local newspaper.

Since 1968, the first floor of the John Mark Verdier House has served as the headquarters of the Historic Beaufort Foundation. The Historic Beaufort Foundation is one of the best places to obtain information about local history.

That history is a rich one. The first European exploration of the area came only twenty-eight years after the voyage of Columbus, when Francisco Cordillo, representing Spain, landed at Port Royal Island in 1520. Cordillo is credited with christening one of the local islands St. Elena. The name evolved to St. Helena over the years.

A group of French Huguenots arrived in 1562, led by Jean Ribaut. Ribaut was so impressed with Port Royal Sound that he claimed it could accommodate "all the shippes of the world." He and his fellow Frenchmen promptly established a colony on Parris Island and called it Charlesfort. When supplies began to dwindle sometime later, Ribaut set sail for France for replenishments, leaving thirty of the colonists behind. He found his homeland in turmoil, and his return to the New World was delayed. Meanwhile, the colonists were suffering. In desperation, they finally built a small boat and sailed for Europe, only to have the wind die and leave them stranded in the middle of the sea. Starvation became a reality, and it is believed the colonists resorted to cannibalism before they were rescued by a British vessel and taken to France.

The English, led by William Hilton, first explored the area in 1660. A British colonization party took a close look at Port Royal Sound in 1669, but local Indians convinced them that better port facilities were to be found to the north along the Ashley River, the site that was soon to become Charleston. It was 1712 before the colonial government laid out plans for the town of Beaufort.

Credit for founding the town belongs to Thomas Nairn and John Barnwell, otherwise known as "Tuscarora Jack" Barnwell for his success in fighting the Tuscarora Indians. The new town of Beaufort did not know peace for long. On Easter Sunday in the year 1715, a group of Indians, mostly from the Yemassee tribe, burned the village and killed as many settlers as they could find. Tuscarora Jack Barnwell was away from home, but his co-founder, Thomas Nairn, was captured and tortured to death, his body pierced with pine splinters and burned over the course of several days. Peace was eventually restored when the Indians were driven south.

Beaufort's first wealth came from the growing of indigo. Indigo brought a high price in Great Britain, so Beaufort-area residents did not view the American cause with much sympathy during the Revolutionary War, feeling that their very livelihood was at stake.

Sea-island cotton brought the town its period of greatest prosperity between 1790 and 1860. In fact, it has been said that Beaufort was one of the wealthiest and most aristocratic towns of its size in the entire country during that time. Most of Beaufort's finest homes date from the years between the Revolutionary War and the Civil War.

The town adopted a strong secessionist stance in the years immediately preceding the Civil War. Local resident Robert Barnwell Rhett supported the Confederate cause so vigorously that he became known as "the Father of Secession." However, once the war was in full swing, Beaufort's resistance to the invaders from the North was short-lived. In November 1861, a Union fleet under Commodore S. F. DuPont passed the forts defending Port Royal Sound and took the town. It remained under Union control for the duration of the war. Much of the white population fled. Some estates were redistributed to freed blacks, while others were confiscated under direct-tax laws. Many were never regained by their former owners. Few Beaufort homes were destroyed during the Civil War, so the town retains a heavy concentration of historical homes and buildings.

The postwar period saw a devastating hurricane in 1893 and the destruction of the cotton crop by the boll weevil after the turn of the century. An era of renewed prosperity had its beginnings in World War I, when the marine base at Parris Island was established. The good times continued with the opening of a major shipping terminal in Port Royal in 1958 and the advent of the local tourist trade in the 1960s and 1970s.

When you leave the John Mark Verdier House and the headquarters of the Historic Beaufort Foundation, head east on Bay Street, crossing Scott Street and Carteret Street at the entrance to the bridge to Lady's Island. Be sure to take a look at the Wallace House, on the left at 611 Bay Street just after you cross Carteret Street.

A tabby house originally stood on the present site of the Wallace House. At one time, the three families living in the 600 block of Bay Street boasted fifteen children *each*, for a total of forty-five offspring. They also had a total of a hundred servants among them. The tabby house and its next-door neighbor were destroyed by fire in 1907. The story goes that two young boys were sneaking cigarettes near the present site of the bridge to Lady's Island. When they heard someone approaching, they hastily discarded their burning cigarettes, which just happened to fall into a loaded hay wagon. The resulting fire claimed some of Beaufort's best homes. The Wallace House was built on the corner before the end of that year.

Continue two houses farther to the Lewis Reeve Sams House, at 601 Bay Street. Before the Civil War, this house had no water supply, and it is said that processions of black children were made to walk back and forth to a well 0.25 mile away. Luckily, a hand pump had been installed in the kitchen by the time of the 1907 fire. While many homes in the vicinity burned, a bucket brigade at the Lewis Reeve Sams House passed water upstairs to drench the second-floor rooms, and blankets were dampened at the hand pump and used to smother the flames wherever they appeared.

Like many other homes in town, the Lewis Reeve Sams House is said to follow the "Beaufort style" of architecture. "Beaufort style" is a catch-all classification encompassing Georgian, Colonial, Greek Revival, and Spanish elements. Perhaps its most characteristic features are its solid foundations of stucco over brick or tabby and its two-story piazzas constructed to catch the prevailing breezes. Unlike classic Charleston homes, Beaufort homes are generally free-standing on large lots.

After you have seen the Lewis Reeve Sams House, turn left off Bay Street onto New Street. On the left at 214 New Street, at the corner of Port Republic Street, is the Thomas Hepworth House. Thomas Hepworth, the chief justice of the colony, built this clapboard cottage around 1717, making it the oldest home in town. The musket slots in the tabby foundation along the north side testify to the fact that the Yemassee Indians were still a real threat to the colonists at the time of the house's construction. The structure served as a private school for boys during the early part of the nineteenth century.

Thomas Hepworth House

Continue 1 block on New Street, then turn right onto Craven Street and follow it across East Street. On your left, the Joseph Johnson House takes up the entire last block of Craven Street. Popularly known as "the Castle," it is one of the most photographed homes in the country, having appeared on posters and in promotional material distributed by both the United States Department of Commerce and the South Carolina Department of Parks, Recreation, and Tourism.

The house was built by Dr. Joseph Johnson around 1850. It rests on a crib of palmetto logs, which were believed to be superior to traditional tabby foundations in surviving an earthquake. The house follows the Italian Renaissance style. Among its many spectacular features are its seventy-nine windows, its four triple chimneys, and its double stairway, one of the widest in the United States. Dr. Johnson was an avid horticulturist. The Castle boasts lush gardens of azaleas and camellias, while giant live oaks protect the house in front and back. The two ancient olive trees on the property were brought from the Mount of Olives in the Holy Land. The bricks used to build the Castle were made at Dr. Johnson's Brickyard Plantation, located on Lady's Island. Covered with a thin layer of plaster, they seem to change color according to the

weather, appearing alternately as shades of tan, gray, and pink. The effect is memorable. Many people feel that if you haven't seen the Castle, you haven't seen Beaufort. The home is not open to the public, but it can be viewed from three sides by walking along Craven, East, and Federal streets.

It is not surprising that such a home should have a ghost. One day while the Castle was under construction, Dr. Johnson was working in his garden when he thought he saw a dwarf walking around the side of the house. He turned to a nearby yardman and inquired about the apparition he had just witnessed. The yardman casually replied that the dwarf lived in the basement.

Dr. Johnson recalled a story that had been around for nearly three centuries. It was said that when Jean Ribaut arrived to colonize the area in 1562, a dwarf called Gauche was among his group of Huguenots. However, when the hungry Frenchmen built their small boat and tried to follow Ribaut back to Europe, Gauche was nowhere to be found. Dr. Johnson saw the mysterious dwarf on other occasions. He suspected it was the ghost of Gauche.

Dr. Johnson's instincts proved correct, though no one has yet come up with a satisfactory explanation of why Gauche should have chosen to haunt the Castle. Subsequent owners of the property have also witnessed the specter.

There is a story about a house guest who had an uncomfortably close encounter with Gauche. After being told about the ghost, the guest was asked whether he would be afraid to sleep in a certain upstairs room with tall windows overlooking the river. The guest replied that no, he was not afraid of ghosts, and that he would be happy to occupy whichever room his hosts selected for him. However, once he was in his bed and just about to be overtaken by sleep, he heard the unmistakable sounds of a small person's footsteps. The door to his room opened quietly, accompanied by a rush of cold air. The guest lay as still as he could. A tiny hand touched his shoulder. Then a small voice—speaking in French, a language the guest understood—said, "Monsieur, this is Gauche." The guest sat upright and asked Gauche to show himself, but the dwarf replied that he did not allow fools to see him. Then came the sound of more tiny footfalls, and the door to the bedroom closed. The guest felt weak, and he had trouble relaxing. The following morning, his hosts did not seem surprised to learn what had happened.

Since those days, furniture has been moved from one place to another within the Castle under mysterious circumstances, and doors have shown a disturbing tendency to open and close of their own accord. All such events are blamed on the ghost of Gauche.

Once you have seen the Castle, retrace your route from the end of Craven Street to East Street and turn right. After 1 block on East Street, turn right onto Federal Street. On the left just past Hamilton Street is the house known as Cassena, at 315 Federal Street.

Cassena was built in the early 1800s by a man named John Blythewood, who passed the property to his daughter and her husband sometime before the Civil War. In 1863, the home was purchased by a former slave of the family's. Cassena remained in the hands of former slaves until it was severely damaged in the hurricane of 1893. In fact, the house played an important role during the hurricane. Its front porch was the highest point in the vicinity, so it was pressed into service as a dock for unloading boatloads of refugees from the islands surrounding Beaufort.

Continue along Federal Street. On the left just before the street ends is the beautiful James Rhett House, at 303 Federal Street. In 1884, James Rhett began construction on this home at the tender age of twenty-three. His intention was to make the house two rooms deep, but he soon discovered that his financial resources would not support such an ambitious project. He had to alter his original plans rather drastically, and the house has been informally known as "Rhett's Folly" ever since. It is difficult to see much folly in James Rhett's work today, as his home presents one of the loveliest facades in town.

Directly across the street from the James Rhett House is the William Fripp House, better known as "Tidewater." Its address is 302 Federal Street. Built

Tidewater

around 1830 by William Fripp, the son of a privateer, Tidewater follows the Federal style. Its two-story portico faces the Beaufort River. William Fripp owned a total of nine plantations in the area. He was noted for his generosity to the poor, a quality that led him to be known all over South Carolina as "Good Billy Fripp."

"Marshlands," the James Robert Verdier House, is located across Pinckney Street from the end of Federal Street; the address is 501 Pinckney Street. Dr. James Robert Verdier is best remembered for his early efforts at treating yellow fever, the scourge of the Low Country. He played an important role in battling the disease in the nineteenth century. His home was built around 1814. Its porch, which runs across the front of the house and around the sides to join the back rooms, is said to have been inspired by Barbadian plantation architecture.

Turn left off Federal Street onto Pinckney Street. After 1 block, turn right onto King Street. Follow King Street to Short Street and turn left, then follow Short Street to Laurens Street and turn right. The Italianate-style home on the

Marshlands

The Oaks

right at 100 Laurens Street is the Paul Hamilton House, known as "the Oaks."

The Oaks was built by Paul Hamilton in 1856, but his family enjoyed it for only five years before they and other wealthy families decided to flee when Beaufort was occupied by Union forces. Following the Civil War, rumor had it that the home was to become a school for blacks, and Hamilton promptly announced that he would bid up to $1 million to regain the property. He understood from authorities that he would be given three days to secure that sum of money, but word subsequently arrived that the house would be sold at sunset on the second day. A group of local people hastily raised the money and purchased the property in Hamilton's name.

Continue along Laurens Street a short distance to view the Edgar Fripp House—known as "Tidalholm"—at 1 Laurens Street. If the house looks familiar, it probably is. Tidalholm was used as a location in the filming of the movies *The Big Chill* and *The Great Santini*. The site is a beautiful one. Tidalholm is situated in a sharp bend in the Beaufort River, which can be seen by looking north, east, or south. An impressive wrought-iron fence surrounds the property.

Edgar Fripp built the home around 1856, but his brother James was the owner by the start of the Civil War. Like its Laurens Street neighbor, the Oaks,

Tidalholm

Riverview

Tidalholm was nearly lost by its former owners after the war, only to be returned thanks to the generosity of others—in this case, thanks to a perfect stranger.

The story is a local favorite. Tidalholm was confiscated by the government, and it was scheduled to be sold at public auction. On the appointed day, James Fripp stood among the crowd with tears running down his face, as he did not have enough money to make a bid. It just so happened that someone in the crowd explained Fripp's predicament to a visiting Frenchman who had been sympathetic to the South during the war. The Frenchman purchased the property, awarded the deed to the surprised Fripp, kissed him on both cheeks, and left for France before Fripp had a chance to thank him properly. A letter in the possession of the descendants of James Fripp verifies the story. So it was that two magnificent homes in the same block of Laurens Street remained with their original families.

Retrace your route to Short Street and turn right. After 1 block, turn left onto Hancock Street. On the right at 207 Hancock Street is "Riverview," the Elizabeth Hext House. Built around 1720, it is believed to be the second oldest home in town. Most visitors find it more intimate than the grand Beaufort mansions constructed in later years.

At the close of the Civil War, there was no benefactor to come forward to help pay for Riverview. The home was sold by the United States Tax Commission for the sum of $640. Actually, the fate of Riverview was the rule, and the fate of places like the Oaks and Tidalholm was very much the exception. Many local homes changed hands during the early postwar days, to the dismay of their former families and the delight of their new owners.

Numerous ghost stories have been connected with Riverview, most of them having to do with pirates. One story tells of a day when the mistress of the house was out walking in the yard. Upon seeing her elderly gardener digging holes in random spots around the property, she asked what he was doing. He replied that he was merely following the instructions of several visitors who had come to see him the previous night. As he went on to describe his visitors' manner of dress, the lady of the house was surprised to learn that they had been nothing less than ancient pirates!

The plot thickened on a subsequent morning, when the excited gardener came to tell his mistress that the pirates had visited him again, this time promising to reveal the location of their buried treasure the following evening. The appointed evening passed, and the gardener failed to perform his regular duties the next morning. The mistress went to his home to investigate. She found that he had suffered a severe stroke. He died shortly afterwards, unable to reveal what he had learned. No pirate treasure has ever been found on the Riverview property, but the tales continue.

After you have seen Riverview, continue west for 2 blocks to view the Chaplin House, on the right at 409 Hancock Street. This home should not be confused with a pre–Revolutionary War house of the same name located a block away, on New Street. The Chaplin House on Hancock Street has a pearl amity button embedded in its balustrade. The button bears the date 1843. It is believed the button signifies that the home was completed to the owner's satisfaction that year. The house came into the possession of John F. Chaplin in 1860, and it has remained with his descendants ever since. To date, members of three generations of the Chaplin family have chosen to hold their weddings on the premises. The Chaplin House was occupied by Union soldiers during the Civil War. Some of their names and regiments, written in chalk, are still faintly visible on the attic door.

Hancock Street ends at East Street. Turn left onto East Street, then turn right onto Prince Street after 1 block. The Henry McKee House, at 511 Prince Street, is on the right at the end of the block. You'll notice that all of its porches face south, the better to catch the prevailing breezes during summer and to retain some measure of warmth during winter. The Henry McKee House is registered as a National Historic Landmark.

The house has had an interesting history. Built by Henry McKee in 1834, it was sold to the De Treville family around 1855. Like so many others, they lost their property after the Civil War. They subsequently sued to regain title. In the meantime, the house had been acquired by Robert Smalls, a former slave born in a small cabin at the rear of the property. Smalls was a talented man who had risen a long way from his humble beginnings. He was a war hero, having captured the ship *Planter* from Confederate forces in Charleston and delivered it to Union authorities in Beaufort. In fact, it was the prize money he received from the sale of the *Planter* that enabled him to purchase the Henry McKee House.

The De Treville family's case against Robert Smalls went all the way to the United States Supreme Court, which decided that Smalls' claim to the property was indeed valid. The decision in the case proved to have a bearing on the dispensation of all wartime tax titles granted in South Carolina. It is interesting to note that no personal animosities lingered after the case was over. One day, an elderly female member of the McKee family—the property's original owners—wandered into Robert Smalls' new home, thinking it was still her own. Smalls' kindly reaction was to allow her to move back into her old room, where she remained until the end of her days.

In later years, Smalls went on to become a National Guard general, a delegate to the South Carolina Constitutional Convention, a legislator at both the state and national levels, and the collector at the port of Beaufort. The Henry McKee House was owned by his family until 1940.

The Arsenal is a must-see on any tour of historic Beaufort. From the Henry McKee House, turn left off Prince Street onto New Street. Follow New Street for 3 blocks, then turn right onto Craven Street. The Arsenal is located a short distance across Carteret Street, on the right at 713 Craven Street. It now houses a small museum.

The original structure on this site was Beaufort's first courthouse. The Arsenal was constructed in 1795, then was completely rebuilt in 1852. A Gothic-style military structure, it boasts massive walls and a gateway with a pointed arch. Two brass trophy guns captured from the British during the Revolutionary War are on the premises. The guns were seized by Union forces during the Civil War but were later returned to their proper home. For many years, the Beaufort Volunteer Artillery, recognized as the fifth oldest military unit in the country, was headquartered in the Arsenal. The unit has taken part

The Arsenal

in all of our major conflicts from the Revolutionary War onward. It is now part of the 713th Armed Cavalry Regiment.

When you reach the Arsenal, you have completed the eastern loop of this tour. You are only 2 blocks north of the starting point, the John Mark Verdier House.

To finish the tour, continue west on Craven Street. Tabernacle Baptist Church, at 907 Craven Street, is on the right 2 blocks from the Arsenal. The structure was originally an adjunct to Beaufort Baptist Church, located approximately 2 blocks to the north. It was used primarily as a meeting house and lecture hall. However, at the close of the Civil War, some five hundred black members of Beaufort Baptist Church decided to break away and start their own congregation, at which time they purchased this structure. Tabernacle Baptist Church was badly damaged in the hurricane of 1893, but it has since been rebuilt. Robert Smalls, the owner of the Henry McKee House, was a member here. His grave is in the churchyard.

Follow Craven Street another 2 blocks to see the Milton Maxcy House, better known as "Secession House." It is on the right at 1113 Craven Street, at the corner of Church Street.

The tabby foundation of Secession House dates to the 1740s. Around the year 1800, Milton Maxcy, a Massachusetts native, acquired the existing house, removed the second story, and replaced it with two stories of wooden siding. Further refinements, such as the marble entrance steps and the marble mantels, were added by Edmund Rhett around 1861. Rhett was a United States senator and one of the leading advocates of secession. Indeed, his home was the site of many heated discussions on the subject of states' rights. It is believed that the last meeting of Beaufort's delegates to the Secession Convention was held at Rhett's home—thus the name Secession House. Legend has it that the fired-up delegates were cheered by a sizable crowd as they left the premises.

Turn right off Craven Street onto Church Street. It is less than 2 blocks to one of Beaufort's principal attractions, St. Helena's Episcopal Church, on the right at 501 Church Street.

St. Helena's Episcopal Church was built in 1724. Most of its bricks were made in England and found their original use as ship's ballast; today, they are covered by a thin coating of plaster. During the Civil War, St. Helena's was

Secession House

St. Helena's Episcopal Church

made to serve as a hospital. Union troops removed the pews, then uprooted tombstones from the churchyard and used them as crude operating tables. The church's organ was destroyed during the war. Its original steeple also suffered badly and was torn down in 1866. The present steeple dates from 1942. St. Helena's survives as one of the oldest churches in continuous use in the United States. To give some perspective on its age, it might be noted that a silver chalice and alms plate donated to the church in 1734 are still used on special occasions.

Many notable persons have been buried at St. Helena's. Tuscarora Jack Barnwell, perhaps Beaufort's favorite son, died in 1724, the same year the church was constructed. He was interred in the graveyard outside the church, but the building has undergone two enlargements since those days, so that his remains now lie under the chancel. And two Confederate generals—Lieutenant General Richard H. Anderson and Brigadier General Stephen Elliott—were also laid to rest here.

Early records at St. Helena's note the curious case of a certain Dr. Perry. Little is known of the man save for the instructions he left for his family at the time of his death. Dr. Perry had a great fear of being buried alive, so he asked that a jug of water, a loaf of bread, and a hatchet be placed in his coffin with him. In the event that he regained consciousness, he intended to keep thirst and

Graveyard at
St. Helena's Episcopal Church

hunger at bay while he hacked his way back to the land of the living.

If you tour the churchyard, you may notice the small, separate section of graves on the north side of the property. Those graves contain the remains of victims of suicide or dueling, as such persons could not be buried in hallowed ground.

When you have seen St. Helena's Episcopal Church, start to retrace your route south on Church Street, but turn right onto North Street before you have traveled a full block. Follow North Street for 3 blocks and turn left onto Monson Street, which ends at Bay Street just before the Beaufort River. Turn left to conclude this tour with a trip past some of the finest homes on Bay Street.

The Edward Barnwell House is located halfway down the first block of Bay Street at number 1405. The home dates from 1785. Edward Barnwell was the great-grandson of Tuscarora Jack Barnwell. He fathered sixteen children, the last of whom was nicknamed Sally Sixteen. The Edward Barnwell House was made to serve as quarters for Union officers during the Civil War. To expedite communications with Federal ships on the Beaufort River, a large platform was erected on the roof. From it, the signal officer could easily flash messages to the vessels at anchor.

The Leverett House, dating from pre–Revolutionary War days, stands at the end of the next block at number 1301. It was originally located on St. Helena Island. Dr. Benjamin Rhett had it moved to its present site around 1850. By the time the Civil War broke out, the home had come into the possession of the Reverend Charles Edward Leverett, who is best remembered for being the last rector of Old Sheldon Church. (For information on Old Sheldon Church, see The Witch Doctor Tour.) Unlike the majority of his neighbors, the Reverend Leverett managed to regain title to his home after the war.

Tabby Manse

The Thomas Fuller House, better known as "Tabby Manse," is located just across Harrington Street at 1211 Bay Street. Thomas Fuller, a wealthy planter, built the home in 1786. It is considered one of the best early homes in Beaufort. The materials used in its construction were of epic proportions. For example, the exterior walls are two feet thick, while hand-hewn structural timbers a foot in thickness extend the full forty-foot width of the house.

The John A. Cuthbert House, number 1203, is located at the end of the block. The home dates from around 1810. Like one of its Bay Street neighbors, the Leverett House, the John A. Cuthbert House was built at another location. Legend has it that the family that owned the home was plagued by disease and untimely deaths. Believing that a nearby pond was responsible for creating an unhealthy atmosphere, they had the house sawed in half and moved to its present site. However, it has not been recorded whether the change of location ended the family's troubles.

Continue 1 block to the William Elliott House, popularly known as "the Anchorage," located at 1103 Bay Street. The home is said to be a beautiful sight to travelers on the Beaufort River, which doubles as the Intracoastal Waterway in this area.

The Anchorage has had a rich history. William Elliott built the house before the Revolutionary War. His grandson, William Elliott III, owned it in the years preceding the Civil War. The younger Elliott was a well-respected agriculturist, sportsman, politician, and author. And though he was both pro-Southern and pro-slavery, he was one of the few men in town who opposed secession, even going so far as to call local firebrand Robert Barnwell Rhett "unscrupulous" and "malignant." However, he quickly dropped his Unionist stance and joined the Confederate cause once the war began, as he had no doubt that his allegiance to South Carolina superseded his ties to the United States.

Around 1891, the Anchorage was purchased by Lester Beardsley, a retired admiral. Beardsley spent $80,000 in modifying the house to suit his taste. Having passed several years of his naval career in Japan, he imported many pieces of Oriental furniture, a few of which are still on the premises. He also added stucco to the exterior and elaborate woodwork to the interior. It is said that Beardsley liked to imbibe. Legend has it that the secret wall panels inside the Anchorage were designed to hide the ingredients used in making his favorite drink, called a Cherry Bounce. And the original circular staircase in the house was supposedly removed in favor of the current L-shaped one so the admiral would be less likely to injure himself in a state of intoxication.

At various times, the Anchorage has seen service as a gambling casino, a tourist home, and an elegant restaurant. It was once threatened by demolition, only to be saved by the efforts of the Historic Beaufort Foundation. It is now protected by a restrictive covenant.

This tour ends at the Anchorage. If you care to visit a house museum before you leave Beaufort, the George Elliott House is 1 block past the Anchorage at 1001 Bay Street. The John Mark Verdier House, where this tour began, is located 2 blocks east of the George Elliott House. And an intersection with U.S. 21, the main route through Beaufort, is 1 block beyond the John Mark Verdier House.

The Anchorage

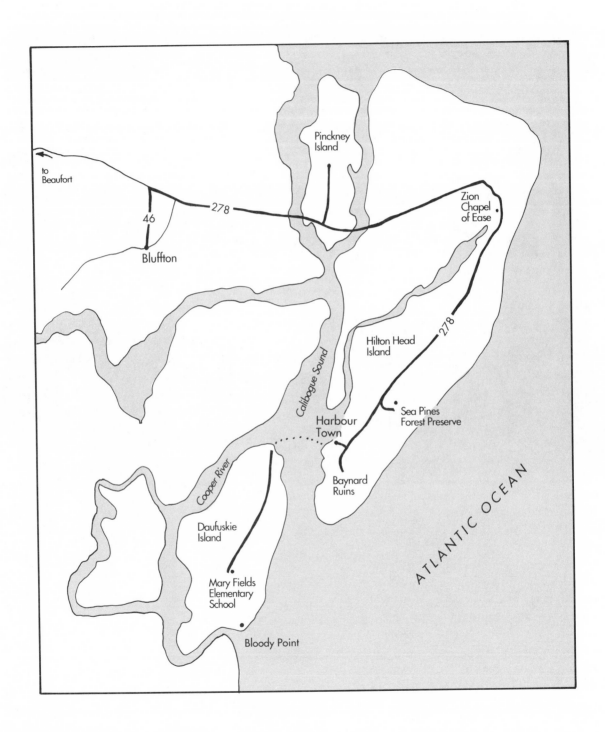

to Beaufort

Pinckney Island

Zion Chapel of Ease

278

46

Bluffton

Hilton Head Island

Calibogue Sound

Harbour Town

Sea Pines Forest Preserve

278

Cooper River

Baynard Ruins

Daufuskie Island

Mary Fields Elementary School

Bloody Point

ATLANTIC OCEAN

The Hilton Head Tour

This tour combines a pleasant drive through the southernmost portion of the South Carolina coast with opportunities for a boat ride, a few short walks, and a tour in a topless bus. It begins at the village of Bluffton, then heads across Pinckney Island to exclusive Hilton Head Island; travelers should be forewarned that a fee is charged to visit the southern section of Hilton Head Island. The tour then heads by boat across Calibogue Sound to end at storied Daufuskie Island, the site of the Strachan Mansion and Mary Fields Elementary School.

Total driving mileage: approximately 27 miles.

This tour starts at the intersection of U.S. 278 and S.C. 46 approximately 15 miles south of Beaufort. Head down S.C. 46 the 1.6 miles into Bluffton, a small village located on the May River. S.C. 46 begins at U.S. 278, so there is no danger that you will be headed in the wrong direction.

As its name would suggest, Bluffton is situated on a high bluff. The town was known as Kirk's Bluff in former days. Among the early settlers in the area were Revolutionary War fighter William Pope and Andrew Verdier, a Huguenot refugee who arrived in America in 1732. Andrew Verdier was the father of John Mark Verdier of Beaufort.

By 1825, Kirk's Bluff was attracting a summertime influx of wealthy planters from along the Savannah and May rivers. The visiting families found that the village offered a welcome respite from the intense heat of the plantations. Swimming, boating, fishing, and gathering crabs, shrimp, and oysters were among their favorite vacation pastimes. Calhoun Street was an important thoroughfare in the village even in those days, running down to a large wharf where steamers bound for Beaufort, Hilton Head Island, and Georgia stopped to take on passengers, mail, and freight.

In 1844, a town meeting was called for the purpose of choosing a new name for the village. It was at that meeting that the name Bluffton was selected. The choice still rings true today.

Entering the village, you will come to an intersection with a four-way stop. Follow S.C. 46 as it bears to the right. After 1 block, turn left onto Calhoun Street. Continue 7 blocks to the Church of the Cross Episcopal, on the right.

Originally established in 1767, the Church of the Cross Episcopal is the loveliest and most historic building in Bluffton. It is also the most photo-

Historic marker at Bluffton

graphed church in the entire state of South Carolina, having appeared numerous times in national publications. It was designed by a French architect named Dimmick, who selected black cypress for the exterior. Note the fan motif of palmetto fronds over the windows. If anything, the church has grown more beautiful over the years. Before you leave the vicinity, make sure you take the time to stroll along the river to see the birdhouse that is shaped exactly like the church. It even has a small cross on its roof.

After you have seen Bluffton, retrace your route to U.S. 278 and turn right. As you drive the 5.3 miles to Pinckney Island, you are entering an area owned for many years by one of South Carolina's most prominent families.

A man named Alexander Mackay received two proprietary grants for local land in 1710. The land was later acquired by Charles Pinckney. Pinckney was a London-educated lawyer, a legislator, a judge, and an adviser to the governor. His wife was the former Eliza Lucas, the woman who pioneered indigo growing in the Low Country. (For more information on Eliza Lucas Pinckney and indigo production, see The Georgetown Tour.) Charles and Eliza had little time for Pinckney Island. They lived at Belmont Plantation on the Cooper River and kept a mansion in Charleston, and they also had considerable landholdings in England.

TOURING THE COASTAL SOUTH CAROLINA BACKROADS

The couple had three children. Their daughter, Harriott, went on to marry Daniel Horry and become the mistress of Hampton Plantation. (For more information on Harriott Pinckney Horry and Hampton Plantation, see The Santee Plantations Tour.) It was one of Charles and Eliza's sons, Charles Cotesworth Pinckney, who inherited Pinckney Island after his father's death in 1758.

Charles Cotesworth Pinckney was like his father in many ways. He, too, was a legislator and lawyer; he even practiced out of the same Charleston office formerly used by his father. And he, too, had little time for Pinckney Island, at least during his working years. He was simply too busy. In addition to practicing law, he was one of the founders of the Charleston Museum, and he played the violoncello well enough to perform at the St. Cecilia Ball, a major social event in Charleston. He was even too busy to accept an appointment to a national office offered by George Washington himself, though he did find time to travel with his family to Philadelphia to attend the Constitutional Convention in 1787.

Historic marker for Pinckney Island

SOUTH CAROLINA

PINCKNEY ISLAND

Inhabited for some 10,000 years, Pinckney Island was known as Espalanga, Look-out, and Mackey's prior to about 1775. Alexander Mackey received two Proprietary grants for land on the island in 1710. Charles Pinckney later owned the island and willed it in 1769 to his son, Charles Cotesworth, who became a successful planter here.

It wasn't until he gave up his law practice and retired to Pinckney Island in 1801 that Charles Cotesworth Pinckney discovered how much he had in common with his mother, the indigo pioneer. He found his interest drawn to agricultural experimentation. He cleared land and planted exotic seeds from all over the world, as well as some conventional crops. He also bred extraordinary strains of sheep, in addition to raising cattle, hogs, chickens, and horses. Indeed, living on Pinckney Island and following in his mother's footsteps seemed to restore him to the energy he had possessed as a younger man. His mansion on the island boasted a library filled with books on scientific subjects, some of them written in foreign languages. The property also contained a nursery filled with exotic plants and a laboratory equipped to conduct a variety of chemical experiments.

Charles Cotesworth Pinckney died in 1825. He had built his mansion in the best-protected area on the island, near a group of century-old trees that promised to lend stability. But despite his efforts, the mansion was swept away by a violent hurricane sometime after his death.

Today, Pinckney Island has reverted to its natural state. It is the site of Pinckney Island National Wildlife Refuge. If you care to make a brief side trip to tour the premises, move into the left-hand lane as you approach the J. Wilton Graves Memorial Bridge—the bridge leading across the Intracoastal Waterway to Hilton Head Island—and follow the signs for the refuge. The road into Pinckney Island National Wildlife Refuge ends after less than 1 mile. For those interested in hiking, there is a 1-mile nature trail that leads through some of the heaviest tropical foliage imaginable. Other activities permitted in the refuge are hiking, bicycling, and saltwater fishing.

When you reach the far end of the J. Wilton Graves Memorial Bridge, you are on Hilton Head Island. U.S. 278, otherwise known as the William Hilton Parkway, is the island's main thoroughfare. Hilton Head Island is a year-round resort that hosts millions of visitors annually. It is nearly 12 miles long and up to 4 miles wide in places, encompassing about 42 square miles.

In the 1560s, when Jean Ribaut and his group of French Huguenots were looking to escape religious persecution in their homeland by coming to the New World, they spent some time on Hilton Head Island before establishing their colony near Beaufort. (For more information on Jean Ribaut's colony, see The Historic Beaufort Tour.)

A century later, Captain William Hilton, the man for whom Hilton Head Island is named, arrived from Great Britain. He was greeted by Spanish-speaking Indians from the Yemassee tribe, which had migrated north from

Florida during Jean Ribaut's day. Captain Hilton wrote glowingly of the natural abundance on the island: the oaks, walnuts, bays, and pines; the grapes, figs, and peaches; and the deer, turkeys, quail, plovers, herons, and ducks. He also noted the abundance of oysters.

Hilton Head Island is by no means devoid of wildlife today, but all the same, the attention of first-time visitors is likely to be drawn to the island's phenomenal development, rather than the kind of natural features noted by Captain Hilton. The modern-day Hilton Head Island had its beginnings in the 1950s, when Yale graduate Charles Fraser developed Sea Pines Plantation. Fraser worked tirelessly to attract both visitors and permanent residents to the island, and his philosophy of providing golf courses, bike paths, marinas, and the like proved highly successful. The fruits of his farsightedness are everywhere. Fraser still lives at Sea Pines Plantation, and his sailing yacht is berthed at Harbour Town Yacht Club.

Immediately upon entering the island, you will see golf courses, seafood restaurants, and shopping centers galore. Upscale housing developments with the word *plantation* in their names abound on both sides of the highway. Most of them occupy the former sites of sea-island cotton plantations, though little is left of the actual plantations today. Some twenty-four cotton plantations were in operation on the island at the start of the Civil War.

The William Hilton Parkway crosses Matthews Drive twice. At the second intersection with Matthews Drive, after a drive of approximately 6.7 miles on the island, you will see the former site of the Zion Chapel of Ease on the right. A cemetery and the Baynard Mausoleum are all that remain today.

There is some interesting history connected with the Zion Chapel of Ease, which was built in 1788. One member of its congregation was a planter named William Eddings Baynard, who came to Hilton Head Island in 1840. Baynard was locally famous because of the way he acquired land on the island. It seems he was something of a gambler. One night when he was playing cards with some of his wealthy friends, he hit upon the idea of a poker game with the plantations owned by the players as the stakes. His fellow players were astonished at his suggestion, but Baynard was persistent. They finally agreed to play the game according to his rules, though they had some serious misgivings. Baynard's boldness paid off richly, as he won Braddocks Point Plantation from Colonel John Joseph Stoney before the night was out. The plantation encompassed more than a thousand acres on Hilton Head Island.

Baynard lived at Braddocks Point Plantation until he died of yellow fever in 1849. His body was removed from the plantation in a carriage draped in black. It was laid to rest in the Baynard Mausoleum at the Zion Chapel of Ease. His coffin was an unusual one, shaped just like his body.

Since the time of Baynard's death, there have been numerous reports of the specter of a carriage draped all in black. The carriage moves slowly from the former site of Braddocks Point Plantation to the mausoleum. It is said that the carriage's passenger holds his hands over his face, though it is not known why. As the carriage moves along the William Hilton Parkway, it stops at the former sites of the old plantation gates, perhaps so William Eddings Baynard can chat with the ghosts of his card-playing friends. When the carriage reaches the mausoleum, it disappears.

The Zion Chapel of Ease was ransacked during the Civil War, and its lovely chalices were stolen. Many years later, an antique buff saw a chalice set in a pawnshop window and recognized it as something of special value. He purchased the set, scrubbed off the tarnish, and found an inscription that read, "Zion Chapel of Ease, Hilton Head, South Carolina 1834." The buyer was interested enough to do some research on the chapel, which he discovered was no longer in existence. He then decided to donate the chalices to St. Helena's Episcopal Church in Beaufort, with the stipulation that should the Zion Chapel of Ease ever be rebuilt, the set would be returned to its proper home. One of

Baynard Mausoleum

the chalices is now kept at the Church of the Cross Episcopal in Bluffton.

It is another 5.1 miles on the William Hilton Parkway to the entrance to Sea Pines Plantation. A fee is charged to tour farther south on the island. Continue straight once you have passed the entrance; the road is now called Greenwood Drive. On your left is Heritage Farm, a farmers' cooperative where residents of Sea Pines Plantation may rent space to grow flowers, herbs, and vegetables. Its separate garden plots with their abundant crops of watermelons, okra, corn, tomatoes, and the like make it look like a patchwork quilt.

The tour now veers off to the east side of Hilton Head Island for a rare look at an Indian shell ring. Approximately 2.1 miles past the entrance to Sea Pines Plantation, turn left off Greenwood Drive onto Tupelo Road. After 0.3 mile on Tupelo Road, turn left onto Lawton Drive, where you will see signs for Sea Pines Forest Preserve. Turn left off Lawton Drive onto Lawton Canal Road after 0.2 mile, and you will soon come upon the entrance to the preserve.

Getting to the Indian shell ring requires a round-trip walk of nearly 2 miles, but it is well worth the effort. The walk begins at the parking lot and meanders on a rich carpet of pine needles through a dense forest of native shrubs and trees. You are likely to spook a deer somewhere along the route. A sign warns that alligators and snakes also live in the vicinity, so be sure to watch your step.

It is believed that the Indian shell ring on Hilton Head Island was built around the same time as the great pyramids of Egypt. Scientists suggest that it was intended as a refuse heap. The Indian shell ring contains the shells of oysters, clams, and mussels, as well as the bones of deer, raccoons, bear, and fish. Numerous nutshells have also been found on the site.

When you first lay eyes on the Indian shell ring, you will probably be surprised at its size. A circular arrangement of oyster-shell mounds, it is about 150 feet in diameter and several feet deep. The Indian shell ring at Sea Pines Forest Preserve is one of only twenty of its kind in existence. It seems a miracle that it remains undamaged so many centuries after its construction. It is also a bit ironic that what probably began as a refuse heap is now protected by law and listed on the National Register of Historic Places.

After you have seen the Indian shell ring, retrace your route to Greenwood Drive. Turn right and follow Greenwood Drive for approximately 0.5 mile, then turn left onto Plantation Drive. Plantation Drive ends after 1 mile, then begins again 1 block to the east; you will have to turn left onto Lighthouse Road, then make a quick right to continue south on Plantation Drive.

Approximately 0.7 mile past Lighthouse Road, you will reach a parking area for Baynard Ruins Park, on the right. An easy, ten-minute walk leads to the

Baynard Ruins

Harbour Town Lighthouse

tabby ruins of William Eddings Baynard's manor house at Braddocks Point Plantation, the magnificent property he won in the poker game in 1840. Baynard and his wife, Catherine, raised their four children here. The manor house was evacuated when Union forces invaded Hilton Head Island in 1861, though it was seized back by a Confederate raiding party the following winter. After the war, it took members of the Baynard family fifteen years to pay the $500 in back taxes they owed the United States government. It was only then that they regained the plantation.

When you have seen Baynard Ruins Park, retrace Plantation Drive to Lighthouse Road and turn left. After 0.4 mile on Lighthouse Road, you will reach Harbour Town Yacht Club. The section of Hilton Head Island called Harbour Town is decidedly elegant. Its marina, a popular stop for yachts traveling the Intracoastal Waterway, is considered one of the finest in the Southeast. If you have the time, you may want to take advantage of the local bicycle-rental service and enjoy a ride along the paved bike trails located throughout the area. You are almost in the shadow of the famous Harbour Town Lighthouse. Harbour Town Golf Links, where the lighthouse is located, is a frequent stop on the professional golf tour. If you watch much golf on television, the distinctive lighthouse with its red and white stripes is likely to be familiar to you.

Several boat tours leave from Harbour Town Yacht Club. To complete this

tour, leave your car in the vicinity of the yacht club and arrange for passage to Daufuskie Island. The island is accessible only by boat, but it should not be missed. A fee is charged for the trip.

Daufuskie Island is the southernmost island off the coast of South Carolina. It is 5 miles long and 3 miles wide, encompassing a total of 6,720 acres. It is bordered by Calibogue Sound, the Atlantic Ocean, the Intracoastal Waterway, and Mongin Creek. The highest elevation on the island is a mere thirty feet.

The island's name has seen a variety of peculiar spellings, among them Dawfoskee, D'Awfoskee, and Da-fus-key. Some people believe the name came about because the island is "the first key" to the entrance of the Savannah River.

Daufuskie Island was granted to Captain John Mongin by King George II in 1740. During the Revolutionary War, island residents supported the British cause. Following the war, sea-island cotton brought great wealth to the plantations on the island. At the start of the Civil War, some of the local planters announced that their sympathies were with the Union. Their decision paid off handsomely in the years that followed. Unlike planters in other areas along the coast, they had no difficulty retaining their holdings after the end of hostilities.

The boat ride across Calibogue Sound to Daufuskie Island takes about forty minutes. Almost as soon as you leave the dock at Harbour Town Yacht Club, you will be able to see Georgia's Tybee Island and other sea islands. Once your

Haig Point Lighthouse

attention turns to Daufuskie Island, the first thing you will notice is the Haig Point Lighthouse, which is said to be haunted. Many people claim to have seen a ghost atop the lighthouse when the moon is full. In fact, some visitors have witnessed the phenomenon from the tour boat on which you are riding.

During the 1870s, lighthouses were built on the northern and southern ends of Daufuskie Island. The Haig Point Lighthouse is located on the northern end, facing Hilton Head Island; it was named for the Haig family, which once owned more than a thousand acres on the island. The Bloody Point Lighthouse, on the southern end, overlooked the open sea in the direction of Savannah, Georgia. Bloody Point's name had its origin in the period before the Revolutionary War. Indian parties from Georgia were in the habit of making raids on the white settlements on the islands south of Beaufort, and the southern tip of Daufuskie Island, just across the Savannah River, was usually their first stop on their bloody missions.

A shipwreck on Daufuskie Island

Cotton was the leading crop on the island for many years, but the boll weevil brought the entire industry to a screeching halt by 1921. Indeed, conditions were so bad that many planters had to sell their landholdings, and the population of the island dwindled. However, things began to look up during the 1940s and 1950s, when local residents turned to oystering for their living.

TOURING THE COASTAL SOUTH CAROLINA BACKROADS

The oysters were sold at Bluffton, after which the shells were brought back to Daufuskie Island and piled along the shore, where they served as a protective seawall. The seawall will come into view as your tour boat gets closer to the island; from a distance, it appears to be a sandbank. You will also begin to get a look at the island's considerable marshlands. South Carolina ranks second in the nation in wetlands acreage, surpassed only by Georgia.

Today, Daufuskie Island is a mixture of Hilton Head Island–style development and back-country roots. The exclusive Haig Point resort community is the centerpiece of development efforts on the island. Work on it began in 1984. Some 950 homes are planned. Haig Point residents enjoy golf, tennis, swimming, horseback riding, and private ferry service.

You will see the fabulous Strachan Mansion as you approach the ferry landing. The mansion serves as the clubhouse for the golf club at Haig Point.

The Strachan Mansion has an interesting story behind it. Though it was built in 1910, it is a newcomer to Daufuskie Island. In its previous existence, it served as a vacation home for the Strachan family on St. Simon's Island, Georgia. Several years ago, it fell into disrepair and was scheduled for demolition. However, the International Paper Company came to the rescue when they realized what a terrific bargain the home was—the purchase price was only $1! Their solution was to put the mansion on a barge and float it 100 miles up the Intracoastal Waterway to Daufuskie Island, where it would be completely restored.

Strachan Mansion on Daufuskie Island

The engineering task was a monumental one. Network television crews were on hand to take footage of the mansion as it was squeezed under low bridges or as it sat in the mud waiting for the tide to rise. The move was successful, though the new owners didn't realize quite the bargain they'd anticipated—they may have paid only $1 for the mansion, but they spent nearly $1 million in moving it! The building of the railroad track on Daufuskie Island from the water to the site where the home rests today cost $300,000 alone. Still, the restored mansion is a thing of considerable beauty, and the preservation efforts of the International Paper Company are to be applauded.

The Strachan Mansion is said to be haunted. While the mansion was being restored, workmen reported a variety of noises they couldn't explain. Some of them even quit their jobs in fear. Finally, the supervisor recognized that he would have to tell a little white lie if the job was ever to be completed. He decided to assure the workers that he himself had discovered the ghost and gotten rid of it. His solution worked splendidly. The strange noises continued, but the workmen no longer complained about them. It remains to be seen

Tour buses leave from the dock to take visitors for a ride around the island.

whether the house will ever be silent again.

As your boat pulls in at the dock, you will notice the tour buses with their tops cut off that wait to take visitors for a ride around the island. A tour is highly recommended, though you may have to scramble to beat your fellow visitors to the best seats. If you've ever been to the Caribbean and ridden one of the ramshackle buses that travels the unpaved roads of islands like Curaçao or Grenada, the topless buses on Daufuskie Island will bring back fond memories. Motorbikes may also be rented, but visitors who pursue that option do not benefit from a guided tour.

There is much to see on the island. The road that extends from one side of the island to the other through heavy stands of oak, pine, wild magnolia, and holly is jokingly called "I-95." If you're lucky, you may get a quick view of the home owned by golfing great Jack Nicklaus. Nicklaus designed the course at Melrose Golf Club, located along the eastern edge of the island. Among the most popular stops on the tour is Driftwood Beach, at the southeast end of the island. Huge pieces of driftwood protrude from the windswept sand. If you like to collect sand dollars, you'll love the selection at Driftwood Beach.

The island's three cemeteries are not among the regular tour stops, but they

Driftwood Beach

deserve a brief mention all the same. In days gone by, two of the cemeteries were reserved for blacks, while the remaining one was reserved for whites. There is an interesting story about Mary Dunn Cemetery, the cemetery for whites, located at the southern tip of the island. Mary Dunn Cemetery features a brick crypt that houses two long, narrow cast-iron coffins. The coffins most likely contain the remains of a husband and wife named Martinangle, though that is not certain; tradition holds that Tories from Hilton Head Island shot and killed Mr. Martinangle during the Revolutionary War. An unusual feature of the cast-iron coffins is that they have glass windows placed directly over the faces of the deceased.

Many years after the husband and wife were laid to rest, vandals broke into the crypt, opened the coffins, and stole whatever personal items they found among the dusty bones. They left without closing the coffins. Several more years passed before the crypt was broken into by a different set of vandals. This time, no sooner had the first of the unwelcome visitors crawled into the crypt when he saw a large black snake beginning to uncoil from where it rested in one of the open coffins. The vandal immediately began screaming and clawing his way back out. Needless to say, his partner reconsidered participating in the misdeed they'd planned. It is worth noting that the couple's remains have been left in peace during the many years since the story of the black snake was first circulated.

First Union African Baptist Church, built around 1863, is a must-see on the tour. The white frame church is situated close to the road. You'll notice that it has two front doors. At the time of the church's construction, one door was intended for men and the other for women and children. The roof of First Union African Baptist Church is made of tin. The bell in the steeple still works.

Another must-see is Mary Fields Elementary School, located in the south central part of the island. Constructed in 1936 for the education of black children, it is the oldest public school in Beaufort County still in operation. Its two rooms serve the needs of grades one through five; children in grades six through twelve take a school boat to a facility on Hilton Head Island. At the time I visited, the total enrollment was nine boys and two girls.

Note the wire stretched between two trees near the entrance to Mary Fields Elementary School. Those are indeed dried snakeskins hanging on the wire. One of the earliest and most important lessons students are taught at the school is the identification of snakes, since three species of rattlesnakes live on Daufuskie Island.

Mary Fields Elementary School has one teacher and one teacher's assistant.

First Union African Baptist Church

Mary Fields Elementary School

TOURING THE COASTAL SOUTH CAROLINA BACKROADS

Since the school isn't big enough to warrant having a principal, the teacher serves in that capacity and is paid a principal's salary. However, there are definite drawbacks to teaching on Daufuskie Island. Chief among them may be loneliness. It takes a person with strong ideals and a firm sense of purpose to teach at a place where even the simplest of tasks—like buying groceries—can be accomplished only by boat and with considerable difficulty.

National attention was first focused on the island thanks to the efforts of a teacher at Mary Fields Elementary School. Former Beaufort resident Pat Conroy came to teach on Daufuskie Island in 1969. He went on to chronicle his experiences in *The Water Is Wide*. Conroy's book later served as the basis for the movie *Conrack*. Conrack was the name his students called him. Pat Conroy has since achieved widespread literary acclaim on the strength of such novels as *The Great Santini, The Lords of Discipline*, and *The Prince of Tides*.

Today, Daufuskie Island is a blend of local traditions like Mary Fields Elementary School and modern development like the homes at Haig Point. The Strachan Mansion, which is both old and new, embodies a little of both worlds. Development on the island has been tasteful and restrained to this date, but long-time residents are understandably concerned about what the future might hold. A good many local landowners value their lifestyle so dearly that they have shown little interest in the vast sums of money offered by potential developers.

This tour concludes with your ride on one of Daufuskie Island's topless buses. As you board the boat for the trip back across Calibogue Sound to where you left your car on Hilton Head Island, perhaps you can decide for yourself whether you prefer the concentrated development of places like Hilton Head Island or the lonely isolation of the traditional portions of Daufuskie Island. As residents all along South Carolina's sea islands have found, the choice is not always an easy one.

Appendix

Federal Agencies

Cape Romain National Wildlife Refuge
Department of the Interior
United States Fish and Wildlife
Service
390 Bulls Island Road
Awendaw, S.C. 29429
803-887-3330

Fort Moultrie National Park
Drawer R
Sullivan's Island, S.C. 29482
803-883-3123

Fort Sumter National Monument
Drawer R
Sullivan's Island, S.C. 29482
803-883-3123

Francis Marion National Forest
Wambaw Ranger District
P.O. Box 788
McClellanville, S.C. 29458
803-887-3257

Parris Island Marine Corps
Recruit Depot
Parris Island, S.C. 29905-5002
803-525-2111

State Parks and Agencies

Edisto Beach State Park
6377 State Cabin Road
Edisto Island, S.C. 29438
803-869-2156

Hampton Plantation State Park
Route 1, Box 47
McClellanville, S.C. 29458
803-887-3982

Hunting Island State Park
1775 Sea Island Parkway
St. Helena Island, S.C. 29920
803-838-2151

Huntington Beach State Park
Murrells Inlet, S.C. 29576
803-237-4440

Myrtle Beach State Park
Highway 17 South
Myrtle Beach, S.C. 29577
803-238-5660

**South Carolina Wildlife and
Marine Resources Department**
P.O. Box 12559
Charleston, S.C. 29422-2559
803-762-5000

County Parks and Agencies

Beachwalker Park
P.O. Box 12043
Charleston, S.C. 29412
803-762-2171

**Charleston County Park and
Recreation Commission**
P.O. Box 12043
Charleston, S.C. 29412
803-762-2172

Folly Beach County Park
P.O. Box 12043
Charleston, S.C. 29412
803-762-2171

James Island County Park
871 Riverland Drive
Charleston, S.C. 29412
803-795-7274

Palmetto Islands County Park
444 Needlerush Parkway
Charleston, S.C. 29464
803-884-0832

Chambers of Commerce

Beaufort Chamber of Commerce
1006 Bay Street
P.O. Box 910
Beaufort, S.C. 29901
803-524-3163

**Charleston Chamber
of Commerce**
P.O. Box 975
Charleston, S.C. 29402
803-577-2510

Edisto Chamber of Commerce
P.O. Box 206
Edisto Island, S.C. 29438
803-869-3867

**Georgetown Chamber
of Commerce**
Drawer 1776
Georgetown, S.C. 29442
803-546-8436

**Hilton Head Island
Chamber of Commerce**
P.O. Box 5647
Hilton Head Island, S.C. 29938
803-785-3673

**Little River Chamber
of Commerce**
2229 Highway 17 North
Little River, S.C. 29566
803-249-6604

**Myrtle Beach Chamber
of Commerce**
1301 North Kings Highway
Myrtle Beach, S.C. 29571
803-626-7444

Others

Boone Hall Plantation
P.O. Box 254
Mount Pleasant, S.C. 20465
803-884-4371

Brookgreen Gardens
Murrells Inlet, S.C. 29576
803-237-4218

The Citadel
Military College of
South Carolina
Charleston, S.C. 29405
803-792-5000

Drayton Hall
3380 Ashley River Road
Charleston, S.C. 29414
803-766-0188

**Hobcaw Barony Tour
Bellefield Nature Center**
Route 5, Box 1003
Georgetown, S.C. 29440
803-546-4623

Litchfield Plantation
P.O. Box 290
Pawleys Island, S.C. 29585
803-237-9322

Magnolia Cemetery
P.O. Box 6214
Charleston, S.C. 29405
803-722-8638

Magnolia Gardens
Route 4, Highway 61
Charleston, S.C. 29414
803-571-1266

Middleton Place
Ashley River Road
Charleston, S.C. 29414
803-556-6020

Patriots Point
40 Patriots Point Road
Mount Pleasant, S.C. 29464
803-884-2727

Tom Yawkey Wildlife Center
Route 2, Box 181
Georgetown, S.C. 29440
803-546-6814

Bibliography

Allston, Susan Lowndes. *Brookgreen-Waccamaw*. Charleston, S.C.: Southern Printing and Publishing Company, 1956.

Alpert, Hollis. *The Life and Times of Porgy and Bess*. New York: Alfred A. Knopf, 1990.

Baruch, Bernard M. *My Own Story*. New York: Henry Holt and Company, 1957.

Black, J. Gary. *My Friend the Gullah*. Columbia, S.C.: The R. L. Bryan Company, 1974.

Bull, Henry deSaussure. *All Saints Church, Waccamaw: 1739–1968*. Columbia, S.C.: The R. L. Bryan Company, 1968.

Christophersen, Merrill G. *Biography of an Island*. Fennimore, Wis.: Westburg, 1976.

Dabbs, Edith M. *Sea Island Diary: A History of St. Helena Island*. Spartanburg, S.C.: The Reprint Company, 1983.

Epps, Florence Theodora, ed. *The Independent Republic Quarterly*. Conway, S.C.: Horry Printers, 1970.

Ewen, David. *A Journey to Greatness: The Life and Music of George Gershwin*. New York: Henry Holt and Company, 1956.

Fitzpatrick, John C, ed. *The Diaries of George Washington*. 4 vols. New York: Houghton Mifflin Company, 1925.

Glen, Isabella C. *Life on St. Helena Island*. New York: Carlton Press, Inc., 1980.

Graydon, Nell S. *Tales of Beaufort*. Beaufort, S.C.: Beaufort Book Shop, Inc., 1963.

A Guide to Historic Beaufort. Beaufort, S.C.: Historic Beaufort Foundation, Inc., 1970.

"Information for Guides of Historic Charleston." This useful work is available through the Reference Department of the Charleston Public Library. It is the reference used by Charleston tour guides.

Lachicotte, Alberta Morel. *Georgetown Rice Plantations*. Columbia, S.C.: The State Printing Company, 1955.

Lewis, Catherine H. "History of Little River." Unpublished history written for the Little River Chamber of Commerce.

Lewis, Oscar. *The Big Four*. New York: Alfred A. Knopf, 1938.

McTeer, J. E. *Beaufort Now and Then*. Beaufort, S.C.: Beaufort Book Company, 1971.

———. *Fifty Years as a Low Country Witch Doctor*. Beaufort, S.C.: Beaufort Book Company, 1976.

Messmer, Catherine Campani. *South Carolina's Low Country: A Past Preserved*. Orangeburg, S.C.: Sandlapper Publishing, 1988.

Petit, James Percival. *South Carolina and the Sea*. Vol. 2. Isle of Palms, S.C.: La Petit Maison Publishers, Inc., 1986.

Prevost, Charlotte Kaminski, and Effie Leland Wilder. *Pawleys Island: A Living Legend*. Columbia, S.C.: The State Printing Company, 1972.

Pringle, Elizabeth Allston. *Chronicles of Chicora Wood*. New York: Scribner's, 1922.

Proske, Beatrice Gilman. *Archer Milton Huntington*. New York: The Hispanic Society of America, 1963.

Rogers, George C. J. *The History of Georgetown County, South Carolina*. Columbia, S.C.: University of South Carolina Press, 1970.

Wallace, David Duncan. *The History of South Carolina*. New York: The American Historical Society, Inc., 1934.

Willcox, Clarke R. *Musings of a Hermit*. Charleston, S.C.: Walker Evans and Cogswell Company, 1968.

Issues of the following newspapers and magazines were of use in preparing this book:

Atlanta Constitution
Bridgeport (Connecticut) *Sunday Post*
Charlotte Observer
Georgetown Semi-Weekly Times
Georgetown Times
Horry Herald

Myrtle Beach Sun News
New York Times
San Francisco Examiner
South Carolina Historical and Genealogical Magazine

Index

Adam, James, 133
Adam, Robert, 133, 168–69
Adams Run, 199
Adjer, James, 168
Adjer, Robert, 164
Aiken, Robert Ingersoll, 218
All Saints Parish, 89
All Saints Waccamaw Episcopal Church, 74
Allston, Francis Withers, 70
Allston, Robert Francis Withers, 100, 175
Alston, Aaron Burr, 92–93
Alston, Charles Cotesworth Pinckney, 175
Alston, Emma Pringle, 175
Alston, Joseph, 61, 92–93
Alston, Theodosia Burr, 61–62, 91–93
Alston, William, 82, 166
Altman, Jesse, 214
Alvin Theater, 191
American Classic Tea, 195
Anchorage, the. See William Elliott House
Anderson, Richard H., 238
Anderson, Robert, 171, 188–89
Andrews, Mike, 59
Anglican church, 89, 99, 120
Annandale Plantation, 111–12
Arcadia Plantation, 79–80, 81, 82
Arsenal, the, 235–36
Arthur Smith King Mackerel Tournament, 10
Ashley Hall, 167
Ashley River, 182, 185, 225
Atalaya, 68
A-10 Thunderbolt II, 52
Atkinson, Sam, 98
Atlantic Beach, 30–33
Atlantic Coast Lumber Company, 104

Baba, Meher, 33
Ball, John, 187
Bannockburn Plantation, 79
Barnwell, Edward, 239
Barnwell, John Gibbes, 221
Barnwell, John "Tuscarora Jack," 225, 238, 239
Barnwell family, 221
Barrett, Billy, 48

Barrett family, 48
Baruch, Belle, 81
Baruch, Bernard M., 81, 114
Basket making, 131–32
Basket women, 131–32
Battery Creek, 217, 219
Battery, the, 167, 171
Battery White, 107–8
Baynard, Catherine, 250
Baynard, William Eddings, 247–48, 250
Baynard family, 250
Baynard Mausoleum, 247–48
Baynard Ruins Park, 249–50
"Be Young, Be Foolish," 27
Beach music, 26–27, 45
Beachwalker Park, 197
Beardsley, Lester, 240
Beaty, Cora, 5
Beaty, Freddie, 15
Beaty, Mary, 14
Beaufort, 208, 223–225, 235
Beaufort Baptist Church, 236
Beaufort County, 208
Beaufort National Cemetery, 208
Beaufort River, 208, 239, 240
"Beaufort style," 226
Beaufort Volunteer Artillery, 235
Beauregard, Pierre G. T., 167, 188–89
Beck family, 4
Beese, Welcom, 65
Bell, Alexander Graham, 172
Belle Isle Museum, 108
Belle Isle Plantation, 107, 108, 127
Belle Isle Villas and Yacht Club, 107, 108
Belle W. Baruch Foundation, 81
Bellefield Plantation, 81
Bellinger, Elizabeth, 206
Belmont Plantation, 244
Berry, C. B., 7, 29
"Bess, You Is My Woman Now," 191
Besselieu, George, 66
Bessent, Tom, 9
Best Friend of Charleston, 146, 149
Big Chill, The, 232
Bigham, Edmund, 15–17
Bigham, Leonard Smiley, 16
Bigham family, 15–16

Black Maria, 43
Black River, 85, 86, 128
Blackbeard. *See* Teach, Edward
Bloody Point Lighthouse, 251
Bluffton, 243, 253
Blythewood, John, 229
Boll weevil, 200, 252
Bonnet, Stede, 172
Boone Hall Plantation, 132–33
"Bosoms, the," 166–67
Botkin, Henry, 190
Boundary House, 6
Braddocks Point Plantation, 247–48, 250
Branford, William, 162
Brewton, Miles, 165
Brick Church, 211
Brick House, 200
Brickyard Plantation, 227
Brightwaters, 48
Brookgreen Gardens, 61, 64–67
Brookgreen Plantation, 61, 62–65, 92
Brown, P. P., 108
Bryan, George Miller "Buster," 37
Buck, Georgia, 21
Buck, Henry, 19, 21
Buck, Henry Lee, 21
Buck family, 19, 21
Buck family cemetery, 19
Bucksport, Maine, 19
Bucksport, S.C., 21
Bucksville, 19–20
Bull, Stephen, 167. *See also* "Stephen Bull
    of Sheldon"
Bull, William, 167
Bull family, 167, 205, 206
Bulls Island, 82
Burr, Aaron, 61, 92
Burr, Theodosia. *See* Alston, Theodosia
    Burr
Burroughs, Adeline Cooper, 44
Burroughs, Don, 34
Burroughs, Frank A., 34, 43, 49
Burroughs and Collins, 43, 47
Butler, Herbert J., 114
Buzzard, Dr., 161, 212

Cabbage Row, 176, 190
Calabash, Mrs., 3
Calabash, N.C., 3–5

Calabash River, 3, 4–5
Calabash Seafood Hut, 4
Calhoun, John C., 152, 169
Calhoun Lemon House, 78
Calhoun Mansion, 169
Calibogue Sound, 251, 257
Cameron, J. M., 213–14
Campbell, Carroll, 123
Campbell, Lord William, 167–68
Cape Fear River, 99, 172
Cape Romain National Wildlife Refuge,
    82, 123, 130
Capers Island, 82
Captain Sam's Inlet, 197
Caravelle, 37
Carr, Minnie S., 169
Carriage House Restaurant, 73
Cassena, 229
Castle, the. *See* Joseph Johnson House
Cat Island, 109
Catfish Row, 176, 190
Cedar Creek, 23
Chandler, Genevieve, 64, 65
Chapin, Simeon B., 33–34, 47
Chapin Department Store, 34
Chapin Foundation of South Carolina, 34
Chapin Memorial Library, 34
Chapin Memorial Park, 34
Chaplin, John F., 234
Chaplin House, 234
Charles I, 145
Charles II, 134, 145
Charles Town Tea Party, 146
Charlesfort, 224
Charleston, 143, 145–47, 149, 150, 159, 177,
    190, 216
Charleston City Hall, 159, 160
Charleston County, 143
Charleston County Courthouse, 159, 161
Charleston double house, 162, 172
Charleston Harbor, 171
Charleston Museum, 150–52, 176, 245
Charleston Naval Base, 187
Charleston single house, 150, 168
Charleston Tea Plantation, 194–95
Charleston Visitor Center, 149–50
Cherry Grove Beach, 23–24, 31
Cherry Grove Pavilion, 24
Chesterfield Inn, 47–48

Chew, Robert L., 188
Chisholm House. *See* Middleton Plantation
Christ Church Episcopal, 199
Christ Church Parish, 132
Chronicles of "Chicora Wood," 77
Church of the Cross Episcopal, 243–44, 249
Churchill, Winston, 81
Citadel, the, 155–56
Citadel Memorial Military Museum, the, 155
City Market (Charleston), 153–54
"City of the Silent," 145
Civil War, 107–8, 147, 150–51, 171–72, 173–74, 187–89, 208, 209, 225, 237–38
Clamagore, 143
Clarendon Plantation, 207
Clemson University, 64
Clifton Plantation, 79, 81, 82
Clinton, Henry, 135, 165
Clover, 108
Cochran, James, 8
Coffin, Thomas A., 172, 213
Coffin Point Plantation, 212–15
Coke, Edward, 118
Colonial Theater, 191
Congaree River, 118
Congdon family, 102
Conrack, 257
Conroy, Pat, 257
Continental Congress, 116, 128, 181
Conway, Robert, 14, 15
Conway, 14, 44, 51
Conway City Hall, 14
Conway Chamber of Commerce, 14
Conwayborough. *See* Conway
Cooper River, 143, 173, 187
Cooper River Bridge. *See* John P. Grace Memorial Bridge
Cordillo, Francisco, 224
Corning family, 207
Cornwallis, Lord, 165
Cotton cultivation, 198–99, 200, 252
Cowan Creek, 208
Cox family, 207
Crawford, Levi, 27
Crescent Beach, 23, 28–29, 31
Crows, the, 26
Cuthbert House, 239

Da-fus-key. *See* Daufuskie Island
Daggett, T. W., 102, 108
Dahlgren, John A., 107–8
Daisy Bank Plantation, 112–13
D'Angelo, Jimmy, 37
Daufuskie Island, 251–55, 257
David, 173
Davidson, Chalmers G., 103
Davis, Jefferson, 188
Dawfoskee. *See* Daufuskie Island
D'Awfoskee. *See* Daufuskie Island
Daytona Beach, Fla., 26
De Treville family, 235
Dealy, Mary, 97
Delano, Sara, 19
deSaussure, Lewis, 172
deSaussure House, 172
Diana, 67
Dimmick (French architect), 244
Dock Street Theatre, 176–77
Doolittle, James, 52
Dover Plantation, 108
Drayton, Dr., 185–86
Drayton, John, 185, 186
Drayton, Thomas, 185
Drayton family, 185
Drayton Hall, 185–86
Driftwood Beach, 254
Drunken Jack Island, 70
Dunbar, Elishua, 19
Dunes Club. *See* Dunes Golf and Beach Club
Dunes Golf and Beach Club, 34, 35, 37
DuPont, Eugene, 114
DuPont, S. F., 225
Durante, Jimmy, 3
Dusenbury, Corrie, 60

Eden, Charles, 217
Edgar Fripp House, 232–33, 234
Edisto Beach State Park, 202–3
Edisto Island, 195, 199–203
Edisto Island Baptist Church, 202
Edisto Island Historic Preservation Society, 199
Edisto Island Presbyterian Church, 200–202
Edisto River, 89

Edistow Indians, 199
Edmonston-Alston House, 175
Edward Barnwell House, 239
Egg Island, 213
Elfe, Thomas, 176
Elizabeth Hext House, 233–34
Elliott, Stephen, 238
Elliott, William, 240
Elliott, William II, 240
Elliott House, 240
Emanuel, Sol, 102
Emerson, Isaac E., 63, 79–80
Emmons, Robert, 52
End of the Trail, The, 67
Engelmayer, Reinhold, 40
English Santee, 120
Epps, Dr., 48
Estherville Plantation, 109, 111

Faith Memorial Episcopal Church, 65
Farley, James, 189
Farrow-Porter House, 100
Fat Harold's Pad, 27
Fat Jack Band, 27
Federal Writers' Project, 56
Female Mite Society of Edisto and
    Wadmalaw Island, 202
Fenwick, John, 193–94
Fenwick Hall, 193
First Scots Presbyterian Church, 176
First Union African Baptist Church, 255
Fisher Boy, The, 73
Flagg, Alice, 57–59, 74
Flagg, Allard, 57–58
Flagg, Arthur, 74
Flagg, Georgeanna, 74
Fleming, Captain, 38
Fleming, Mack, 195
Floral Beach. *See* Surfside Beach
Folly Beach, 189–90
Folly Beach County Park, 192
Folly River, 192
Footlight Players of Charleston, 177
Ford, Henry, 172
"Forever Charleston," 150
Forlorn Hope Plantation, 79, 81
Fort Johnson, 171, 187–89
Fort Moultrie, 134–35, 137, 188

Fort Moultrie, Battle of. *See* Sullivan's
    Island, Battle of
Fort San Marcos, 219
Fort Sumter, 147, 152, 171–72, 188–89
Forten, Charlotte, 210
Four Corners of Law, the, 146, 159
Fox, Gustavus V., 188
Francis Marion National Forest, 128, 130
Fraser, Charles, 247
Fraser, James Earle, 67
Freeda A. Wyley, 40
French Huguenot Church, 91, 177
French Santee, 120
French Tavern, the, 91
Friendfield House, 81
Fripp, Edgar, 232
Fripp, James, 233
Fripp, Johanne, 215
Fripp, John, 215
Fripp, John II, 215
Fripp, William "Good Billy," 230
Fripp family, 215
Fripp Island, 215–17
Frogmore, 211–12
Frogmore Stew, 212
Fuller, Thomas, 239

Gable, Clark, 116
Gallivants Ferry, 11
Garden City Beach, 56, 71
Garden Club of Charleston, 176
Gardens Corner, 205, 207
Gauche, 228–29
Gautier, Catherine, 219
Gay Dolphin Gift Shop, 41
Gaye, Jean de la, 219–21
"Gee," 26
George II, 89, 116, 251
George III, 146
George, Prince of Wales, 89
George Hill Plantation, 79
Georgetown, 51, 85, 88–91, 97–99, 103–5,
    108, 112
Georgetown County, 85
Georgetown County Courthouse, 101–2
Georgetown Steel Corporation, 103
Gershwin, George, 176, 186, 190–92
Glennie, Alexander, 74

"Gold Bug, The," 137
Golf Holiday, 37
Gone With the Wind (book), 164
Gone With the Wind (movie), 133
Grace Chapel, 195
Grand Strand, the, 23, 26, 34–35, 45, 48, 51–52
Gray, John W., 221
Great Santini, The (book), 257
Great Santini, The (movie), 232
Greenwich, 134
Greer, Michael, 86
Griffith, Melanie, 196
Guggenheim, Solomon R., 174
Gullah, 191
Gwynne, Alice Claypoole. *See* Vanderbilt, Alice Claypoole Gwynne

Hagley Plantation, 99
Haig family, 252
Haig Point, 253
Haig Point Lighthouse, 253
Half Moon Battery, 146
Hall, Bill, 195
Hamilton, Alexander, 92
Hamilton, Paul, 232
Hammock Shops, 75
Hampton, Wade, 155
Hampton House, 116, 117, 118–19
Hampton Park, 154–55
Hampton Plantation, 116–18, 126
Hand (community), 11
Harbor Island, 215
Harbour Town Lighthouse, 250
Harbour Town Yacht Club, 247, 250
Harold Kaminski House, 102–3
Harrietta Plantation, 118
Harriott Pinckney, 152
Harvest Moon, 102, 107–8
Hasell, Lewis, 63
Hatch, General, 166
Hawkins, Maxine, 59
Hayne, Robert Y., 167
Hazard family, 169
Heath, Robert, 145
Hebron United Methodist Church, 17, 19
Henning-Stearns House, 102
Henrietta, 19–21

Henry Erben organ, 177
Henry McKee House, 234–35
Hepworth, Thomas, 226
Heriot-Tarbox House, 95
Heritage, Jim, 155
Heritage Farm, 249
Hermitage, the, 57, 58–59
Heyward, Daniel, 176
Heyward, DuBose, 176, 186, 190–91, 192
Heyward, Thomas, 168
Heyward-Washington House, 176
Hibben, James, 134
Hibbens Ferry Tract, 134
Hilliardsville, 134
Hilton, William, 224, 246–47
Hilton Head Island, 209, 246–47, 249, 257
Historic Beaufort Foundation, 224, 240
Historic Charleston Foundation, 175
Hitler, 38
Hobcaw Barony, 80–81, 82, 88
Hobcaw House, 81
Holliday, Flora, 55
Holliday, George, 55
Holliday, J. W., 11, 30
Holliday, John Monroe, 11, 30
Home by the River, 118
Hopley, George A., 163
Hopsewee Plantation, 115–16
Horry, Ben, 56
Horry, Daniel, 116–17, 119, 120
Horry, Elias, 108, 116
Horry, Harriott Pinckney, 117–18, 245
Horry, Judith, 116, 119
Horry, Peter, 14, 108, 127
Horry County Courthouse, 16–17
Horry County Museum, 15
Hot and Hot Fish Club, 23, 68, 70–71
Housatonic, 151
Huger, Benjamin, 79
Huger, William Elliott, 168
Huger family, 168
Huguenots, 116, 120, 177, 219, 224, 246
Hunley, 150–51
Hunting Island, 215
Huntington, Anna Hyatt, 61, 63–64, 65–67
Huntington, Archer Milton, 63, 64–65
Huntington, Collis P., 63
Huntington Beach State Park, 67–68

Huntington family, 63, 68
Hurl Rock, 49–50
Hurricane Fishing Fleet, 10
Hurricane Hazel, 24, 33
Hurricane Hugo, 24, 48, 60, 123–24, 127, 128, 130, 144

"Independent Republic of Horry, the," 29–30
Indian shell ring, 249
Indigo cultivation, 89–91
"I–95," 254
International Paper Company, 103–5, 253
Intracoastal Waterway, 4, 5–6, 123, 253
Iron Mike, 218
Isle of Palms, 82, 137, 138

James, George S., 189
James Island, 147, 176, 186
James Island County Park, 192–93
James Island Presbyterian Church, 186
James Rhett House, 229
James Robert Verdier House, 230
Jefferson, Thomas, 92
Jennewein, C. Paul, 64, 66
Jeremy Creek, 123, 127
Joan of Arc, 67
John Mark Verdier House, 223–24
John P. Grace Memorial Bridge, 143–44
Johns Island Presbyterian Church, 196
John's Oak, 194
Johnson, Don, 196
Johnson, Joseph, 227–28
Johnson, Nathaniel, 146
Johnson, Robert, 89, 172
Johnson Creek, 215
Johnstone, Andrew, 111
Johnstone family, 108
Jones, Edward C., 144
Jordan, Daniel W., 23
Jordan, I. C., 28
Joseph Johnson House, 227–29
Juel, Frank, 10

Kaminski, Harold, 102–3
Kaminski, Heiman, 102
Kaminski, Julia, 102–3
Kaminski family, 102
Kelley, Dr., 13

Key-war. *See* Kiawah Island
Kiawah Island, 196–98
Kiawah River, 197
King, Benjamin, 98
King, Martin Luther, Jr., 210
Kings Highway, 8
Kingston. *See* Conway
Kingston Presbyterian Church, 14–15
Kinloch, Francis, 114
Kinloch Gun Club, 114
Kinloch House, 114
Kinloch Plantation, 113, 114
Kirk's Bluff. *See* Bluffton
Kuka, Saudi "Doc," 31

Lachicotte, A. H., 75
Lachicotte, A. H. "Doc," Jr., 75
Lady's Island, 208, 227
Lafayette, Marquis de, 223–24
Lafayette House, the. *See* John Mark Verdier House
Laffey, 141
Lance, Maurice Harvey, 9
Laurel Hill Plantation, 61, 63
Lee, Eford, 61
Lee, Jeanette, 132
Lee, Pearl, 61
Lee, Robert E., 159
Lee's Inlet Kitchen, 61
Legare, Solomon, 163
Legare family, 201–2
Legare Mausoleum, 201–2
Leland, Elizabeth, 124
Leverett, Charles Edward, 239
Leverett House, 239
Lewis, James, 31
Lewis Reeve Sams House, 225
Liberty Lodge, 78
Lincoln, Abraham, 147, 188
Lipton Tea Company, 195
Litchfield Country Club, 73
Litchfield Plantation, 73
Little Hampton, 126–27
Little Pee Dee River, 29
Little River, 7, 23
Little River (village), 7–10
Little River Neck, 9
Long Bay, 28
Lords of Discipline, The, 257

Lower Mill. *See* Bucksport, S.C.
Lowndes, Rawlins, 113
Lucas, Eliza. *See* Pinckney, Eliza Lucas
Lucas, George, 90
Lucas, Henry, 114
Lucas, Jonathan, 115
Lucas, Jonathan, Jr., 115
Lucasville, 134
Luff, Walter, 37–39, 52
Lumber River, 29
Lusitania, 80
Lynch, Thomas, 90, 116, 120
Lynch, Thomas, Jr., 116

Macbeth Art Gallery, 93
McClellan, Gerald, 123
McClellanville, 123–24, 126–27
McGahan, Mrs. Thomas R., 164
Mackey, Alexander, 244
McTeer, J. E., 214–15, 217
McTeer Memorial Bridge, 217
Magnolia Cemetery, 144–45
Magnolia Farm, 144
Magnolia Gardens, 183, 185
Magnolia Plantation, 183, 185
Magnolia Umbria Plantation, 144
Major, Evangeline, 211
Manigault, Gabriel, 155
Marine Biological Laboratory, 187
Marine Research Laboratory, 187
Marion, Francis, 108, 117, 127–28, 130
Marion, Gabriel, 61
Marion, Isaac, 6
Marion's Men, 128
Marsh Harbour Golf Links, 5–6
Marshall, George, 135
Marshall Reservation, 135
"Marshlands." *See* James Robert Verdier
    House
Marshlands Plantation House, 187
Marsh-Wright House, 100
Martin, Chlotilde, 224
Martinangle, Mr. and Mrs., 255
Mary Dunn Cemetery, 255
Mary Fields Elementary School, 255, 257
Masonic Lodge (Georgetown), 101
Maxwell, Walter, 24
May River, 243
Maynard, James T., 116

Mayrant's Bluff. *See* Battery White
Meade, General, 166
Meher Spiritual Center, 33–34
Methodist Episcopal Church of
    Georgetown, 100
Metropolitan Opera, 190
Michaux, André, 183
Middle Mill. *See* Bucksville
Middleton, Arthur, 113, 182
Middleton, Henrietta, 182
Middleton, Henry, 181–82, 183
Middleton, Mary, 206
Middleton family, 181
Middleton Place, 181–83
Middleton Plantation, 200
Midway, Battle of, 141
Miles Brewton House, 164–66
Mill Swamp, 11
Millbrook Plantation, 111–12
Milldam Plantation, 114
Mills, Robert, 14, 101
Milton Maxcy House, 237
Mineola. *See* Little River (village)
"Miss Grace," 27
Mongin, John, 251
Monroe, James, 79
Moore's Landing, 130
Morrall, John, 57
Morris, George, 163
Morris Island, 188
Motte, Rebecca Brewton, 165
Moultrie, William, 135, 137, 146, 155, 188
Mount Pleasant, 134, 143
Mount Pleasant Basket Makers of
    Charleston County, 132
Murrells Inlet, 56–57, 61, 71
Muster Shed School, 11
Myrtle Beach, 37–39, 41, 43–47, 48, 51–53,
    124
Myrtle Beach Air Force Base, 51–53, 56
Myrtle Beach Army Air Field. *See* Myrtle
    Beach Air Force Base
Myrtle Beach Convention Center, 40
Myrtle Beach Farms Company, 34, 47
Myrtle Beach Pavilion, 41, 43, 44–47
Myrtle Beach State Park, 55
Myrtle Bush Plantation, 221
Myrtle Square Mall, 47

Nairn, Thomas, 225
Nathaniel Russell House, 175–76
National Fisheries Center, 187
National Sculpture Society, 67
National Trust for Historic Preservation, 211
Naval stores production, 29
Navarro, Elizabeth, 114
Neptune, 146
New Ironsides, 173–74
New Town. *See* Myrtle Beach
Nicaraqua Victory, 144
Nichols, Jonathan, 19
Nicklaus, Jack, 254
Nixonville, 11
Norburn Cottage, 79
Normie, 176
"North and South," 169
North Beach Lighthouse, 215
North Edisto River, 199
North Island, 109
North Jetty, 71
North Myrtle Beach, 23, 27, 31
North Santee River, 110–11. *See also* Santee River
Nullification, 147
Nymph and Fawn, 66

Oak Hill Plantation, 79
Oak Island Plantation, 200
Oak Tavern, 91
Oaks, the (Beaufort). *See* Paul Hamilton House
Oaks, The (Murrells Inlet), 61, 63, 92, 93
Ocean Drive Beach, 23, 24, 26–28
Ocean Forest Hotel, 39–40
Ocean Forest Villa Resort, 39, 40
Ocean Lakes Campground, 5
O'Connor, Michael P., 167
"O.D." *See* Ocean Drive Beach
O'Donnell, Patrick, 164
O'Donnell's Folly, 164
Old Citadel, the, 152
Old Sheldon Church, 205–6, 239
Old Town. *See* Conway
Oliver, William L., 59
Oliver's Lodge, 59–60
Operation Desert Storm, 52–53
Ordinance of Secession, 98

Oristo. *See* Edisto Island
O'Sullivan, Florentia, 134
Oyster Point, 169

Palmetto Islands County Park, 133
Paradise, 196
Parker, Peter, 135, 146
Parris Island, 213, 217–19, 224
Pate, Lucille Vanderbilt, 80
Pate family, 80
Patriot, 61–62, 92–93
Patriots Point, 141, 143
Patterson, Elizabeth, 33
Paul Hamilton House, 232
Pawley, Anthony, 76
Pawley, George, 74, 76
Pawley, Percival, 76
Pawley, Percival II, 76
Pawley House (Georgetown), 103
Pawley House (Pawleys Island), 77
Pawleys Island, 75–79
Peace Corps, 211
Pee Dee River, 71, 85, 128
Pelican Inn, 78
Penn Center, 209–11
Penn School, 210, 211, 213
Perrin, J. W., 28
Perry, Dr., 238
Perry, Edgar A. *See* Poe, Edgar Allan
Petigru, Thomas, 72
Phillips, Mrs., 134
Pickens, Governor, 187
Pig Pen Bay Schoolhouse, 11
Pinckney, Charles, 90, 117, 244–45
Pinckney, Charles Cotesworth, 153, 154–55, 245–46
Pinckney, Eliza Lucas, 90, 117, 244–45
Pinckney, Josephine, 164
Pinckney Island, 244–46
Pinckney Island National Wildlife Refuge, 246
Pine Lakes Country Club, 39
"Pineapple Gates." *See* Simmons-Edwards House
Pipe Down Plantation, 72
Pitch production. *See* Naval stores production
Planter, 235
Planters' Hotel, 177

Plyler, Justin, 41
Poe, Edgar Allan, 137
Poetry Society of South Carolina, 164
Ponce de Leon, 187
Pope, William, 243
Poplar, 11
Porgy, 176, 186, 190, 192
Porgy and Bess, 176, 186, 190–92
Port Royal (village), 217, 225
Port Royal Experiment, 209–10
Port Royal Island, 224
Port Royal Sound, 224, 225
Powers, Hiram, 67
Pregnell's Wharf, 152
Prince Frederick Parish, 89
Prince George Winyah Episcopal Church, 98-100
Prince George Winyah Parish, 89, 99
Prince of Tides, The, 257
Pringle, Elizabeth Allston, 77
Prioleau, Julia M., 217
Prospect Hill, 79
Provincial Congress, 128
Provost, Augustine, 206
Provost, Charlotte Kaminski, 79
Provost House, 79
Pulaski, Count Casimir, 217

Ravenel, John, 173, 174
Ravenel, St. Julien, 173
Ravenel, William, 174
Rawdon, Lord, 165
Red Bluff, 11
Red Store–Tarbox Warehouse, 91, 92
Reesor, Annette Epps, 48
Rennet, Henri Le. *See* Poe, Edgar Allan
Restaurant Row, 34
Retreat Plantation, 219, 221
Revolutionary War, 99, 128, 135, 137, 146, 165–66, 187–88
Reynolds, Nancy DuPont, 113
Rhett, Benjamin, 239
Rhett, Edmund, 237
Rhett, James, 229
Rhett, Julia Emma, 113
Rhett, Robert Barnwell, 225, 240
"Rhett's Folly." *See* James Rhett House
Rhoda H. Shannon, 188

Ribaut, Jean, 219, 224, 228, 246
Ribaut Monument, 219
Rice cultivation, 62–63, 85–86, 95–96, 114
Rice Hope Plantation, 114–15
Rice Museum, 95, 96
Riley, Joseph J., 150
Rivers, William, 190
Riverview. *See* Elizabeth Hext House
Road's End, 21
Robertson, John, 169
Rockville, 195
Roosevelt, Eleanor, 142
Roosevelt, Franklin Delano, 81
Root Man, 212
Roper, Robert William, 174
Rose Hill Plantation, 79, 81
Royal family, 197
Russell, Nathaniel, 175
Russell, William P., 169
Rutledge, Archibald, 95, 118–19, 120
Rutledge, Edward, 182
Rutledge, Frederick, 118
Rutledge, Harriott Horry, 118
Rutledge, Henry, 126
Rutledge, Irvine, 127
Rutledge, John, 118

St. Cecilia Society, 147, 245
St. Elena Island. *See* St. Helena Island
Saint-Gaudens, Augustus, 67
St. Helena Episcopal Chapel of Ease, 211
St. Helena Island, 209–10, 212, 213, 215, 224
St. Helena's Episcopal Church, 211, 237–39, 248
St. James Chapel of Ease, 124
St. James Santee Episcopal Church, 120
St. John the Evangelist Chapel, 77
St. Mary's Chapel, 99
St. Michael's Episcopal Church, 149, 159–60, 177, 179
St. Philip's Episcopal Church, 149, 159, 177, 179
Sampit River, 85, 98, 107
Sandy Island, 71–73
Santee Coastal Reserve, 82
Santee River, 99, 123, 128. *See also* North Santee River; South Santee River

Savannah, 141
Savannah River, 243, 252
Sculptured Oak Nature Trail, 55
Sea Pines Forest Preserve, 249
Sea Pines Plantation, 247, 249
Sea Side Inn, 43, 44
Seabrook Island, 195
Secession Convention. *See* South Carolina
   Secession Convention
Secession House. *See* Milton Maxcy House
Second Avenue Fishing Pier, 48–49
Serre, Noe, 116
Shaftesbury, earl of, 199
Shag, the, 26–27, 45
Sheldon, Gilbert, 206
Sheldon Hall Plantation, 205
Sheldon Plantation, 167
Sherman, William Tecumseh, 137, 221
Silas N. Pearman Bridge, 143
Simmons-Edwards House, 164
Simms, William Gillmore, 145
Simonds, Andrew, 172
Singleton Swash, 34–35, 37
Skene, Alexander, 14
Smalls, Robert, 235, 236
Smalls, Sammy, 176, 186
Smith, Benjamin, 6
Smyth, Thomas, 168
Society of Shaggers, 27
S.O.S. *See* Society of Shaggers
S.O.S. Weekend, 27
Sousa, John Philip, 114
South Carolina Arts Commission, 67
South Carolina Constitutional Convention,
   235
South Carolina Hall of Fame, 40–41
South Carolina Institute of Archaeology
   and Anthropology, 219
South Carolina Inter-State and West
   Indian Exposition, 155
South Carolina Jockey Club, 147, 154
South Carolina Jockey Club Ball, 155
South Carolina Railway Freight Depot
   Building, 149
South Carolina Secession Convention, 147,
   237
South Carolina Welcome Center, 7
South Carolina Wildlife and Marine
   Resources Center, 187
South Carolina Wildlife Commission, 187

South Island, 109
South Jetty, 71
South Santee River, 110, 118. *See also*
   Santee River
South Strand Chamber of Commerce, 56
Speros, Steve, 10
Spillane, Jane Rogers, 60
Spillane, Mickey, 60
Springfield Plantation, 63
Springmaid Beach, 50
Springmaid Villa, 50
Springs, Elliott White, 50
Springs family, 51
Springs Mills, 50
Squash (servant of VanderHorst family),
   199
State interposition. *See* Nullification
Steinmeyer, C. S., 214
"Stephen Bull of Sheldon," 206, 221
Stevens, Cleveland, 31
Stone, Thomas Archibald, 133
Stone, Willie, 9
Stoney, John Joseph, 247
Stoney Landing, 173
Stono Indians, 193
Stono River, 193
Strachan Mansion, 253–54, 257
Sullivan's Island, 134–35, 137–38, 188
Sullivan's Island, Battle of, 137
Sully, Thomas, 103
"Summertime," 191
Sumter National Forest, 128
Surfside Beach, 55–56
"Swamp Field, the." *See* Crescent Beach
Swamp Fox. *See* Marion, Francis
Swamp Fox Hiking Trail, 130
Swinton, William, 89
Sword Gate House, 163–64

Tabby, 187, 211, 219
"Tabby Manse." *See* Thomas Fuller House
Tabernacle Baptist Church, 236
Talbot, Theodore, 188
Talvande, Andrew, 163
Talvande, Rose, 163
Tar production. *See* Naval stores
   production
Tarbox, Frank G., Jr., 64, 65
Tarleton, Banastre, 120
Taylor, W. W., 102

Tea cultivation, 195
Teach, Edward, 172, 216–17
Thomas, Debbie, 124
Thomas Fuller House, 239
Thomas Hepworth House, 226
"Three Sisters, the," 168
Tidalholm. *See* Edgar Fripp House
Tidewater. *See* William Fripp House
Tiffany, Louis Comfort, 169
Tilghman Beach, 24
Tilly Swamp Baptist Church, 11
Tobacco cultivation, 11–12, 30
Tom Yawkey Wildlife Center, 82, 109–10, 123
Tomotley Barony, 206
Towne, Laura, 210, 213
Townsend, Daniel, 202
Townsend, Hephzibah Jenkins, 202
Townshend, Pete, 33
Trapier, Hannah, 86
Trapier, Paul, 86
Travelers Chapel, 12–13
Trenholm, George Alfred, 111
Trinity Episcopal Church, 202
True Blue Plantation, 78
Tucker, Dan, 73
Tucker, Hattie Mae, 73
Tucker, Henry Massingberd, 73
Tucker, John Hyrne, 73
Turner, Ted, 114
Turpentine production. *See* Naval stores production
Tuscarora Indians, 225
Tybee Island, Ga., 251
Tyson, George, 30

United States Air Force, 52
United States Army Air Corps, 51
United States Coast Guard Station (Sullivan's Island), 134–35
United States Custom House, 153
United States Fish and Wildlife Service, 130
United States Forest Service, 128, 130
United States Marine Corps Station. *See* Parris Island
United States Post Office (Charleston), 159, 161
Upper Mill, 19

Vanderbilt, Alfred Gwynne, 79–80
Vanderbilt, Alice Claypoole Gwynne, 79
Vanderbilt, Cornelius, 79
Vanderbilt, George, 80, 114
Vanderbilt, Margaret Emerson, 79–80
Vanderhorst, John, 114
VanderHorst family, 198–99
VanderHorst Mansion, 198, 199
Varin (Frenchman), 7
Verdier, Andrew, 243
Verdier, James Robert, 230
Verdier, John Mark, 223, 243
Vereen, Jeremiah, 34
Vereen family, 6–7
Vereen Memorial Historical Gardens, 6
Villa Margherita, 172

Waccamaw Arts and Crafts Guild, 51
Waccamaw River, 57, 71, 85
Wachesaw, 61
Wadmalaw Island, 194
Waite, Ezra, 164–65
Walker, Edward Tabb, 221
Wall, E. Craig, 39, 52
Wallace House, 226
Wampee, 11
Ward, Joshua, 74–75
Ward, Joshua John, 62–63, 65, 70, 74, 79
Warren, Russell, 101
"Warthog." *See* A-10 Thunderbolt II
Washington, George, 5, 7, 8, 34, 62, 82, 103, 119, 159, 176
Washington, Philip, 72
Washington Race Course, 147, 154–55
Water Is Wide, The, 257
Wateree River, 118
Waterman, Eleazer, 100
Waterman-Kaminski House, 100
Waterway Hills Golf Course, 34
Wedgefield Plantation, 85, 86
Weldon, Felix de, 218
Werner, Christopher, 163
Weston, Plowden, 74, 78
Whaley, Maria, 163
White, Edward Brickell, 91, 177, 179
White, Robert, 39
White Point Gardens, 169
White Point Swash, 33
Whitfield, George, 8
Wicklow Hall Plantation, 114

William Bull House, 167
William C. Gatewood House, 164
William Elliott House, 240
William Fripp House, 229–30
William Hilton Parkway, 246
William Ravenel House, 174
William Washington House, 172
Williams, George W., 169
Williamson, Atkin, 179
Wilmington, Chadbourn & Conway Line, 14
Windsor House, 86, 88
Windsor Plantation, 85, 86
Windy Hill Beach, 23, 31, 33
Winyah Bay, 85, 88–89, 90, 128
Winyah Indigo Society, 89, 90
Winyah Indigo Society Hall, 88, 91
Winyah tribe, 88
Winyaw tribe. *See* Winyah tribe
Woodland, 60
Woodmason, Charles, 206
Woodside brothers, 39
World War I, 218, 225
World War II, 37–39, 51–52, 135, 141–42, 161
Wragg, Samuel, 86
Wurlitzer organ, 46

Yawkey, Tom, 109–10
Yellow fever, 186
Yemassee Indians, 225, 226, 246–47
Yorktown, 141–43
Young, Bruce, 13
Young, Emory, 13
Young, George, 114

Zeigler, J. A., 16
Zion Chapel of Ease, 247, 248–49